Second Language Acquisition

General Editors: Paul Meara and Peter Skehan

Theories of Second-Language Learning

Barry McLaughlin

Professor of Psychology,
University of California, Santa Cruz

Edward Arnold

First published in Great Britain 1987 by
Edward Arnold (Publishers) Ltd, 41 Bedford Square, London WC1B 3DQ

Edward Arnold (Australia) Pty Ltd, 80 Waverley Road, Caulfield East,
Victoria 3145, Australia

Edward Arnold, 3 East Read Street, Baltimore, Maryland 21202, U.S.A.

British Library Cataloguing in Publication Data

McLaughlin, Barry
    Theories of second language learning.——
    (Second language acquisition).
    1. Second language acquisition
    I. Title   II. Series
    418'.07'15   P118.2

    ISBN 0 7131 6513 8

To my mother, Dorothea McLaughlin

Text set in 10/11 pt Times Compugraphic
by Colset Private Limited, Singapore

Printed and bound in Great Britain by
Biddles Ltd, Guildford and King's Lynn

Contents

vi *Contents*

Preface

This book is about theory and the role of theory in research on adult second-language learning. My principal goal is to examine what position theory plays in this growing subfield of applied linguistics and to evaluate present theories. Particular attention is paid to methodological issues and to the question of how theoretical concepts are translated into empirical procedures. The book is oriented toward an informed audience but does not assume extensive background.

The introductory chapter is devoted to discussion of the nature of theory and to the question of how theories are evaluated. I begin by assuming that science, like other knowledge processes, involves the proposing of theories, models, hypotheses, etc. and the acceptance or rejection of these on the basis of some external criteria. In a strict sense, I argue, theories are not 'accepted' or 'proven' – rather the successful theory is tested and escapes being disconfirmed. This point of view is compatible with those philosophies of science that emphasize the impossibility of deductive proof for inductive laws (Hanson, Popper). Varying degrees of "confirmation" are conferred upon a theory through the number of plausible rival hypotheses available to account for the data; the fewer such plausible rival hypotheses, the greater the degree of 'confirmation'.

This approach to evaluating theory is applied to the theories and models treated in subsequent chapters. In chapter 2, the most ambitious, 'grand' theory of adult second-language learning is discussed: Krashen's Monitor Model. This theory is treated first because it was, in its essentials, formulated earlier than the other theories discussed in the book. Krashen's Monitor Model provides, in my view, an example of an unsuccessful theory of second language. It purports to account for extensive empirical data and to have broad implications for language instruction, but its claims, discussed in detail in this chapter, are unwarranted and the Monitor Model fails to meet the canons of theoretical sufficiency.

The next four chapters deal with 'intermediate' theories that are more limited in perspective than the Monitor Model. The first of these is Interlanguage theory, which applies a linguistic perspective to second-language phenomena. Then follow chapters on Linguistic Universals and Acculturation/Pidginization theory, both of which also are essentially linguistic theories, though the acculturation notion represents an attempt to incorporate social-psychological considerations. The next chapter, on Cognitive theory, takes a different perspective and treats second-language learning as the acquisition of a complex cognitive skill. The contribution of each of these approaches is examined and evaluated.

The final chapter discusses what it is that a satisfactory theory of second-language learning must explain. In this chapter I also examine various methodologies used in second-language research and the relationship of theory to practice.

Not all theoretical approaches to second-language phenomena are discussed in this book. Neurolinguistic approaches are but briefly mentioned, because at present they have generated little systematic research in the field. Approaches that focus on discourse processes are thought to contribute more to methodology than to theory, and so are not treated here. Other approaches are excluded as not in the mainstream of second-language research. Such judgements are subjective; I include a chapter on Cognitive theory because I see this approach to be important – others may disagree.

I would like to thank Paul Meara for his encouragement and his comments on the manuscript at various stages. Lydia White, Patsy Lightbown, Mike Sharwood-Smith, John Schumann, and Kevin Gregg all provided helpful comments on parts of the manuscript. Above all, I express my gratitude to my wife, Sigrid, for patience and understanding.

1

Introduction

Over the past two decades or so, the number of studies concerned with second-language learning has increased exponentially, as has the number of journals, anthologies, and textbooks dealing with this topic. One reason is practical: there are more people than ever whose economic aspirations depend on their learning a second language. In European countries there are large numbers of immigrants and 'guest-workers' who have to learn the language of the home country. A similar situation exists in the United States, which has recently witnessed a huge influx of immigrants, legal and illegal. Consequently, there is a growing need for second language teachers of both children and adults, for pedagogical information, and for research on the process of second-language learning.

A second reason for the increase in research on second-language learning is that advances in the areas of general linguistics, psycholinguistics, and cognitive psychology have prepared the groundwork for the study of second-language learning. During the past two decades there has been an enormous increase in our knowledge of the process of language learning in young children. All over the world, researchers follow young children with their tape recorders or video recorders, gathering information on their linguistic and cognitive development. As more is learned about the process of first-language development, hypotheses are generated that stimulate research on second-language learning in children and adults.

This volume is concerned primarily with second-language learning in adults (I have discussed second-language learning in children elsewhere: McLaughlin 1984, 1985). The focus here is on theory – how theory informs and guides research and how theory is evaluated on the basis of research. To begin, I would like to discuss three assumptions that are basic to the scientific research enterprise, including the field of adult second-language learning.

1

Three assumptions

In a thoughtful review of research on adult second-language learning and its application to teaching practice, Patsy Lightbown (1985) identified three broad categories of research based principally on methodological differences. The first type of research consists of *descriptive studies*. Such studies begin by collecting speech samples from second-language speakers – either of spontaneous speech or through various elicitation procedures – and then compares these samples to target-language norms. The goal is to account for consistencies or discrepancies between the second-language learners' use of certain linguistic forms and native use. For example, there have been a large number of studies comparing second-language learners' acquisition of certain morphemes in obligatory contexts to acquisition patterns observed in native speakers.

Another type of research on adult second-language learning that Lightbown identified consists of *experimental pedagogical studies*. These are studies in which the attempt is made to manipulate certain variables experimentally to determine their effect on classroom learning. Thus, for example, researchers modify the presentation of linguistic forms to second-language learners, compare subjects learning under different conditions of instruction (e.g., rule-learning versus conversation-based instruction), or attempt to control the complexity of the input language.

A third category of research refers to *hypothesis-testing studies*. This is Lightbown's term for research in which the investigator, rather than beginning from a language sample or testing certain variables for their effect on classroom learning, begins with a specific hypothesis based on the findings of previous research or theory. Thus an investigator might test the hypothesis that there exist linguistic universals that shape language development in its early stages. Or a researcher might have found certain error patterns in a sample of speech drawn from speakers of a particular first language, and may conduct a study to determine whether these patterns are found in the speech of speakers of other first languages.

Lightbown's classification scheme is helpful in understanding recent developments in the field of adult second-language learning. However, while acknowledging the usefulness of this typology, there is a sense in which all research fits into the last category. That is, in a most fundamental sense all research involves hypothesis testing, whether this is explicitly acknowledged or not. Every investigator begins with some hypotheses about the phenomena being studied, although these hypotheses may not be stated formally. Even the researcher involved in descriptive research of the most rudimentary nature is testing hypotheses. These hypotheses originate in some theory about the data. In trying to impose order on the data, the researcher organizes the data according to some cognitive schema or theory. Without a theory there can be no hypotheses. This brings us to the first assumption:

Assumption 1. Research is inseparable from theory.

It is important to be clear about what one means by theory. The term 'theory' is used here to refer to a way of interpreting, criticizing, and unifying established generalizations. A theory is flexible and pliant, in that it allows its generalizations to be modified to fit data unforeseen in their formulation. And theory is heuristic, in the sense that the theory itself provides a way of guiding the enterprise of finding new and more powerful generalizations.

The generalizations that constitute the basis of a theory derive initially from regularities or constancies in our experience of natural phenomena. Whitehead wrote:

> Recognition is the source of all our natural knowledge. The whole scientific theory is nothing else than an attempt to systematize our knowledge of the circumstances in which such recognitions will occur. (Cited in Kaplan 1964, 85)

Thus the first step in the scientific enterprise is the marking of enduring or recurrent events in the flow of experience

Hypotheses serve to carry forward the scientific inquiry. They are the scientist's best hunches about the regularities or constancies characteristic of the phenomena in question. To test an hypothesis, the scientist organizes the inquiry so as to facilitate a decision as to whether the hunch is correct. Once an hypothesis has been established, it is said to constitute a 'fact' or a 'law', according to whether it is particular or general in content. These facts and laws, in turn, are the stuff of theory.

In a most fundamental sense, then, a theory is a system of facts and laws. But by being brought together in a theory, the facts and laws are altered, reformulated, reinterpreted. The theory is more than the aggregate of the facts and laws; it gives each of them a new meaning. The facts and laws take on a new light from the theory: the theory illuminates facts and laws. Further, good theory is always open, for the set of generalizations making up a theory is never complete. The value of a theory derives not only from the explanations it is constructed to provide, but also from its unanticipated consequences. This is the sense in which theory is heuristic: theory provides guesses as to how the uncontrolled and unknown factors in the area under study are related to known facts and laws. Theory guides the search for further data and further generalizations.

In fact, all observation involves theorizing. One does not simply read and record nature's protocol. Inferences occur even at the perceptual level. As Popper (1959) argued, there is no purely 'phenomenal language' distinct from 'theoretical language'; there is no way of talking of something sensed and not interpreted. We cannot free ourselves from theories; theories are part and parcel of the human cognitive makeup.

Thus the researcher concerned with adult second-language learning is inevitably testing hypotheses about a theory. The theory may be vaguely or not at all described. But just as on the perceptual level there is no uninterpreted intuition or bare sensation, the researcher is never unencumbered by expectancies and beliefs about the phenomena in question. And even if we could free ourselves from theory, it would be unwise not to make use of theory to interpret what we observe and to generate new hypotheses.

We come now to the second basic assumption:

Assumption 2. There is no one scientific method.

Earlier the point was made that theoretically-derived hypotheses are tested via a scientific inquiry designed to facilitate a decision as to whether a given hypothesis is correct. This inquiry process can take many forms. There is no one 'scientific method'. Thus the traditional research cycle – proceeding from description to correlation to experimentation – assumes that experimental research is the *sine qua non* for establishing the validity of research. But science does not progress only in the laboratory. It is true that experimentation allows for degrees of control not possible in other situations, yet there are the attendant perils of trivialization of the phenomenon under investigation and lack of motivation on the part of the subject. Experimentation should obviously have its place in the researcher's repertory, but it is no panacea.

Hypotheses may be tested via any of the methods Lightbown identified. To use one of her examples, Huebner (1979) examined the patterns of use of the English article by a Hmong speaker and found that this second-language learner's use of the article was strongly influenced by his mistaken assumption that English, like his native language, uses what might be called pragmatic (topic prominence) rather than syntactic (subject prominence) rules for marking definiteness. This confirmed the hypothesis that for some learners there are internal consistencies in language use that may occur without regard to target language norms.

The Huebner study was descriptive and longitudinal. It involved a single case. Yet the results are theoretically significant. There is no need to take the research further to confirm Huebner's hypothesis. One does not need to carry out an experiment to 'prove' the point. Further research may provide further confirmation (or disconfirmation) of Huebner's hypothesis, but careful descriptive-analysis research can stand on its own. It represents an important scientific contribution; just as important as experimental research. Observation and descriptive-analytic work need not be the first steps on a journey where experimentation is the end of the road.

In research on adult second-language learning, as in all scientific research, there is the danger of fadism. Abraham Kaplan (1964) has identified what he termed *the law of the instrument*, which may be formulated as follows: Give a small boy a hammer and he will find that everything he encounters needs pounding. Second-language research has had its instruments, its ways of doing research, and it can happen that the methods researchers use set limits on the questions they can answer. Worse than that, some successful techniques have come to be applied mechanically and other approaches have been denied the name of science.

Another danger comes from the *mystique of quantity*. Numbers have no magical powers; they do not have scientific value in and of themselves. Yet often one senses an exaggerated regard for the significance of measurement, so much so that complex statistical analyses are used to salvage sloppy observation or bad experimentation. Statistics are tools of thought, not substitutes for thought. I have argued strongly for the use of more sophisticated statistical procedures in research on second-language learning (McLaughlin 1980), but if such techniques as multivariate regression analyses are used to mystify, the field will move quickly into the realm of the occult.

My own preference is for a multimethod approach, where a number of different methodologies are employed to test theoretical hypotheses. A catholicity of outlook is needed in research on adult second-language learning. This is not to say that one approach is as good as another in a particular context or that all should be used in any single inquiry. A multimethod approach moves the field along; it may not serve the purposes of a given researcher. Data triangulation is achieved most often through the work of different researchers with different interests getting a fix on the same phenomenon from different angles:

Assumption 3. There is no single scientific truth.

The kind of methodological openness advocated in assumption 3 runs contrary to a natural tendency to feel that one's own approach and one's own point of view is better than other people's. Disciplines tend to become fragmented into 'schools', whose members are loath to accept, and are even hostile to the views of other schools using different methods and reaching different conclusions. Each group becomes convinced that it has a corner on 'truth'.

It can be argued, however, that it is counterproductive to believe that there is a single truth that can be known directly and objectively by the application of scientific methods. One philosophical position contends that truth can never be known directly and in its totality. All knowledge, the argument runs, is mediated by the symbol systems used by scientists. If one adopts this epistemological stance, scientific truth can be known only as it is mediated by the perspectives of the scientists and thus there are multiple accounts of what is seen. Multiple ways of seeing result in multiple truths.

From this point of view, scientific progress is achieved as we come to illuminate progressively our knowledge in a particular domain by taking different perspectives, each of which must be evaluated in its own right. The symbol system or metaphor used by a particular scientist may help us see more clearly, but it does not constitute ultimate truth. Nor does the combination of all partial representations of truth add up to ultimate truth. Ultimate truth, it is argued, is only approximated in the shadows cast by the metaphors of our theories.

In an insightful discussion of the way in which symbol systems are used by investigators of adult second-language learning, Schumann (1983a) identified a number of metaphors underlying the work of various researchers. These include Krashen's (1981) use of the 'affective filter', Selinker and Lamendella's (1976) highly metaphorical neurofunctional perspective, and Adjemian's (1976) notion of the 'permeability' of the interlanguage system. In fact, as we shall see in the course of this book, metaphors abound in the theories that have been developed to account for various aspects of adult second-language learning.

This is not to say that all metaphors are equally valid or that all ways of looking at second-language phenomena are equally veridical. Criteria for evaluating the adequacy of different theoretical points of view can be specified, and in the final section of this chapter, such criteria will be spelled out. The point is simply that, regardless of one's epistemological beliefs about the nature of truth, it is useful to look at adult second-language learning from as many perspectives as possible. At least in the present stage of the development of our knowledge, it seems premature to argue for the 'truth' of one theory over another.

The nature of theory

Earlier in this chapter theory was defined as a way of interpreting, criticizing, and unifying established generalizations. In addition, it was argued that a theory is pliant, in that it allows its generalizations or 'laws' to be modified to fit data unforeseen in their formulations, and heuristic, in that the theory itself provides a way of finding new and more powerful generalizations. These last two characteristics of a good theory are especially important in considering how theory operates.

The functions of theories

A theory is both a summary of known facts and laws and a conjecture about the relationships among them. The purpose of theory is in part to further *understanding*. Theories help us understand and organize the data of experience. They permit us to summarize relatively large amounts of information via a relatively short list of propositions. In this sense, theories bring meaning to what is otherwise chaotic and inscrutable.

A second function of theories is *transformation*. New theories change the relationship between laws and facts. They enable us to use the empirical data to draw conclusions that are not evident from the data taken in isolation. In this sense, theories transform the meaning of what is known. They go beyond the information given and change both the content and form of our knowledge.

Theories also guide *prediction*. Good theories stimulate research. They are the ground from which hypotheses spring: theories generate new hypothetical laws to be put to empirical test. These hypotheses embody predictions about where the theory is leading. They are not a guess at an answer to a riddle, but an idea about the next step that is worth taking.

These functions of theory can be illustrated by an example from research on adult second-language learning. One of the leading theories of second-language learning for many years was what can be called the structural–behaviourist theory. According to this theory, language learning was viewed as a process of habit development to be inculcated by varying contingencies of reinforcement. Behaviourist theories were invoked to justify such principles as sequential control of the learning process, specification of learning goals, and immediate reinforcement. Structural theory was invoked to justify the use of contrastive analysis: it was felt that by being aware of the structural differences between languages, the teacher could foresee student errors and help in overcoming them.

Thus the structural–behaviourist theory provided a framework for *understanding* the process of second-language learning. Principles such as reinforcement and habit formation and the method of contrastive analysis *transformed* thinking about second-language learning phenomena, or at least made more explicit old ways of thinking about second-language learning. Furthermore, the theory led to specific *predictions* about learning. For example, according to structural–behaviourist theory, the errors that learners make in a second language should reflect the structures of their first language. This turned out not to be the case in many instances (see McLaughlin 1984), nor were structural–behaviourist predictions about classroom learning supported in experimental pedagogical studies (see McLaughlin 1985).

Ultimately, structural–behaviourist theory was abandoned or modified so extensively as to be nonrecognizable. The theory was useful, however, for although we now think of second-language learning in very different terms, we have evidence that allows us to reject a position that at first glance agrees with common sense. If one asked the proverbial 'man on the street' for his view of the process of learning a second language, the theory would most probably look something like structural–behaviourist theory. That such notions can be rejected as insufficient is a step forward.

Types of theories

There are at least two different dimensions that can be used to classify theories. One can examine their form or their content. From the formal point of view, many different distinctions can be made (see Einstein 1934; Kaplan 1964; Nagel 1961). For the most part, these distinctions correspond to the difference between more 'deductive' and more 'inductive' approaches (Table 1.1). The *deductive approach* characterizes formal theories in which the concepts of the theory are related to each other in a set of propositions that are assumed to be true without proof (though they may be empirically testable). These constitute the axioms of the theory. Ideally, these axioms are as few as possible, so that the theory is simple and parsimonious.

Table 1.1　Deductive and inductive theories

	Deductive theories	Inductive theories
Beginning point	Interim solutions	Empirical data
Network	Theoretical concepts and constructs	Relationships between laws
Ultimate goal	Explanation	Explanation
Advantage	More interesting claims	Close to data
Disadvantage	Remote from data	Limited claims

Given these basic axioms or assumptions, laws of logic are applied to obtain new propositions. This procedure is called 'deducing the consequences of the theory'. The new propositions that follow from the assumptions of the theory are called 'hypotheses'. If the hypotheses of the theory are empirically supported, they become the laws and facts of the theory. In a deductive theory, there are fewer and more general laws at the top of the pyramid, and a greater number of more specific laws as we move to the base.

In contrast to the deductive approach, the *inductive approach* progresses from the accumulation of sets of facts and sets of laws to theory.

Rather than beginning from sets of premises or axioms that are assumed to be true, the inductive approach is tightly empirically based. There is no jump to theoretical statements until a large number of empirical relationships have been established.

In the inductive approach, hypotheses are derived from the theory as in the deductive approach, but they are the result of gaps in the network of empirical relationships, rather than the consequence of logical deductions. Hypotheses do not come from logical reasoning, but are the investigator's best hunch about a new relationship, given certain empirical facts. The theory guides the investigator, but hypotheses are not as tightly and logically formulated as in the deductive approach.

In practice, it is often difficult to determine whether the approach taken is more deductive or inductive. There are few well-developed formal theories outside of the natural sciences, and in each case it is a question of emphasis. Some theorists are more 'top-down' or deductive in their orientation, while others stay closer to the data and are therefore more 'bottom-up' in approach. Both are approaches to theorizing and so both aim at explanation: inductive approaches tend to offer more cautious and descriptive accounts, whereas deductive approaches tend to provide more general causal statements. But here again we are dealing with a continuum along which theories can be placed, rather than with a dichotomy.

From the point of view of the content of theories, there are *micro* or *macro* theories, depending on the range of phenomena the theory is thought to accommodate. Thus macroeconomics is concerned with the workings of an economy or industry, whereas microeconomics focuses on the behaviour of individual participants in the economic process. The distinction is a relative one and what is micro to one theorist can be macro to another. In the field of adult second-language learning, a macro theory might attempt to deal with the whole range of phenomena involved in the language-learning process, as does Krashen's Monitor Model, treated in chapter 2, whereas micro theories might concentrate on specific phenomena of limited scope, as do the theories of intermediate range discussed in chapters 3 to 6.

It is often argued that micro theories are intrinsically more satisfactory, and in many fields, such as sociology and psychology, the tendency of researchers is to shy away from macro theory. It may be true that at a particular stage in the development of a field of research it is overly ambitious to attempt to articulate a macro analysis. The length of the reduction chain connecting the theoretical terms with observable ones can be too long. This is why many theorists restrict themselves to 'miniature theories'.

In the end, however, an adequate theory will have to be 'macro' enough to encompass more than a limited range of phenomena. A satisfactory theory of adult second-language learning must go beyond accounting for how people form relative clauses. A theory of the formation of the relative clause among second-language learners – one that distinguishes different kinds of relative clauses in different second languages – might be very useful indeed. But eventually one would like to incorporate this micro theory into a broader and more extensive theoretical context.

The construction of theories

How have researchers gone about constructing theories in thinking about adult second-language learning? I have argued that in the most general sense, research is inseparable from theory. But theories can be more or less systematic. In the initial phase of a discipline's development, research is often guided by a *proto-theory*. This corresponds to what Long (1985b) has called theory of the 'storehouse' variety. It consists of a collection of (often unrelated) generalizations about phenomena.

In the domain of second-language learning these generalizations might consist of statements such as:

(1) Learners who begin a second language after puberty acquire language structures more quickly than do children, but attain lower levels of ultimate proficiency.
(2) Learners of certain structures (such as the interrogative or the negative) in a particular language pass through a specific developmental sequence before attaining the target version.
(3) The errors made in acquiring certain structures in a particular language are similar for learners of different language backgrounds.

Each of these generalizations is a conclusion based on research evidence (or more correctly, the interpretation of research).

Although the generalizations that make up a proto-theory may appear to be unrelated, it is usually the case that they reflect an underlying perspective. Thus researchers who adhere to the above propositions are likely to advocate other beliefs about language learning, such as the belief in universal grammar or in an innate pre-programmed language-learning device of the type postulated by Chomsky. At first, the connection between the generalizations and their broader theoretical implications may not be clear. As more research accumulates, however, and researchers begin to think more about the meaning of their results, the proto-theory begins to evolve into a true theory.

In and of itself, the proto-theory suffers from several disadvantages. If its generalizations are left unrelated, it leads nowhere. It does not further understanding because it does not provide any coherent account of the phenomena it seeks to explain. One would like to know why one finds developmental sequences and why learners from different language backgrounds make similar errors. Nor does a proto-theory lead to new hypotheses. The danger is that researchers will simply accumulate information. Indeed, much research on adult second-language learning is proto-theoretic in the sense that it is concerned with single generalizations in isolation from any more general theoretical context.

There is usually, however, a broader theoretical context within which even the most restricted and myopic research is carried out. Perceptive researchers can articulate their theoretical biases, and the best research addresses specific theoretical questions. These questions arise as researchers try to fit together the pieces of the puzzle. As is indicated in Figure 1.1, theory develops out of a collection of apparently unrelated generalizations. A theory evolves once it is observed that the relationships (A–B) and (C–D) are consistent with Theory I. If, however, the relationship (E–F) is inconsistent with Theory I but consistent with relationships (A–B) and (C–D) in a new theoretical framework, then Theory II replaces Theory I. As other relationships are tested and found to be inconsistent with Theory II, it becomes replaced by a new theory.

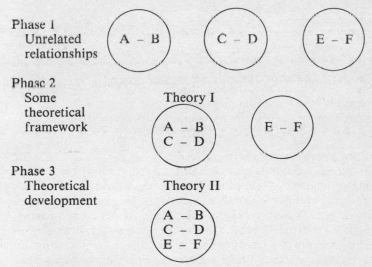

Phase 1
Unrelated
relationships

Phase 2
Some
theoretical
framework

Phase 3
Theoretical
development

Figure 1.1. Phases in the development of theory.

No theory stands or falls on the basis of a single observation or experiment. Only the pattern of multiple tests determines the goodness of fit between theory and data, and a theory is not replaced until a better one is found. As a field progresses, existing theories are replaced by better ones. This evolution has occurred in the field of second-language research, although there is a tendency to build up from scratch, rather than building on what has already been established. This is unfortunate, because progress in science requires taking into account the achievements of one's predecessors. Even scientific revolutions preserve some continuity with the old order of things.

There is also a tendency in the field of second-language research to limit the range of theory to specific phenomena. In the short run, this has the advantage that the theory can be built and tested within a restricted domain. But in the long run, small-scale theories of limited scope – theories of transfer, of communicative competence, of discourse processing, of the role of input – need to be made part of the larger picture.

Evaluating theory

The final topic in this introductory chapter concerns the criteria whereby theories are to be evaluated. Kaplan (1964) argued that norms of validation could be grouped in three categories: norms of correspondence, norms of coherence, and pragmatic norms. Norms of correspondence are most basic and correspond to the semantic level. Norms of coherence refer to the interrelation of the elements of the theory or the syntactic level. Norms of pragmatics refer to the functional or practical application of the theory.

Correspondence norms

There are two issues to be discussed here: (1) the correspondence of the concepts of the theory to some external reality, and (2) the correspondence of the theory to the facts the theory is to explain. The first issue refers to *definitional adequacy*; the second to *explanatory power*.

If a theory is to tell us anything about the world, it must contain empirical elements. There must be some connection to the intersubjective world of observation and experience, or the theory is indistinguishable from fantasy. In this sense theory construction is a social enterprise. Observations need to be described, analyses justified, and experiments replicated. Philosophers may argue about the possibility of intersubjectivity, but the enterprise of science presupposes some way out of solipsism.

The concepts of a theory need to be defined in a way that clarifies their meaning; that is, in such a manner that different persons will interpret them in the same way. The theorist may select terms from everyday language or may coin a new term for purposes of the theory. If the term is drawn from everyday language, the surplus meaning must be pared away, so that the ambiguity of everyday language is eliminated. If the term is a neologism, it can be precisely defined, but risks being misunderstood. For example, although most of the concepts used in theorizing about adult second-language learning are drawn from everyday language, there are some neologisms, such as the concept 'intake'. The problem is that this term has taken on a number of different meanings, and it is not always clear what a particular investigator means in using it. This, of course, is also a problem with terms drawn from everyday language – witness the confusion that surrounds the use of the term 'interference' in second-language research.

One attempt to overcome the vagueness of theoretical terms is the use of *operational definitions*. The idea is that a concept is synonymous with the operations that are necessary for its measurement. For example, an operational definition of 'language proficiency' is the score a learner achieves on a test designed to measure language proficiency. One problem with this approach is that of determining why one set of operations is chosen rather than another: why measure language proficiency in this way, with these instruments, rather than some other way? A more serious, and related, problem with operationalism is that there may legitimately be two, or more, different ways of measuring a concept. For example, 'reading ability' in a second language can be measured by the speed with which a text is read, by the number of errors a reader makes, or by scores on a test of comprehension. Thus, the same concept may have two or more operational definitions, and, presumably, two or more meanings.

Another problem with operationalism is that many concepts in a theory have only indirect reference to experience. Their empirical meaning depends on their relation to other concepts as fixed by their place in the theory. It is these other concepts that have a sufficiently direct application to experience to allow for specifying operations. For example, 'negative transfer' is something not directly observable; rather, one examines the errors that second-language learners make for evidence of negative transfer. Negative transfer is a *construct*, in that it is not directly observable, but may be inferred from an observation. Even more remote from experience are *hypothetical constructs*, which are not defined by reference to observables, but derive their meaning from the whole theory in which they are embedded and from their role in the theory. Thus, in social science, terms such as 'castration complex' and 'Protestant ethic' derive their meaning only from the specific theory in which they are embedded. There is no castration complex outside Freudian theory.

The possibility of theoretical constructs may make a strict operationalism impossible (in the sense that not all concepts in the theory will be tied directly to observable operations), but this does not deny the utility of tying the theory, at some level, to observables. If terms are not clearly defined, it is difficult to evaluate the theory's internal consistency, agreement with data, and testability. The more precisely the terms in a theory are defined, the more possible it becomes for the scientific community to determine the adequacy of the theory.

Theoretical adequacy, however, requires more than definitional precision. The theory must have explanatory power. It must fit the facts and go beyond them. Fitting the facts sometimes means restricting the theory to a more limited domain than was originally envisioned. The theorist's task is to construct a theory that includes as much as can be adequately handled by the set of theoretical principles, but that does not suffer from overgenerality. In the initial phases of theory development, in particular, there may be a tendency to extend the theory too far. Later research may show that the theory's range of applicability is more limited.

Going beyond the facts means that the theory cannot be so restricted that it simply explains the facts it was introduced to explain. Ad hoc theories do not move us to new predictions about new data. Good theories have generality: they extend to situations and events not specifically included in the phenomena that the theory was first set up to explain.

To explain phenomena is to do something more than to describe them in other terms. It is not enough to say that in learning a second language the learner moves from controlled to automatic processing (see chapter 6). Cognitive theory uses these concepts to say something about why some learning tasks are more difficult than others and about why the learning process takes the form it does. The concepts of controlled and automatic processing have meaning only in the context of the whole theory. In a sense, to explain is to illuminate the whole by reflecting light from the parts. It is the combination of all of the elements of the theory that makes us see or understand something in a new way.

Explanation gives insight into the 'why' of experience. This is not to say that one explanation is 'true' and all others 'false'. The insight provided by a good theory is not the only possible insight. Even the best of theories are restricted in their applicability and truth-value. Good theory meets the norms of correspondence when the 'why' it provides applies to a specified range of phenomena and when the conditions suitable to its application are met.

Norms of coherence

Here we come to the question of how the parts relate to each other and to the whole. Generally speaking, the more simple the theory, the greater its appeal to our understanding. The propositions, corollaries, and hypotheses of the theory should be stated in clearly understandable terms so that the theory is easily communicable to others in the field. Predictions should be straightforward and unequivocal.

The problem is that the phenomena in question might be complex and may require a complex explanation. As Poincaré put it:

If we study the history of science, we see happen two inverse phenomena, so to speak. Sometimes simplicity hides under complex appearances: sometimes it is the simplicity which is apparent and which disguises extremely complicated realities. (1913, 35)

Thus the search for simplicity needs to be tempered by a certain scepticism.

On the other hand, any theoretical enterprise needs the judicious use of Occam's razor. There needs be the commitment not to multiply variables unnecessarily. As Popper (1959) argued, the more complicated the theory, the less it says – because it becomes all the more difficult to falsify. Good theory is economical. A theory that accounts for given phenomena with fewer propositions is preferable to a theory that requires a greater number. *Ad hoc* explanations that apply to a specific instance or phenomenon complicate the theory and make it suspect. Furthermore, there are more escape hatches in more complicated theories: disconfirming facts are transformed into confirming evidence by the appeal to arguments that allow the theorist to have it both ways.

This is not to say that new principles and new concepts should not be added for the theory to account for new data. These modifications should be recognized as such, however. They may add complexity to the system, but the phenomena to be explained may require this complexity. On the other hand, it may be that a more simple theory will eventually replace an elaborated and complex theory, as the phenomena under study become better understood. Another possibility is that simpler theories of more limited scope come to be preferred to more general ones. I will argue in this book that this is the tendency in the field of second-language research.

There is another sense in which the norm of coherence may be applied. Certain theories may be discounted because they are inconsistent with what is presently known. Good theory usually fits in with the body of knowledge that is already established and is consistent with related theories that have gained acceptance. If a theory is inconsistent with related acceptable theories, it has relatively less antecedent probability of being valid. Kaplan (1964) gave the example of telepathy. Apart from the question of the reliability of the evidence in support of this notion, there is the problem that telepathy is wholly at variance with everything else we know about the transmission of information. For instance, unlike the transmission of all other forms of information, the propagation of telepathic information appears to be quite independent of the distance it traverses.

Again, there is a need for caution, because reliance on the test of consistency precludes the possibility of paradigm shifts – those cases in the history of a discipline when a totally new way of looking at the phenomena under study became acceptable. Rigid application of norms of coherence rules out the possibility of scientific revolutions. The shift from Skinner's view of language learning to that of Chomsky would have been impossible if the test of a theory's validity hinged on is consistency and continuity with past theories.

In short, the norm of coherence should be applied with care. The danger is that the search for simplicity and clarity will leave unexplained what may be most interesting in the data. Theories need to be open: they need to be capable of modification if the facts are stubborn. And sometimes theories and entire ways of thinking need to be abandoned. Theories are confirmed only to a certain degree. That a theory is validated does not mean that it is true, but only that it is more probable, at present, than other explanations. The history of science is one of successive approximations and occasional restructuring.

Pragmatic norms

We come now to the question of whether a theory is useful in any practical way. Kurt Lewin's famous dictum: 'There is nothing as practical as a good theory' needs to be read cautiously. Theory may not translate into practice for a number of reasons. For example, the theory may specify conditions that are not present in real situations. Language teachers who are careful to provide 'comprehensible input' (see chapter 2) to their students, may find their students, nonetheless, overwhelmed by the task of learning the target language because they are subject to so many other sources of input, such as TV and native speakers with whom the learner comes in contact in everyday life.

Furthermore, the tentative and open nature of theories of adult second-language learning makes most proponents nervous about spelling out practical implications. At this stage in our knowledge, it is a long step from theory to classroom practice. There are, as we shall see, some definite practical lessons to be learned from theories of language learning, but researchers who claim that their theories have been definitively substantiated by research are misleading practitioners.

More important than practical implications – especially in the early development of a field – is the question of how effectively the theory serves our scientific purposes. The role that a theory plays is largely dependent on how it guides and stimulates the ongoing process of scientific inquiry. If the theory is a dead end, it is bound to be abandoned. Thus the theory of language learning advocated by Skinner and the behaviourists was abandoned when it became recognized, not only that the answers it provided were inadequate, but also that it raised no new questions.

Thus, a theory is validated as much by what it suggests and hints at as by what it affirms explicitly. Validation is not merely a question of the theory's correspondence to the facts and internal coherence; there is also the question of the predictions the theory makes. Without rich heuristic value, the theory will eventually be deserted as researchers look to other theories that generate more hypotheses.

Confirmation

In addition to Kaplan's three norms for validity, there is another condition: falsifiability. A theory can fit the data well, can be consistent with related theory and elegant in its formulation, and it can be heuristically rich – without being falsifiable. That is, the theory can meet the criteria of norms of correspondence, norms of coherence, and pragmatic norms – and still be of little value. Theories that are self-contained cannot be tested. The theory may survive, though at best it will survive as an impervious fortress, perhaps invincible but in splendid isolation.

My favourite example from the social sciences is psychoanalytic theory. How does one test, for example, the psychoanalytic notion of repression? If a person recalls a traumatic incident from the past, the person is not repressing it. If the incident is not recalled, the person is repressing it. Therefore, both recall and failure to recall agree with the theory. The problem is that the theory is not falsifiable.

In any scientific endeavour the number of potentially positive hypotheses very greatly exceeds the number of hypotheses that in the long run will prove to be compatible with observations. As hypotheses are rejected, the theory is either disconfirmed or escapes being disconfirmed. But it is never confirmed. The results of observation 'probe' but do not 'prove' a theory. An adequate hypothesis is one that has repeatedly survived such probing – but it may always be displaced by a new probe (Campbell and Stanley 1963). This is the logic of statistical inference as well. The 'null hypothesis' cannot be accepted; it can only be rejected or fail to be rejected.

This leads to the question of how advances are made if hypotheses are never proven or confirmed. They do gain acceptability, however, as rival hypotheses are disconfirmed. The fewer the number of plausible rival hypotheses available to account for the data, the more confidence one has in the validity of the theory. Note, however, that in any stage in the accumulation of evidence – even in the most advanced physical sciences – there are numerous possible theories compatible with the data. Theories are 'well established' when few rivals are practical or seriously proposed.

But even theories that are 'well established' in this sense are limited in their truth value. Other perspectives and other 'symbol systems' may be equally valid. Each helps us to understand the phenomena better, but no one theory has a monopoly on truth. Scientific knowledge in any field grows when the phenomena to be accounted for are viewed from diverse perspectives.

To conclude, I have argued in this chapter that scientific progress is achieved as we come to illuminate progressively our knowledge by taking different perspectives and by utilizing diverse methods of research. Good theories fit the data well, are consistent with related formulations, are clear in their predictions, and are heuristically rich. Perhaps most important, they are capable of disconfirmation. In the remainder of this book, leading theoretical approaches to adult second-language learning will be reviewed and evaluated against the criteria discussed in this chapter.

2

The Monitor Model

The most ambitious theory of the second-language learning process is Stephen Krashen's Monitor Model. The theory evolved in the late 1970s in a series of articles (Krashen 1977a, 1977b, 1978a, 1978b), and was elaborated and expanded in a number of books (Krashen 1981, 1982, 1985; Krashen and Terrell 1983). Krashen has argued that his account provides a general or 'overall theory' (1985, 1) of second-language acquisition with important implications for language teaching. According to Krashen, the theory is supported by a large number of scientific studies in a wide variety of language acquisition and learning contexts. This research is seen to provide empirical validation for a particular method of elementary language instruction – the Natural Approach (Krashen and Terrell 1983).

Krashen's theory has achieved considerable popularity among second-language teachers in the United States. This is due in large measure to his ability to package his ideas in a way that makes them readily understandable to practitioners. On the other hand, the theory has been seriously criticized on various grounds by second-language researchers and theorists (Gregg 1984; Long 1985b; McLaughlin 1978; Taylor 1984). Indeed, 'Krashen-bashin' has become a favourite pastime at conferences and in journals dealing with second-language research.

In this chapter the limitations of the theory will become apparent. I have been critical because I believe that excessive claims have been made for a theory that fails to meet the criteria discussed in chapter 1 for good theory. Krashen should be given credit, however, for attempting to bring together research findings from a number of different domains. One can disagree with the interpretation of these findings and still admire the ingenuity and insightfulness of the theorist.

Krashen's theory can be placed on the deductive side of the inductive–deductive continuum. That is, the theory begins with a number of assumptions, from which hypotheses are derived. These assumptions are not clearly stated by Krashen, but will be discussed in the following pages. The theory also has a number of metaphors, one of which, as we shall see, is the Monitor, or mental editor, that utilizes conscious grammatical knowledge to determine the form of produced utterances. The Monitor is thought to play a minor role in the second-language process, however, and in recent years Krashen has apparently abandoned the term 'Monitor theory'. Nonetheless, because this term remains generally used in the literature, it will be retained here.

Krashen argued that experimental and other data are consistent with a set of five basic hypotheses, which together constitute his theory. In this chapter, I will discuss these five central hypotheses:

(1)   The Acquisition–Learning Hypothesis
(2)   The Monitor Hypothesis
(3)   The Natural Order Hypothesis
(4)   The Input Hypothesis
(5)   The Affective Filter Hypothesis

In each instance, I will look at whether the data support the hypothesis. The concluding section reviews the argument of the chapter and evaluates the success of the theory in meeting the criteria for good theory discussed in chapter 1.

The Acquisition–Learning Hypothesis

Krashen maintained that adult second-language learners have at their disposal two distinct and independent ways of developing competence in a second language: *acquisition*, which is 'a subconscious process identical in all important ways to the process children utilize in acquiring their first language' (1985, 1) and *learning*, which is 'a conscious process that results in "knowing about" language' (1985, 1). Acquisition comes about through meaningful interaction in a natural communication setting. Speakers are not concerned with form, but with meaning; nor is there explicit concern with error detection and correction. This contrasts with the language learning situation in which error detection and correction are central, as is typically the case in classroom settings, where formal rules and feedback provide the basis for language instruction.

Nonetheless, for Krashen it is not the setting *per se*, but conscious attention to rules that distinguishes language acquisition from language learning. In the natural setting an adult can obtain formal instruction by asking informants about grammar and by receiving feedback from friends. Similarly, language can be acquired in the classroom when the focus is on communication – for example, through dialogues, role-playing, and other forms of meaningful interaction.

But if setting is not the distinguishing characteristic of acquisition and learning in Krashen's sense, it is important for him to make clear what he means by 'conscious' and 'subconscious'. Krashen has not provided a definition of these terms, although he did operationally identify conscious learning with judgements of grammaticality based on 'rule' and subconscious acquisition with judgements based on 'feel' (Krashen *et al*. 1978). The difficulty with such an approach is that it is impossible to know whether subjects in this experiment were actually operating on the basis of rule or feel. Krashen and his colleagues had their subjects state the rule when they made judgements on the basis of rule, but they may have done so because the demand characteristics of the situation emphasized rule articulation. Moreover, subjects may have given feel answers because they were not quite sure as to how to articulate the rule on the basis of which they had operated. Aside from this attempt, Krashen has provided no way of independently determining whether a given process involves acquisition or learning.

Does learning become acquisition?

The slipperiness of the acquisition–learning distinction becomes more apparent when one considers the evidence for the first corollary of the distinction (and one of the central tenets of Krashen's theory): that 'learning does not "turn into" acquisition' (1982, 83). That is, according to Krashen, what is consciously learned – through the presentation of rules and explanations of grammar – does not become the basis of acquisition of the target language. The argument that conscious learning does not become unconscious acquisition is based on three claims (Krashen 1982, 83–7):

(1) Sometimes there is 'acquisition' without 'learning' – that is, some individuals have considerable competence in a second language but do not know very many rules consciously.
(2) There are cases where 'learning' never becomes 'acquisition' – that is, a person can know the rule and continue breaking it, and
(3) No one knows anywhere near all the rules.

All of these arguments may be true, but they do not constitute evidence in support of the claim that learning does not become acquisition. Kevin Gregg (1984) pointed out that such a claim runs counter to the intuitive belief of many second-language learners, for whom it seems obvious that at least some rules can be acquired through learning. He gave the example of having learned the rules for forming the past tense and gerundive forms of Japanese verbs by memorizing the conjugation chart in his textbook. In a few days his use of these forms was error-free, with no input but a bit of drill. Gregg's point is that he – and his classmates – had 'learned' the rules and these rules had become 'acquired' – in the sense of meeting the criterion of error-free, rapid production – without meaningful interaction with native speakers.

Krashen argued that the experience that Gregg described merely 'looks like' (1981, 117) learning causes acquisition. He gave the example of an individual who had learned in a classroom a rule such as the third person singular morpheme for regular verbs in English. This individual was able to apply this conscious rule at Time 1, but it was only later, at Time 2 – after meaningful input from native speakers – that the rule was acquired. Krashen contended that the learner was 'faking it' until his acquisition caught up, or until he arrived at the rule 'naturally' (1981, 118). Until Time 2, he was outperforming his acquired competence. He was able to apply the rule when given enough time and when focusing on form, but had not yet 'acquired' it.

At issue here is Gregg's subjective sense that he, and learners like him, apply the rule rapidly and without making mistakes regardless of context versus Krashen's contention that such application occurs only when certain conditions are met. Krashen's argument has a suspicious *ad hoc* ring to it, but the most troubling aspect of this disagreement is that it is difficult to support one position or the other until it is clear what is meant by 'acquisition' and 'learning'. I had raised this issue in my critique of Krashen's theory (McLaughlin 1978) in commenting on my own inability to determine whether acquisition or learning was involved in my production of certain German sentences. Remarkably, Krashen, in his reply (1979), was able to specify how much of each was involved in the utterances. This was not the point, however. The point is that there needs to be some objective way of determining what is acquisition and what is learning. This Krashen did not supply.

Krashen (1979) argued that the acquisition–learning distinction is an abstraction that predicts many observable and concrete phenomena. He compared his hypothesis to hypotheses in cognitive psychology that are based on abstractions used to predict measurable phenomena. But the abstractions used in cognitive psychology, as Krashen correctly pointed out, are defined by special experimental conditions. If the acquisition–learning hypothesis is to be tested, one needs to know what experimental conditions are necessary to bring out the differences between these two processes.

Can adults 'acquire' a language as children do?

As was noted above, Krashen maintained that acquisition is 'a subconscious process identical in all important ways to the process children utilize in acquiring their first language' (1985, 1). Indeed, Krashen argued that adult acquirers have access to the same 'Language Acquisition Device' (LAD) that children use (1982). As Gregg (1984) has pointed out, Krashen appears to be giving the LAD a scope of operation much wider than is normally the case in linguistic theory. Krashen seemed to equate LAD with unconscious acquisition of any sort; in contrast, Chomsky (1980), who invented the LAD notion, saw the mind as modular, with the LAD as but one of various 'mental organs' that interact with each other and with the input to produce linguistic competence.

According to Chomsky, the LAD is a construct that describes the child's initial state, before the child receives linguistic input from the environment. The LAD is constrained by innate linguistic universals to generate grammars that account for the input. It is not clear how the concept of LAD can be applied to an adult (Gregg 1984). The adult is no longer in the initial state with respect to language and is also endowed with more fully developed cognitive structures.

In fact, Chomsky stated at one point (1968) that he believed that whereas first-language acquisition takes place through the essential language faculty, which atrophies at a certain age, it is still possible to learn a language after that age by using such other mental faculties as the logical or the mathematical. This suggests that for Chomsky, the ability to use LAD declines with age and that adult second-language learners must rely on other 'mental organs'.

More recently, however, Chomsky has made some statements about second-language performance that seem compatible with Krashen's argument that adults and children have access to the same LAD. Chomsky maintained that 'people learn language from pedagogical grammars by the use of their unconscious universal grammar' (1975, 249). If one assumes that the LAD is constrained by an innate universal grammar that enables the child or adult second-language learner to project grammars to account for the input from speakers of the target language, then Universal Grammar theory appears to be consistent with Krashen's notions. Indeed, Krashen argued that Chomsky's (1975) distinction between to 'cognize' and to 'know' 'is quite similar, if not identical, to the acquisition–learning distinction' (1985, 24). It seems, however, that Chomsky's concepts are not coterminous with Krashen's, because for Chomsky one can 'cognize' both what is accessible to consciousness and what is not (1975, 165), whereas for Krashen 'acquisition' refers only to what is subconscious.

On closer examination, it is difficult to fit Krashen's notions within contemporary Universal Grammar theory. As Flynn (1985) noted, Universal Grammar theory is focused on abstract and linguistically significant principles that are assumed to underlie all natural languages. These principles are argued to comprise the essential language facility with which all individuals are in general uniformly and equally endowed. The application of this theory to second-language learning in adults will be discussed in more detail in chapter 4. As we shall see, principles of the Universal Grammar are hypothesized to involve properties described as parameters. Language acquisition is seen as a process of setting the values of the parameters of these universal principles, and not as a problem of acquiring grammatical rules. This is a very different enterprise from the one that concerns Krashen.

Thus the second corollary of the acquisition–learning distinction cannot be supported on the basis of the arguments advanced by Krashen. The claim that adults acquire languages in the same way as children do rests on a faulty understanding of the LAD. Like the first corollary – that learning does not become acquisition – no empirical evidence is provided in support of the claim. In fact, both corollaries are not falsifiable because the central concepts to be tested – acquisition and learning – are poorly defined.

The Monitor Hypothesis

According to Krashen, 'learning' and 'acquisition' are used in very specific ways in second-language performance. The Monitor Hypothesis states that 'Learning has only one function, and that is as a Monitor or editor' and that learning comes into play only to 'make changes in the form of our utterance, after it has been "produced" by the acquired system' (1982, 15). Acquisition 'initiates' the speaker's utterances and is responsible for fluency. Thus the Monitor is thought to alter the output of the acquired system before or after the utterance is actually written or spoken, but the utterance is initiated entirely by the acquired system.

This hypothesis has important implications for language teaching. Krashen argued that formal instruction in a language provides rule isolation and feedback for the development of the Monitor, but that production is based on what is acquired through communication, with the Monitor altering production to improve accuracy toward target-language norms. Krashen's position is that conscious knowledge of rules does not help acquisition, but only enables the learner to 'polish up' what has been acquired through communication. The focus of language teaching, for Krashen, should not be rule-learning but communication.

One interesting implication of Krashen's argument is that learning is available only for use in production, not in comprehension. Krashen provides no evidence for this claim and, indeed, as Gregg pointed out, this is a rather counter-intuitive notion. Gregg, who lives in Japan, gave an example from his own experience:

The other day while listening to the radio, I heard the announcer announce *wagunaa no kageki, kamigami no kasoware*. Knowing that *kageki* = 'opera' and that *kami* = either 'god' or 'hair' or 'paper', and knowing that there is a (fairly unproductive) rule in Japanese for pluralizing by reduplication, I concluded that *kamigami* must be the plural of *kami*, 'god', that therefore *wagunaa* must be Wagner and *kasoware* must mean 'twilight', and that I was in danger of hearing *Die Götterdämmerung*. Of course I was not quite right: there is no word *kasoware*, it's *tasogare*. But the point is that I was using a rule that I had 'learned' (and never used productively), and using that rule consciously (and quickly enough to turn the radio off in time). . . . Which suggests that 'learning' can indeed be used in comprehension, as no one before Krashen would have doubted. (1984, 82–3).

The three conditions for Monitor use

As we have seen, the Monitor acts as a sort of editor that is consciously controlled and that makes changes in the form of utterances produced by acquisition. Krashen has specified three conditions for use of the Monitor:

(1) *Time*. In order to think about and use conscious rules effectively, a second language performer needs to have sufficient time. For most people, normal conversation does not allow enough time to think about and use rules. The over-use of rules in conversation can lead to trouble, i.e., a hesitant style of talking and inattention to what the conversational partner is saying.

(2) *Focus on form*. To use the Monitor effectively, time is not enough. The performer must also be focussed on form, or thinking about correctness . . . Even when we have time, we may be so involved in *what* we are saying that we do not attend to *how* we are saying it.

(3) *Know the rule*. This may be a very formidable requirement. Linguistics has taught us that the structure of language is extremely complex, and they [sic] claim to have described only a fragment of the best known languages. We can be sure that our students are exposed only to a small part of the total grammar of the language, and we know that even the best students do not learn every rule they are exposed to. (Krashen 1982, 16)

Krashen seems unsure of the first condition, time. In his latest book he mentioned only the last two conditions (1985, 2). His thinking in this respect was modified by results of a study by Hulstijn and Hulstijn

(1984), who independently manipulated focus on form and time with adult second-language learners (English speakers learning Dutch). When the subjects were focused on form without time pressure, there were gains in accuracy, as the Monitor theory predicts. But when there was no focus on form, giving subjects more time did not make a difference in their performance. Krashen agreed that this was evidence that the availability of extra time does not, alone, involve the Monitor.

The second condition for use of the Monitor, focusing on form, is also problematic. In several studies, focusing subjects on form by having them correct spelling and grammar in written composition did not result in use of the Monitor (Houck *et al*. 1978; Krashen *et al*. 1978). Krashen's solution to this problem was to add another condition: the subject must be focused on form and the test must be an 'extreme' discrete-point test that centres on just one item or rule at a time. Even this condition does not, however, suffice to produce the Monitor. Fathman (1975) and Fuller (1978) found that instructions to focus on form did not result in the gain in accuracy that use of the Monitor should produce. The test they used to elicit language seems to meet the criterion of an extreme discrete-point test in that subjects were shown pictures and asked such questions as *Here is a ball. Here are two* ——. with the expectation that they would produce the plural.

It appears to be rather difficult to demonstrate the operation of the Monitor in such studies and Krashen's repeated failures to do so are explained away by changing the requirements. As he put it, 'Again, I do reserve the right to change my hypothesis in the light of new data' (1979, 155). This is true, but for the researcher attempting to test the theory, the constant modifications are frustrating. Seliger (1979) concluded that the Monitor is limited to such specific output modalities and requires such carefully confined conditions for its operation that it cannot be thought to be representative of the learner's internal, conscious knowledge of the grammar.

The third condition, that the learner knows the rules, has also been challenged by the research of Hulstijn and Hulstijn (1984). In their study, subjects' rule knowledge, as assessed in an interview, did not relate to how much subjects gained in performance from focus on form and absence of time pressure. Focus on form and time had the same effect on learners who could correctly verbalize the rules, for learners who could not state any explicit rules at all, and for learners who stated partly correct, or even incorrect, rules. Krashen's attempt to explain away these findings as due to 'inter-stage fluctuation' (1985, 22) is shamelessly *ad hoc*. Once such explanations are invoked, the theory becomes completely untestable.

In short, Krashen has not been able to demonstrate that the putative conditions for Monitor use do in fact lead to its application. What research on this issue has demonstrated is either (1) that the Monitor is rarely employed under the normal conditions of second-language acquisition and use, or (2) that the Monitor is a theoretically useless concept. Krashen has argued lately for the first conclusion (1985), but if the Monitor is the only means whereby conscious knowledge of the rules of a second language ('learning') is utilized, then why make the learning–acquisition distinction? If learning occurs only under such rarified conditions, what role can it possibly have in gaining competence in a second language?

Individual differences

In spite of the difficulties of demonstrating Monitor use under experimental conditions, Krashen has based his explanation of individual differences in second-language performance on the Monitor concept. He distinguished three types of Monitor users:

(1) *Monitor over users*. These are people who attempt to Monitor all the time, performers who are constantly checking their output with their conscious knowledge of the second language. As a result, such performers may speak hesitantly, often self-correct in the middle of utterances, and are so concerned with correctness that they cannot speak with any real fluency. . . .

(2) *Monitor under-users*. These are performers who have not learned, or if they have learned, prefer not to use their conscious knowledge, even when conditions allow it. Under-users are typically uninfluenced by error correction, can self-correct only by using a 'feel' for correctness (e.g., 'it sounds right'), and rely completely on the acquired system. . . .

(3) *The optimal Monitor user*. Our pedagogical goal is to produce optimal users, performers who use the Monitor when it is appropriate and when it does not interfere with communication. Many optimal users will not use grammar in ordinary conversation, where it might interfere. . . . In writing, and in planned speech, however, when there is time, optimal users will typically make whatever corrections they can to raise the accuracy of their output. . . . (1982, 19–20)

According to Krashen, Monitor over-users are either individuals who have been 'victims' of a grammar-only type of instruction or individuals who are inclined by personality to learn languages by consciously applying rules. In contrast, under-users are those individuals who are thought to make no, or very little, use of conscious rules. The evidence for these different types of performers is based on case studies.

How is one to know, however, when an individual is consciously applying a rule? As Gregg (1984) noted, Krashen made the serious mistake of equating 'rules' with the rules of the grammarian. But these are usually not the rules that individuals learning a second language apply in their speech. Language learners have inchoate and not very precise rules that guide them in forming utterances. They may not be able to articulate these rules with any accuracy and resort to them more or less consciously. Nonetheless, speech is a rule-governed process, and a person trying to communicate in a second language will not get far by throwing words together at random. From a linguist's point of view, the rules that speakers use may be incorrect and inadequate, but they are often sufficient to get the right sounds uttered in the right order.

The question of how conscious these rules are is difficult (perhaps impossible) to answer. It can be argued that most of the rules with which language learners operate are informal rules of limited scope and imperfect validity. These rules lead to conscious decisions in processing language:

> We know *something* that seems right or wrong, even when we don't think of or know the proper rule from a formal system. (Dulany *et al*. 1984, 554)

It may be that rules that were once conscious continue to control at an unconscious level. But the automatic processing that such rules allow is not the product of an internalized Monitor that applies formal rules, but rather is the automatized residue of informal rules the learner once had consciously in mind (Dulany *et al*. 1984). Be that as it may, once one allows that learners operate with informal and inchoate rules, it becomes much more difficult to determine whether the rules are being consciously employed in any specific case.

What does it mean, then, to say that some people are 'over' users and some 'under' users of the Monitor? Everyone uses rules; the differences Krashen observed in his case studies seem to relate to differences in ability to use and articulate the specific grammatical rules that were learned in the classroom. It is not necessary to invoke the Monitor to account for such differences, and because the concept has such little empirical justification, it seems unwise to do so.

Adult–child differences

The Monitor also plays an important role in Krashen's explanation of adult–child differences in language learning:

> Formal operations are hypothesized to be responsible for the birth of the extensive conscious Monitor (granting that children may have some meta-awareness of language). . . . Formal operations also have certain affective consequences, which may be aggravated by biological puberty. These affective changes affect

our ability to acquire (they strengthen the 'affective filter' . . .). (1979, 153)

Children are therefore thought to be superior language learners, because they do not use the Monitor and are not as inhibited as older learners. The second claim, relating to the Affective Filter Hypothesis, will be discussed later. At issue here is what evidence there is that lack of the Monitor in childhood leads to superior competence in a second language.

The first question is whether children are indeed superior in language-learning ability. Krashen (1979) argued that the research evidence is that adolescents and adults are faster language learners in the initial stages, but that young children do better in terms of their eventual attainment. That is, he distinguished *rate* and *ultimate attainment*. I have argued elsewhere (McLaughlin 1984) that there is no evidence in support of this argument. Instead, research on syntactic and semantic variables consistently supports the argument that older learners are better both in terms of rate and ultimate attainment. It is only in the area of phonological development that younger children do better, although even here the evidence is not unequivocal. In any event, the Monitor notion has not been applied by Krashen to phonological development.

What research shows is that early adolescence is the best age for language learning – both in terms of rate of learning and ultimate attainment. Particularly impressive is the evidence that Canadian English-speaking 12- and 13-year-old children in 'late' French immersion programmes do just as well as children from the same background who were in 'early' French immersion programmes beginning in kindergarten and who had twice as many hours of exposure to French (McLaughlin 1985). If Krashen's argument is correct, young adolescents who are at the stage of formal operations in Piaget's sense would be expected to be heavy Monitor users and therefore poor performers. But their performance seems even better than that of young children.

A second problem with Krashen's argument is that it assumes that the use of the Monitor interferes with performance. Hence children who have not developed the Monitor have, a priori, an advantage in language learning. But is it necessarily true that using the Monitor (i.e., applying conscious knowledge of the rules of a language) interferes with performance? Many learners would argue that knowing and applying the rules helps them perform better, though they might be slowed down. Perhaps using the Monitor actually leads to better performance and this is why adolescents do so well.

Certainly there is a sense, which many learners share, that what they have consciously learned becomes the basis for unconscious and automatic performance. According to Krashen, this is illusory, because conscious learning can never be transformed into unconscious acquisition. Learning, through the Monitor, acts only as an editor on utterances that are initiated through acquisition. The problem is that it is impossible to prove this argument either way. We simply cannot unequivocally identify the knowledge source in any utterance.

Furthermore, Krashen's argument leaves unexplained well-documented cases of self-taught learners who gained facility in a language without any opportunity for 'acquiring' it. In many cases these were individuals with knowledge of several other languages who learned with great rapidity and to a remarkable level of proficiency – without contact with native speakers.

To conclude this section, the Monitor Hypothesis has been criticized on a number of scores. First, it has proven rather difficult to show evidence of Monitor use. The Monitor requires such restricted conditions for its operation that it cannot be thought to be representative of the learner's internal, conscious knowledge of the target language. Even if one posits a Monitor as representing conscious knowledge of a language, that knowledge is quite different from what Krashen attributed to the Monitor. People have rules for language use in their heads, but these rules are not those of the grammarian. People operate on the basis of informal rules of limited scope and validity. These rules are sometimes conscious and sometimes not, but in any given utterance it is impossible to determine what the knowledge source is. Thus in a real sense, the Monitor Hypothesis is untestable. Finally, the argument from adult–child differences is based on two unproven assumptions: that children are, ultimately, superior to adults in language performance, and that Monitor use interferes with performance.

The Natural Order Hypothesis

The Natural Order Hypothesis states:

> that we acquire the rules of language in a predictable order, some rules tending to come early and others late. The order does not appear to be determined solely by formal simplicity and there is evidence that it is independent of the order in which rules are taught in language classes. (Krashen 1985, 1)

In addition, Krashen argued that those whose exposure to second language is nearly all outside of language classes do not show a different order of acquisition from those who have had most of their second-language experience in the classroom. This 'natural' order of acquisition is presumed to be the result of the acquired system, operating free of conscious grammar, or the Monitor.

In this section, I will discuss the evidence for the Natural Order

Hypothesis, some methodological problems with research on this topic, and the question of what the Natural Order Hypothesis tells us about the second-language acquisition process. Because of the amount of research that has been conducted on this question, this discussion will be relatively brief. Fuller treatments appear in Hakuta and Cancino (1977), McLaughlin (1984), and Wode (1981).

Evidence for a 'natural' order

The principal source of evidence for the Natural Order Hypothesis comes from the so-called 'morpheme' studies. In 1974, Dulay and Burt published a study of what they called the order of acquisition of grammatical morphemes or 'functors' in English by five- to eight-year-old children learning English as a second language (1974b). Their work was based on a finding reported by Roger Brown (1973) from research with children learning English as a first language. According to Brown there is a common – 'invariant' – sequence of acquisition for at least 14 functors, or function words in English that have a minor role in conveying sentence meaning – noun and verb inflections, articles, auxiliaries, copulas, and prepositions such as *in* and *on*. Dulay and Burt were interested in whether children who acquire English as a second language learn these functors in the same sequence.

In their research they used an instrument called the Bilingual Syntax Measure (Burt *et al.* 1975), which consists of cartoon pictures and a series of questions. The questions are designed to elicit spontaneous speech that should contain most of the morphemes described by Brown. For example, in response to a picture of a very fat man and the question, 'Why is he so fat?' the child might say, 'He eats too much and doesn't exercise.' Using this instrument, Dulay and Burt looked at the

Table 2.1 Morpheme rank order

Morpheme	Form	Example
Pronoun case	he, him	He doesn't like him.
Article	a, the	The man ate a sandwich.
Copula	be, am, is, are	The dog is angry.
Progressive	-ing	The man is eating.
Plural	-s	His hands are dirty.
Auxiliary	be + verb + -ing	The froggie is drinking milk.
Regular past	-ed	The froggie disappeared.
Irregular past	came, went	He came back.
Long plural	-es	He builds houses.
Possessive	-'s	My friend's bag.
3rd person singular	-s	The man runs fast.

Based on Dulay and Burt 1974b.

accuracy order of eleven morphemes in children's speech, by determining what percentage of times a subject correctly supplied a morpheme in an obligatory context. This accuracy order was assumed to reflect acquisition order. Examination of a small corpora of speech from 60 Spanish-speaking children in Long Island and 55 Chinese-speaking children in New York City revealed that the sequence of acquisition of the functors was virtually the same for both groups (Table 2.1).

Note that Dulay and Burt lumped together children with different amounts of exposure to the second language and measured 'acquisition sequence' by the degree to which the functors were correctly supplied in the speech samples. Their study was not a longitudinal study, and, strictly speaking, they did not measure *acquisition sequence* but rather *accuracy of use* in obligatory contexts. Other cross-sectional studies are open to the same criticism.

Krashen cited the research of Dulay and Burt as well as a number of other studies of second-language acquisition with adults and children. He concluded:

> This survey also found no significant cross-sectional–longitudinal differences and no significant individual differences among acquirers when a minimum of ten obligatory occasions is used for each item and the data are gathered in a 'Monitor-free' condition. (1985, 20)

Unfortunately, Krashen's survey does not tell the whole story.

For one thing, the results of longitudinal studies do not always agree with the results of cross-sectional research. Studies of individual children across time have shown different patterns from those observed in cross-sectional work (Hakuta 1976; Rosansky 1976). It may be that grouping data in cross-sectional research obscures individual variation. Group curves do not necessarily reflect accuracy order for any one individual in the group (Andersen 1978; Huebner 1979), nor, as we have seen, do they necessarily tell us much about order of acquisition.

One source of deviation from a 'natural' order is the learner's first language. Hakuta and Cancino (1977) have argued that the semantic complexity of the morphemes may vary depending on the learner's native language. They cited research that indicates that where a second-language learner's first language does not make the same discriminations as the target language, more difficulty in learning to use these morphemes occurs than is the case for learners whose first language makes the semantic discrimination. Thus, Korean children, whose language has no article equivalents, performed more poorly on the article in morpheme studies than did children whose language, such as Spanish, contains articles. Similarly, longitudinal research showed that a Japanese child had great difficulty with the English definite/ indefinite article contrast, presumably because Japanese lacks this semantic discrimination.

Evidence of transfer from the first language has been obtained in a number of studies dealing with acquisitional sequences (see McLaughlin 1984). Longitudinal studies of child second-language learners provides support for the notion that children will use first-language structures to solve the riddle of second-language forms, especially where there is syntactic congruity between structures (Wode 1981) or morphological similarity (Zobl 1979). Thus Krashen's claim that an invariant natural order is always found is simply not true.

Methodological issues

Aside from the question of whether it is legitimate to infer 'natural' developmental sequences from accuracy data based on cross-sectional research, there are other important methodological issues in the morpheme studies. For example, Hatch (1983) has pointed out that it is possible to score morphemes as acquired when, in fact, the function of the morpheme has not been acquired. Many learners, she contended, produce large numbers of -ing verb forms in the beginning stages of learning. If, as in most morpheme studies, the morpheme is scored as correct when it is used appropriately in an obligatory context, it will look as if the -ing form is being used correctly when it is being used excessively, in correct and incorrect contexts.

Hatch has pointed out another, more subtle issue. In most morpheme research, analyses are conducted on the basis of rank-order data, with the proportion of appropriate uses in obligatory contexts as the index of accuracy of usage. When learners from different language backgrounds are compared, it is assumed that the distance between the ranked morphemes is equal. That is, the distance between the third and fourth morphemes as ranked in accuracy for Chinese subjects is assumed to be the same as the distance between the third and fourth morphemes for Spanish-speaking subjects. But if, say, the third and fourth ranking morphemes for the two groups were the copula and the article, it is conceivable the same ranks conceal large differences in accuracy. The mean scores for the copula and the article might show large differences for the Chinese subjects, but small differences for the Spanish-speaking subjects. These differences are lost when statistics are used that are based on ranked data (e.g., the Spearman rho correlation method, which is normally used in morpheme research).

Another problem is that by adopting the list of morphemes developed by Brown for first-language research, investigators may have inadvertently lumped together morphemes that may differ in difficulty for second-language learners. Thus, for example, the definite and indefinite articles may not be of equal difficulty for all learners of English, but the scoring procedures allow for no distinction. Indeed, this is precisely what Andersen (1978) found to be the case in his research with Spanish-speaking subjects.

Finally, there is the question of whether the finding of a 'natural' order in morpheme accuracy is instrument- and task-specific. This question was raised by Larsen-Freeman (1975), who found a strong relationship between accuracy scores for adult second-language learners and child second-language learners when the data were obtained on the Bilingual Syntax Measure. However, when she looked at other tasks, using other instruments, she did not find that correlations between adult and child accuracy scores were as strong. This led her to conclude that one should be careful about claims of an invariant order of acquisition based on morpheme research.

The Natural Hypothesis and the acquisition process

It should be pointed out that Krashen did not base his claim for the validity of the Natural Order Hypothesis on morpheme research alone. He also maintained that there is a 'natural' sequence for the development of the negative, the auxiliary system, questions, and inflections in English, and for a number of constructions in other languages. He admitted that there is individual variation, but concluded that

> we can certainly speak of some rules as being early-acquired and others as being late-acquired, and of predictable stages of acquisition (1985, 21).

There is a definite need to allow for individual variation in any description of the second-language acquisition process, because evidence on this score is hard to ignore (McLaughlin 1984). The learner's first language can make the acquisition of certain forms in a target language more difficult than they are for learners with other first languages (Wode 1981; Zobl 1979). The frequency of certain forms in the speech the learner hears can affect developmental sequences (Larsen-Freeman 1976). It has even been suggested that, until we know more about developmental sequences in a large number of languages, we cannot rule out the possibility that some systems of a given language will be acquired in predictable sequences whereas others will not be subject to any particular acquisition sequence (Lightbown 1985). Finally, research indicates that different learning strategies can produce different acquisition patterns in individuals acquiring the same target language (Vihman 1982).

Krashen recognized the limitations of a strict linear view of the Natural Order Hypothesis and postulated that 'several streams of development are taking place at the same time' (1982, 53–4). He did not, however, define what he meant by 'streams of development' nor did he say how many 'streams' could flow at once. As Gregg (1984) pointed out, the possibility of more than one stream vitiates the Natural Order Hypothesis.

Evidence for individual variation points to a central problem with the Natural Order Hypothesis as advanced by Krashen: The hypothesis says little or nothing about the *process* of acquiring a second language. Research by Wode *et al.* (1978) has indicated that individual second-language learners take different routes; they decompose complex structural patterns and rebuild them step by step, attaining varying degrees of target-like proficiency. This process cannot be captured by research that focuses on the accuracy of use of specific morphemes in large cross-sectional samples of second-language learners. And longitudinal case studies, when they are carefully done, provide considerable evidence for erroneous premature forms, incomplete intermediate structures, formulaic utterances, avoidance tendencies, and patterns of acquisition that are dependent on affective factors and language contact (Meisel *et al.* 1981; Wode *et al.* 1978; Wong Fillmore 1976). This richness is lost in an analysis that focuses on final form or on superficial developmental similarities.

Thus the case study literature indicates a much greater complexity than Krashen has acknowledged. Commenting on this complexity, Hatch observed:

> if the form is naturally easy, it may be acquired early even though its function is not known. On the other hand, if the function is clear (e.g., plurality), it may *not* be acquired early *if* the affix is not regular. . . . In other words, the naturalness rules for morphology may have to be stated in terms of if/then statements, and orders may have to be assigned to each of these rules as well. (1983, 55)

To conclude, Krashen's argument for the Natural Order Hypothesis is based largely on the morpheme studies, which have been criticized on various grounds and which, by focusing on final form, tell us little about acquisitional sequences. Research that has looked at the developmental sequence for specific grammatical forms indicates that there is individual variation and that there may be several different developmental streams leading to target-like competence. If the Natural Order Hypothesis is to be accepted, it must be in a weak form, which postulates that some things are learned before others, but not always. Lacking a theory of why this is the case, such an hypothesis does not tell us much.

The Input Hypothesis

If we assume, as Krashen does, that learners progress through 'natural' developmental sequences, we need some mechanism to account for how they go from one point to another. This is one role of the Input Hypothesis in Krashen's theory. This hypothesis postulates that

> humans acquire language in only one way – by understanding messages, or by receiving 'comprehensible input'. . . . We move from *i*, our current level, to *i + 1*, the next level along the natural order, by understanding input containing *i + 1*. (Krashen 1985, 2)

Krashen regarded this as 'the single most important concept in second language acquisition today', in that 'it attempts to answer the critical question of how we acquire language' (1980, 168).

There are two corollaries of the Input Hypothesis:

(1) Speaking is a result of acquisition and not its cause. Speech cannot be taught directly but 'emerges' on its own as a result of building competence via comprehensible input.
(2) If input is understood, and there is enough of it, the necessary grammar is automatically provided. The language teacher need not attempt deliberately to teach the next structure along the natural order – it will be provided in just the right quantities and automatically reviewed if the student receives a sufficient amount of comprehensible input. (1985, 2)

Thus for Krashen comprehensible input is the route to acquisition and information about grammar in the target language is automatically available when the input is understood.

In *The Input Hypothesis* (1985), Krashen listed ten lines of evidence in support of this hypothesis. He acknowledged that alternative explanations could not be excluded in every case, but argued that the Input Hypothesis had validity because it provided an explanation for all of these phenomena. This is a typical Krashen strategy, one I have criticized before in discussing an earlier version of his theory (McLaughlin 1978). What Krashen does is not provide 'evidence' in any real sense of the term, but simply argue that certain phenomena can be viewed from the perspective of his theory. In this section, I will review seven of these lines of 'evidence', and in the next section I will turn to the remaining three, which deserve more extended treatment because they are most critical for the theory.

Some lines of evidence for the Input Hypothesis

The silent period
One phenomenon that Krashen saw as evidence in support of the Input

Hypothesis was the silent period. Though not as typical as Krashen would have us believe, this phenomenon has been observed to occur in some children who come to a new country where they are exposed to a new language, and are silent for a long period of time. During this period they are presumably building up their competence in the language by listening. Krashen argued that they are making use of the 'comprehensible input' they receive. Once competence has been built up, speech emerges.

This is hardly evidence for the Input Hypothesis. The mere fact that some learners are hesitant to speak for a time when they are put in a new linguistic environment does not address the question of how language is acquired. Krashen's argument for the role of comprehensible input – plausible as it may at first appear – must compete with other possible explanations for the silent period (anxiety, personality differences, etc.).

In addition, there is a problem with the Input Hypothesis as formulated by Krashen: how, in the silent period, does an individual come to understand language that contains structures that have not yet been acquired; how does speech become comprehensible to a person who initially knows nothing of the language? Krashen's answer to these questions is that acquirers use context, knowledge of the world, and extra-linguistic information to understand the language directed at them. But if the child is in a silent period and says nothing or very little, those directing speech at the child are receiving relatively little feedback about whether the child is using extra-linguistic information successfully. This seems to be an uneconomical model for language acquisition.

Furthermore, the question of how unknown structures ($i + 1$ structures) are acquired cannot be answered by appeals to extra-linguistic sources of information. How can extra-linguistic information convey to the child the rules for yes/no questions or passivization?

> For example, if one has acquired the basic SVO pattern of English sentences, then, being presented with sentences like *John was bitten by the dog*, and with the appropriate contextual evidence – John with tooth marks on his arm, a dog, etc. – one might be able to understand the sentence, and even unconsciously develop a rule of passivization. But understanding that *John was bitten by the dog* means the same thing as *The dog bit John* does not mean that one has acquired the rule of passivization. Such presentation of input would not in itself enable a learner to avoid producing sentences like **I was rained*, **I was died by my father*, or conversely **The river situated the house*. (Gregg 1984, 88)

The way out of this dilemma would be to appeal to some LAD that would provide the acquirer with the means to learn grammatical structures. But although, as we have seen, Krashen paid lip service to the idea of LAD, he insisted repeatedly that comprehensible input is the impetus to the development of the learner's grammar. On one occasion Krashen did suggest that internal mechanisms can affect the development of the grammar:

> the creative construction process . . . produces new forms without the benefit of input by reorganizing the rules that have already been acquired. (1983, 138)

This idea is not developed, however, and the emphasis throughout Krashen's recent writings has been on the role of comprehensible input on the development of a learner's grammar.

Thus evidence of a silent period is not evidence for the Input Hypothesis. Comprehensible input (made meaningful through extra-linguistic information) cannot, in and of itself, account for the development of the learner's grammatical system. Understanding messages is not enough. How does the learner progress from understanding to acquisition? Here the theory is silent.

Age differences

Another argument Krashen (1985) made for the Input Hypothesis was based on age differences. He maintained that older acquirers progress more quickly in the early stages because they obtain more comprehensible input than do younger learners. For one thing, Krashen argued, input to older learners is more comprehensible because their knowledge of the world makes the input more meaningful than it is for a child. He also maintained that older learners are able to participate in conversations earlier than younger learners because they can utilize the strategy of falling back on first-language syntactic rules, supplemented with second-language vocabulary and repaired by the Monitor. Finally, according to Krashen, older learners do better initially because they gain more comprehensible input via their superior skills in conversational management.

These arguments run counter to what we shall see is one of the main claims of the Input Hypothesis – that simpler codes, such as caretaker speech in first-language acquisition, provide ideal input for $i + 1$, because they are readily comprehensible. If this is the case, then younger children should have a great advantage over older children and adults, because speech addressed to them is tied to the 'here and now', is less complex grammatically, contains more repetitions and more frequent vocabulary items, etc.

In any event, the superiority of older learners when compared to young children does not provide evidence for the Input Hypothesis.

Many other explanations for the superiority of older learners are possible (McLaughlin 1984), including the availability of superior mnemonic devices, the need to speak about more complex and demanding topics, and the ability to profit from correction and training in grammar. Krashen's arguments for age differences are imaginative but unconvincing; moreover, they contradict other claims of the Input Hypothesis.

The effect of exposure
Krashen (1985) saw research on the effect of exposure to a second language as support for the Input Hypothesis. Studies show, for example, that the longer people live in a country, the more proficient their language – unless they live in immigrant communities where they use the second language relatively little and rely on their first language. For Krashen, what mattered is not mere exposure, but exposure to comprehensible input, which the immigrant who relies on his first language presumably lacks.

This raises the question of what precisely is 'comprehensible' input. In his earlier writings, Krashen used the term 'intake':

> 'Intake' is, simply, where language acquisition comes from, that subset of linguistic input that helps the acquirer learn language. (1981, 101)

Here Krashen was apparently making a distinction similar to Corder's (1967) between language that is produced in the presence of a learner (input) and language that is actually absorbed by a learner (intake). In more recent writings the term 'intake' has been replaced by 'comprehensible input'. Presumably, however, not all input is comprehensible, and the question left open is when input is comprehensible and when it is not.

Krashen does not define comprehensible input; what he says is that input is comprehensible when it is meaningful to and understood by the hearer. But this is tautological. Krashen has attempted to be more precise by arguing that the only effective input (intake or comprehensible input) is input that contains structures just beyond the syntactic complexity of those found in the current grammar of the acquirer. Thus, if we assume that the learner is at some developmental level i, effective input will contain structures at the $i + 1$ level.

Unfortunately, as Ioup (1984) has pointed out, this presumes that it is possible to define a set of levels and determine which structures constitute the $i + 1$ level. At the present stage of second-language study, both tasks are impossible for researchers, and, above all, for teachers dealing with many students at different levels of ability.

This did not faze Krashen. Although he admitted that it would be 'desirable' to be able to specify the learner's level, he argued:

it would be unwise to wait for this kind of progress before considering application of the Input Hypothesis and the theoretical constructs associated with it . . . the Input Hypothesis has massive empirical support both at the theoretical and the applied levels. (1985, 68)

This manner of argumentation is particularly exasperating, especially when many practitioners accept such assertions uncritically.

Krashen has provided no evidence at all for his assertion that research on the effects of exposure supports the Input Hypothesis. To do so, he would have to provide some way of determining what is comprehensible input for a given learner, because presumably it is not mere exposure that is effective, but exposure to the right kind of input. There is no way of determining what such input would be, and hence no way of testing the hypothesis.

Lack of access to comprehensible input
The argument here is that language learners who do not have access to comprehensible input are held up in their development. Krashen (1985) gave the example of hearing children of deaf parents with little exposure to comprehensible input, who are severely delayed in language acquisition, though they catch up ultimately when they are exposed to comprehensible input. In contrast, hearing children of deaf parents with considerable exposure to comprehensible input through interaction with adults or other children showed little language delay.

The problem with this argument as scientific 'evidence' for the Input Hypothesis is, once again, that it is untestable. There is no way of knowing what is comprehensible input, as was just pointed out. Children do profit in their language development from interacting with native speakers whose language is well-formed. No one would deny this. But the Input Hypothesis states that certain input is helpful because it is 'comprehensible', i.e., understood by learners, and is about to be acquired next, i.e., $i + 1$. There is considerable evidence, however, that first- and second-language learners acquire structures that are neither understood nor due to be acquired next.

This evidence comes from research that has shown that some child second-language learners make considerable use of formulaic expressions during the process of acquisition (see McLaughlin 1984, chapter 6). These expressions function as unanalysed units, stored in memory, and used in what the child considers an appropriate situation. The child does not understand the meaning of the individual words in the expression, nor is the meaning of the whole expression fully, or necessarily correctly, understood. The use of such expressions is a spontaneous strategy that children employ for communicative purposes. Formulaic constructions enable learners to express communicative functions they have not yet mastered and may be far from mastering.

There is evidence that formulaic speech also assists the child in analysing language. Wong Fillmore (1976) has argued that formulas constitute the linguistic material on which a large part of the child's analytic activities are carried out. In her child second-language learners, formulas – learned without the child having to understand anything of their internal structure – were eventually compared with other utterances in the repertory and with the speech of native speakers. In this process, the child learned which parts of the formula varied in different speech situations and which parts were like other utterances. In time the child had acquired an abstract structure consisting of a pattern or rule by which similar utterances could be constructed. Thus, in this view, formulaic speech is an important ingredient in the language-learning process.

Krashen and Scarcella (1978) denied that such a process typically occurs in second-language learning. They argued that Wong Fillmore's subjects were in an atypical situation, where they were exposed to routinized predictable input and were forced to speak. But this is clearly a situation in which many children find themselves. Much second-language acquisition in childhood occurs in play situations with other children where the input is routine and repetitive and where there are definite demands on the child learner to talk. Furthermore, there is evidence from first- and second-language learning that some children have a preference for formulaic speech and learn language by breaking down larger unpacked and unanalysed units of speech into smaller units, in such a way that parts of formulas are freed to recombine with parts from other formulas or new lexical items in productive fashion (Clark 1974; Peters 1983; Vihman and McLaughlin 1982).

If the use of formulaic speech is important in some situations and for some children, there is a problem for the Input Hypothesis. Research has shown that such expressions are only vaguely understood by the child and contain grammatical constructions far in advance of the child's current level of development. The input that serves as a basis for formulaic speech can hardly be described as 'comprehensible input' in Krashen's sense. So, in circumstances where children are forced to talk before they have analysed the language in any detail and for children whose personal style disposes them to use unanalysed chunks of language, something other than comprehensible input is promoting language acquisition. Access to comprehensible input (assuming one could determine what language structures constitute $i + 1$) does not seem to be the only route to acquisition.

Immersion and sheltered language teaching

As additional evidence for the Input Hypothesis, Krashen (1985) cited the success of programmes in immersion and sheltered language teaching. He argued that these methods are effective because they provide learners with comprehensible input through the use of subject-matter instruction they can understand.

If one is to avoid circularity (arguing that the input is comprehensible because it furthers acquisition and that it furthers acquisition because it is comprehensible), one has to show that 'comprehensible input' can be independently assessed. But, as we have seen, Krashen provides no way of doing this. One could just as well argue that immersion and similar programmes work because they provide children with input that is partly understood and partly not understood – i.e., $i + 3$, or $i + 4$. Without a way of measuring the various levels of difficulty in the acquisition of various linguistic structures, we are in a very black forest indeed.

Krashen provides no direct evidence for his claim that immersion and similar programmes support the Input Hypothesis. As was mentioned earlier, the strategy is simply to show that certain phenomena can be viewed from the perspective of his theory. But if it is impossible to test the theory in any meaningful way, such claims have little credibility.

The success of bilingual programmes

Krashen argued (1985) that bilingual education programmes, when they are successful, provide children with comprehensible input that leads to second-language learning. He also maintained that first-language subject-matter instruction assists in this process because it supplies the background information that makes input in English comprehensible.

No evidence was provided for these claims. Furthermore, even if it could be shown that comprehensible input assists children to learn a second language, there is considerable evidence from research on second-language learning in bilingual classrooms that children need to interact actively with the language if they are to become proficient with it (McLaughlin 1985). Understanding the input is not enough for effective language learning in bilingual classrooms.

In addition, the Input Hypothesis, and Krashen's theory generally, address only one kind of language proficiency. In bilingual classrooms, children have to learn face-to-face interpersonal language skills, as well as those skills that are needed to deal with abstract and decontextualized school language. Krashen's theory makes no such distinction and assumes a unitary notion of language proficiency.

The reading hypothesis

Krashen argued that the Input Hypothesis 'may also apply to the acquisition of writing style' (1985, 18). He maintained that writing competence comes only from large amounts of self-motivated reading for pleasure and/or interest. Such reading gives the individual a 'feel' for the look and texture of good writing.

The connection between these assertions and the Input Hypothesis was not made explicit. Presumably, reading provides the 'comprehensible input' for writing. But what is the best type of reading input for writing? Does *i* + *1* input in reading help writing? What would this mean?

Again, we are confronted, not with evidence, but with assertions that have only tangential relevance to the central claims of the theory. There is a certain degree of 'face validity' to much of what Krashen says. But when one looks for direct evidence of the theory, the result is disappointing. The findings of research with immersion or bilingual education are not inconsistent with the claims of the Input Hypothesis, but they provide no evidence for it. The same is true of the other 'lines of evidence' discussed above. One can agree with Krashen that the right kind of input helps second-language learning. But as Gregg (1984) put it, such a claim has no more explanatory power than Molière's doctor's explanation that opium makes one sleepy by virtue of its dormitive powers.

Three key arguments for the Input Hypothesis

The principal arguments for the Input Hypothesis are based on the role of simple codes, research on the effect of instruction on second-language acquisition, and methods comparison research. In this section I will examine each of these in turn.

The role of simple codes

Krashen (1985) argued that simple codes, such as caretaker speech in first-language acquisition, provide ideal input for learners because they are easily comprehensible and not finely tuned to the learner's needs. Fine tuning is assumed to be problematic because language may be finely tuned in a way that is in fact irrelevant. Krashen cited evidence from first-language research that indicated that parents do not necessarily provide the child with precisely the rule the child is ready for – i.e., *i* + *1*. Thus the relationship between the complexity of the input and the child's competence is not perfect.

> The child's 'next rule' need not be covered in every utterance or even in every interchange. Given enough comprehensible input, the necessary grammar is covered in sufficient quantity. (1985, 5)

Krashen (1982) argued that three characteristics of simple codes assist language acquisition: (1) these codes are used to communicate meaning, not to teach language, (2) they are 'roughly tuned,' not 'finely tuned' to the learners' current level of linguistic competence, and (3) they are used in speech that follows the 'here-and-now' principle – that is, directed to what the learner can perceive in the immediate environment.

Krashen was careful not to claim that the use of simple codes by parents, teachers, and others *causes* language acquisition. There is no evidence that this is the case (Hoff-Ginsberg and Shatz 1982). Krashen used such terms as 'will be very useful to the child' (1982, 23), 'might encourage language acquisition on the part of the child', (1981, 124), and 'helps the child in decoding the message' (1985, 5).

There is one line of research that creates serious problems for any appeal, however cautious, to simple codes. For example, Heath (1983) reported that Black children in the working-class community she studied were largely ignored as conversation partners until they became information givers. Parents, older siblings, other family members, and friends simply did not address speech to these children; they learned to speak by taking in and imitating sounds they heard around them. Moreover, the language they heard was well beyond their current level of competence.

Research with children from other cultures (e.g., Ochs 1982) points to the same conclusion. In many societies, parents and other caretakers do not use simpler codes in talking to young children. Simplification is viewed as an inappropriate speech behaviour. There is now considerable evidence that many children in the world learn language in a way that is different from the way that American middle-class White children learn to speak. To argue that there is a single way of learning a language is, as Faltis put it, 'a subtle form of ethnocentrism, the view that one's own group is the best model for whatever it is that we want to establish' (1984, 355).

Krashen's reaction to this cross-cultural research has been to dilute the role of simple codes even further:

> Faltis correctly suggests that the Input Hypothesis should be reconsidered in light of this cross-cultural evidence. In my view, the cross-cultural data does not supply counter-evidence to the Input Hypothesis. It is, in fact, valuable data in that it focuses attention on what is essential for language acquisition: Not simplified input but comprehensible input containing $i + 1$ structures 'slightly beyond' the acquirer's current state of competence. (1985, 6)

So we are back, once again, to comprehensible input.

Essentially, then, Krashen would have it both ways. Simplified input helps language acquisition because it provides comprehensible input, but even if children are not exposed to simplified input, they learn because they have other sources of comprehensible input. There is a problem here, however, because the speech that many children hear from parents and older children is not comprehensible in the $i + 1$ sense. Black children in the American South (Heath 1983) and children in Western Samoa (Ochs 1982) are not exposed to input that provides them with structures that are a bit beyond their current level of proficiency. Adult speech to children in these cultures is not 'finely tuned' or 'roughly tuned' or in any way accommodated to the child's needs. These children seem to learn without simplified input and without comprehensible input as Krashen defined it.

The effects of instruction
Krashen (1985) argued that the Input Hypothesis 'helps to settle' an apparent contradiction in the research literature. Some studies indicate that formal instruction helps second-language acquisition, while others seem to argue that informal environments are superior or just as good. To resolve this contradiction, Krashen proposed that language classes are effective when they are the primary source of comprehensible input. This occurs when beginners find the input from the 'real world' too complex to understand. Language classes are thought to be less helpful when (1) the students are already advanced enough to understand some input from the outside world, and (2) the input is available to them. Thus, Krashen argued, research suggests that ESL classes for foreign students in the United States benefit beginners, but are of little help to more advanced learners who can get comprehensible input from subject matter classes and from social situations.

One problem with such an argument is that comparisons of the amount learned in beginning and advanced ESL classes do not control for the complexity of the material being presented nor for the motivation of the learners. It may be that advanced ESL students benefit less from instruction because what they have to learn is more complex and their motivation to learn is not as great as it is with beginning students. Once students can negotiate meaning in a language, they may be less motivated to refine and polish their grammar.

In addition, not all studies show that instruction does not help more advanced learners. Long (1983) reviewed research dealing with the effect of instruction and found that a number of studies showed that instruction did benefit more advanced learners who were in an environment that provided them with a good deal of comprehensible input. Thus the research evidence is not unequivocal.

Krashen's arguments about the effect of instruction assume that formal instruction in a second language is helpful *only because it is a source of comprehensible input*. Teaching students grammar is seen merely to provide a topic for discussion and is effective because it serves as a carrier of comprehensible input. The main function of the second-language class according to Krashen is to provide learners with good and grammatical comprehensible input that is unavailable to them on the outside, and to bring them to the point where they can obtain comprehensible input on their own in the 'real world'.

Such a position, however, ignores the advanced cognitive development of adults and the advantages of formal teaching and learning. Krashen argued that the best way to learn a second language is to approach the language as children do when they are acquiring their first language. Rather than focusing on form or memorizing vocabulary, the learner needs to understand messages. But consider the time it takes for a child to learn a first language: assuming that young children are exposed to a normal linguistic environment for at least five hours a day, they will have had, conservatively, 9,000 hours of exposure between the ages of one and six years. In contrast, the Army Language School in California regarded 1,300 hours as sufficient for an English-speaking adult to attain near-native competence in Vietnamese (Burke 1974). Clearly, adult learners have cognitive skills that enable them to take advantage of formal instruction.

Another problem for the theory concerns the elimination of incorrect forms. If the learner has learned incorrect intermediate forms, there is no way in Krashen's system for these forms to be changed, except through more comprehensible input. According to the theory, acquisition is not affected by negative data or specific structural teaching. Krashen acknowledged this problem:

> The theory predicts that eradication of fossilized forms that result from the acquisition of intermediate forms will be difficult. . . . The theory also predicts that drill and conscious attention to form will not be a permanent cure – using the conscious Monitor will only cover up the error temporarily, learning does not become acquisition. (1985, 48)

How then are such incorrect forms to be eliminated? The answer is 'large, fresh doses of comprehensible input':

> One possibility is that there may be a way 'around' rather than a way out. While the acquirer may not be able to forget, or 'unacquire' acquired forms, he may be able to acquire a new language, a new version, a new 'dialect' of the target language. (1985, 49)

The absurdity of this explanation is immediately apparent. Would the correction of each incorrect grammatical form mean that the speaker had acquired a new 'dialect'? What happens to the old 'dialect'? Presumably old versions remain, and the learner speaks a new version as well.

More important, how does exposure to more comprehensible input lead to revision? Krashen (1985) suggested that to initiate change the learner must compare *i*, the present state of the system, with any data suggesting that a new rule is required. If there is a discrepancy, the new rule becomes a candidate for acquisition. Unfortunately, there are cases where the inconsistency between the present state of the system and the input data will not be apparent from an examination of the input. White (1985a) has provided a number of such examples. For instance, a French speaker, learning English, must learn that in English, unlike French, an adverb cannot come between a verb and a direct object. In English we cannot say *The dog bit viciously the boy*. Yet adverbial placement in English is relatively free, so that sentences such as *The dog bit the boy viciously*, *The dog viciously bit the boy*, and *Viciously, the dog bit the boy* are all allowed. A native speaker of French who assumes that English is like French in adverbial placement will not receive positive input indicating that this is not the case. Nor will this information come from extra-linguistic sources.

Another example is a Spanish speaker learning English who assumes that empty pronouns are allowed, such as *Is very busy* for *She is very busy*. In Spanish, lexical pronouns and empty pronouns are not mutually exclusive, and the learner is likely to think that the same is true in English. Hearing sentences such as *She is very busy* does not provide the learner with information that *Is very busy* is not allowed. One way adults learn these rules is through formal instruction, where the discrepancy between their intermediate forms and target language norms can be pointed out. Indeed, by learning such rules adult learners can greatly reduce the time it takes to become proficient in a second language.

Method comparison research

Krashen (1985) argued that research comparing the effectiveness of different methods indicates that methods that rely on providing learners with comprehensible input are clearly superior to grammar-based and drill-based methods. In particular, he argued for the superiority of the so-called 'Natural Approach' (Krashen and Terrell 1983).

The Natural Approach is predicated on Krashen's belief that communicative competence, or functional ability in a language, arises from exposure to the language in meaningful settings where the meanings expressed by the language are understood. Rules, patterns, vocabulary, and other language forms are not learned as they are presented or encountered, but are gradually established in the learner's repertory on the basis of exposure to comprehensible input. Rule isolation and error correction are explicitly eschewed in the Natural Approach. If the teacher uses a grammatical syllabus, she is likely to be teaching structures that some learners know already and that are too far beyond other learners. If the teacher corrects errors, her students are not free to experiment creatively with the language.

Curiously, the emphasis on communication can justify any instructional approach (Krahnke 1985). If comprehensible input is the sole source of information about the structure of the second language and if anything encountered in the new language is potentially meaningful, even formal instruction can provide comprehensible input to some learners. Indeed, if second language learners consciously learn the structure of the language and follow the rules carefully in communication, their own speech can provide a source of comprehensible input for structures not yet 'acquired' in Krashen's sense (Sharwood-Smith 1981). Krashen (1982, 1985) acknowledged this possibility and regarded it as an instance of 'learning' indirectly aiding 'acquisition'.

Krashen (1985) also acknowledged that consciously learning a rule could help make input comprehensible and thus help acquisition. Being taught a rule that is not at $i + 1$ will not, according to Krashen, lead to acquisition of that rule, but it may help make context more understandable and hence lead to acquisition of other forms that are at $i + 1$. For example, English-speaking students learning French may be taught the future forms before being ready to acquire them. When reading French they then may recognize that the future is being used, and this may help to learn other forms, even though they may not be ready to acquire the future.

These instances of learning 'indirectly' helping acquisition point to the difficulty of arguing from methods comparison research. If studies show that grammar-based or drill-based instruction is effective, Krashen can say that it is because such methods indirectly provide comprehensible input. This effectively rules out evidence that runs counter to Krashen's claims.

It may be more fruitful to admit that correction and grammar teaching can help to stimulate change and can lead to a different stage in the acquisition process (White 1985a). Rather than looking on grammar teaching merely as a way of improving the monitoring abilities of the learner, it seems reasonable to see correction and grammar teaching as providing a shortcut for learners. This is not to subscribe to language teaching methods that rely heavily on grammar teaching. But it does suggest that there is a role for correction and grammar teaching in language instruction. As Krahnke noted,

> Strategically, much of the effort spent arguing against the teaching of grammar might be better spent on convincing true believers in grammar instruction that grammar has a newly defined but useful role to play in language teaching and in showing them what it is. (1985, 598)

Krashen's polemic against grammar-based methods has done the field of language teaching a service, because he has made teachers and learners aware that there is more to a language than knowledge of its grammar. His writings have made teachers realize the importance of creating an environment in the classroom that promotes realistic communicative use of language. But his dismissal of grammar teaching smacks of pontificating. Most researchers in the field today give grammar-based instruction a wider role than Krashen allowed it (Bialystok 1981; Rutherford and Sharwood-Smith 1985; White 1985a). The question is one that deserves empirical scrutiny, not *ex cathedra* statements.

Other considerations

As we have seen, Krashen regarded the Input Hypothesis as 'the single most important concept in second language acquisition today', in that 'it attempts to answer the critical question of how we acquire language' (1980, 168). Krashen claimed that if input is understood and there is enough of it, the necessary grammar is automatically provided. Speaking is a result of acquisition and not its cause. The ability to communicate in a second language cannot be taught directly but 'emerges' on its own as a result of building competence via comprehensible input. Thus for Krashen comprehensible input is the route to acquisition and information about grammar in the target language is automatically available when the input is understood.

System-internal factors

Indeed, for Krashen, comprehensible input and the level of the affective filter (to be discussed in the next section) are *the causative factors* involved in second language acquisition:

> In order to acquire, two conditions are necessary. The first is comprehensible (or even better, comprehended) input containing $i + 1$ structures a bit beyond the acquirer's current level, and second, a low or weak affective filter to allow the input 'in'. This is equivalent to saying that comprehensible input and the strength of the filter are the true causes of second language acquisition. (1982, 33)

This is a strong claim and one that is not entirely consistent with Krashen's own writings.

At issue here is the role system-internal factors play in the acquisition process. From time to time Krashen has written of the 'creative construction process' and LAD, as system-internal processes that affect acquisition. As we have seen, he maintained that 'adults can access the same natural "Language Acquisition Device" that children use' (1982, 10), and suggested that acquired rules can be reorganized by the creative construction process so that new forms are produced without the benefit of input (1983, 138). This is an interesting suggestion that seems at odds with the argument that comprehensible input and the level of the affective filter are *the* causative factors in acquisition.

Unfortunately, Krashen's theory is vague about the content of system-internal processes (White 1985a). Nor does the theory say anything about how system-internal and system-external factors interact. Krashen has argued that speech becomes comprehensible to a learner who knows little or nothing of a language through extra-linguistic information. As we have seen, however, it is not clear how extra-linguistic information will motivate syntactic change. Nor is it clear that contextual and extra-linguistic sources of information are the only route to grammatical development.

White has argued that various aspects of the input can trigger grammatical change. These include linguistic factors, as well as the non-linguistic factors that Krashen has specified. White showed how it is possible to make specific proposals as to what aspects of grammar will change in acquisition and what kind of input is necessary to bring this change about. She concluded,

> Krashen's assumption that we cannot know what input is relevant to *i* + *1* is due to the fact that he never has any specific proposal as to what *i* and *i* + *1* consist of. (1985, 6)

Again, the conclusion one comes to is that the Input Hypothesis is too vague and imprecise to provide an account of the process of acquisition in second-language learners.

The role of output
Krashen (1985) has argued that speaking is unnecessary for acquiring a second language. In his view, the only role that the speaker's output plays is to provide a further source of comprehensible input. Other researchers would argue that *understanding* new forms is not enough; the learner must be given the opportunity to *produce* the new forms. Swain (1985) has argued for the importance of 'comprehensible output'. Other authors (including Krashen) stress the importance of 'negotiating meaning' to ensure that the language in which the input is heard is modified to the level the speaker can manage.

Long and Porter (1985) have provided evidence for the usefulness of what they termed 'interlanguage talk', conversation between non-native speakers in which they negotiate meaning in groups. Such group work has been found to increase the communicative abilities of the group members and to motivate students to learn. It provides evidence that learners can benefit from talking, although Krashen would probably argue that this is because of the comprehensible input they receive from their own speech and that of other group members.

It is questionable, however, whether comprehensible input alone can account for how learners correct and adjust their hypotheses about the language. Unless learners try out the language, they are unlikely to get the kind of feedback they need to analyse the structure of the language.

Wong Fillmore described this process in the school children she studied:

> Second language learning in a school context thus requires the active participation of both the learners and those who provide them with appropriate 'input'. Learners have to work actively on this input, guessing at what is being talked about and continually trying to sort out relationships between observed speech and experiences. Unless the speakers use the language in ways that permit the learners to figure out what is being talked about, the learners will not be able to perform the necessary analyses on the language. Unless the learners try to sort things out and provide feedback to the speakers to aid them in making the necessary adjustments, learning will not occur. (1982, 9)

Krashen did not deny the importance of this hypothesis-testing process, but argued that it 'does not require production' (1985, 36). In principle, this may be true and may account for how children whose speech is physiologically impaired learn the language. Nonetheless, for most normal children and adults learning a language, one's own speech is a valuable source of information about the language. As Gregg put it, 'there is no a priori reason to assume that a learner systematically ignores his own utterances' (1984, 88).

To conclude, the Input Hypothesis makes a strong claim – that acquisition is *caused* by understanding the input to which the learner is exposed. Internal factors are given little emphasis; in Krashen's recent (1982, 1985) writings there is almost no mention of the role of system-internal factors. The importance of output is also de-emphasized, and understanding a new language is given far greater stress than speaking it. A more balanced view of the second-language learning process gives equal weight to internal and external factors and to production and comprehension.

The Affective Filter Hypothesis

As we have seen, Krashen argued that comprehensive input was a necessary, but not a sufficient condition for successful acquisition. Affective factors are also seen to play an important role in acquiring a second language. According to the Affective Filter Hypothesis, comprehensible input may not be utilized by second-language acquirers if there is a 'mental block' that prevents them from fully profiting from it (Krashen 1985). The affective filter acts as a barrier to acquisition: if the filter is 'down', the input reaches the LAD and becomes acquired competence; if the filter is 'up', the input is blocked and does not reach the LAD (Figure 2.1). Thus

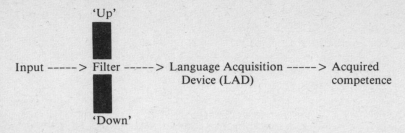

Figure 2.1. The operation of the 'Affective Filter' (based on Krashen 1982). Only when the filter is 'down' or low is input thought to reach the Language Acquisition Device and become acquired competence.

> input is the primary causative variable in second language acquisition, affective variables acting to impede or facilitate the delivery of input to the language acquisition device. (1982, 32)

Krashen maintained that acquirers need to be open to the input and that when the affective filter is up, the learner may understand what is seen and read, but the input will not reach the LAD. This occurs when the acquirer is unmotivated, lacking in confidence, or concerned with failure. The filter is down when the acquirer is not anxious and is intent on becoming a member of the group speaking the target language.

For Krashen, the affective filter is the principal source of individual differences in second-language acquisition:

> The Affective Filter Hypothesis captures the relationship between affective variables and the process of second language acquisition by positing that acquirers vary with respect to the strength or level of their affective filters. Those whose attitudes are not optimal for second language acquisition will not only tend to seek less input, but they will also have a high or strong affective filter – even if they understand the message, the input will not reach that part of the brain responsible for language acquisition, or the Language Acquisition Device. Those with attitudes more conducive to second language acquisition will not only seek and obtain more input, they will also have a lower or weaker filter. (1982, 31)

Thus the argument is that a strong or high affective filter blocks input from reaching the LAD.

There is general agreement that affective factors play a critical role in second-language learning. There have been numerous studies in the literature dealing with the sources of individual differences (see McLaughlin 1984, ch. 6; 1985, ch. 7). What is questionable is whether it is necessary to postulate an affective filter to explain the research findings in this field. There are two issues that deserve examination: (1) the role of the affective filter in language acquisition, and (2) the need for an affective filter to explain individual variation in second-language learning.

The affective filter and language acquisition

The affective filter was first proposed by Dulay and Burt (1977) to account for how affective variables affect the process of second-language learning. The concept was given its most extensive treatment in Dulay, Burt, and Krashen. In this work the affective filter was defined as follows:

> The filter is that part of the internal processing system that subconsciously screens incoming language based on what psychologists call 'affect': the learner's motives, needs, attitudes, and emotional states. (1982, 46)

The filter is described as having four functions:

(1) It determines which language models the learner will select.
(2) It determines which part of the language will be attended to first.
(3) It determines when the language acquisition efforts should cease.
(4) It determines how fast a learner can acquire a language.

Thus the filter is thought to limit what it is that the learner attends to, what will be learned, and how quickly the language will be acquired.

This limiting or restrictive role of the affective filter is left rather vague in the writings of Krashen and his colleagues on the topic. There is no explanation, for example, of how the affective filter determines which 'part of the language' to attend to first. How is this selective function to be performed unless there is some possibility of comparing various 'parts' against each other? But do beginning learners have the necessary discriminatory facility? Can they separate out different 'parts' for comparison and select appropriate ones to learn first?

> The notion 'part of a language', in so far as it has any meaning at all, presupposes some sort of grammatical theory that the filter must have access to. Even in the most extremely unlikely, simpleminded interpretation of [Krashen's argument] – say, a morbid fear of adjectives – The filter must 'know' what an adjective is, and such knowledge can by no stretch of the imagination be called 'affective'. (Gregg, 94)

There is no account in Krashen's writings of how this knowledge would reach the filter.

This problem becomes serious when one considers concretely what it would mean for the affective filter to operate. Take, for example, an individual whose accent in German was quite good except for /r/ and /l/ sounds. Does such an individual have an unconscious aversion to German /r/ and /l/ sounds? Why would the filter prevent the acquisition of these sounds and not others? Or why would the filter make it difficult for Japanese speakers of English to learn the definite and indefinite articles? As Gregg put it, 'Once we move from the general to the particular, once we try to put a little content, a little specificity into the hypothesis, we run into difficulty' (1984, 93).

Similarly, the Affective Filter Hypothesis provides little information as to why learners stop where they do. If one asks what kind of predictions this hypothesis is capable of making regarding success in second-language acquisition, one draws a blank. Presumably, learners who suffer from a great deal of self-consciousness, lack motivation, and are anxious, are not likely to learn very much. Those who are motivated but self-conscious and anxious would be expected to learn more. Those who are indifferent would be expected to learn even more because their filter is not blocking input. Indeed, the theory does not differentiate between the indifferent and the highly motivated, because the filter is essentially described as a limiting and restrictive mechanism.

In short, the Affective Filter Hypothesis is not precise enough about how a filter would operate, no attempt has been made to tie the filter to linguistic theory, specific predictions are impossible, and some predictions that are possible are blatantly absurd. Nor is it clear what kind of a mechanism could carry out all of the functions assigned to the filter. The role of the affective filter in Krashen's theory appears to be that of *deus ex machina*, allowing for any and all results. But appeals to poorly defined mechanisms do little to further understanding.

The affective filter and individual differences

According to Krashen, the reason why children ultimately reach higher levels of attainment in language development than are achieved by individuals who begin the language in adulthood is 'due to the strengthening of the affective filter at about puberty' (1982, 44). That is, children have an advantage in language development because their affective filter is lower. Adult learners, on the other hand, are likely to have higher affective filters because of events that occur in adolescence. Following Elkind (1970), Krashen (1981) argued that during adolescence the individual goes through the stage of 'formal operations', which leads to the ability to conceptualize the thoughts of others. Unfortunately, adolescents tend to think that other people are concerned with the same thing that concerns them: themselves. This leads to increased self-consciousness, feelings of vulnerability, and a lowered self-image – all of which, presumably, interfere with language learning.

On the basis of the Affective Filter Hypothesis, therefore, one would predict that adolescence is the worst period for language learning. Unfortunately for the hypothesis, there is considerable evidence that early adolescence is the *best* time to learn a second language (McLaughlin 1985, ch. 7). Krashen consistently ignored the evidence on this issue and has made a 'younger-is-better' argument that is contradicted by available data (see McLaughlin 1984, ch. 3).

Furthermore, people do not remain adolescents forever. Eventually many of the feelings of self-consciousness, vulnerability, and insecurity that mark adolescence disappear in mature adults. Is Krashen arguing that insecure and more vulnerable adults will make poorer language learners? Are adults who are secure and self-confident necessarily superior language learners? There is no research evidence to support a causal relationship between these personality variables and language learning. Indeed, research on individual differences in second-language learning has proven to be a methodological Armageddon. It is extremely difficult to show any relationship between personality factors and language learning. The issue of the characteristics of the 'good language learner' is likely to puzzle researchers for some time to come. It seems extremely premature to posit an affective filter without specifying its nature and how one is to assess its strength.

Another question relates to children. Are children who are more insecure and less self-confident less likely to learn their first language? Surely children differ in these affective states. Yet there is no evidence that highly insecure and anxious children make poorer language learners. Krashen has not allowed the affective filter to play a role in first language development, though there is no a priori reason why it should not.

To conclude, Krashen has provided no coherent explanation for the development of the affective filter and no basis for relating the affective filter to individual differences in language learning. Nor does the hypothesis bear detailed linguistic scrutiny. Although most researchers in the field of second-language acquisition would admit that affective variables play a critical role, few would see a need to postulate an affective filter that is vague in its origin and function.

Evaluation

In chapter 1 four criteria were specified for evaluating theory: (1) the theory must have definitional precision and explanatory power, (2) the theory must be consistent with what is currently known, (3) the theory must be heuristically rich in its predictions, and (4) the theory must be falsifiable. It should be obvious that Krashen's theory does not score well against such criteria. In fact, I have argued in this chapter that

Krashen's theory fails at every juncture. By way of summary, I will itemize what I see to be the central problems with the theory.

(1) The acquisition–learning distinction is not clearly defined and it is impossible to determine which process is operating in a particular case. Hence a central claim of the theory, that 'learning' cannot become 'acquisition', cannot be tested empirically. Nor is the theory of acquisition consistent with current linguistic theory.

(2) Krashen has been forced by empirical evidence to place severe restrictions on the conditions required for use of the Monitor. Because the Monitor is so restricted in its application, 'learning', which is thought to involve the use of the Monitor, can easily be dispensed with as an integral part of gaining facility in a second language.

(3) The case for the Natural Order Hypothesis is based largely on the morpheme studies, which are of questionable methodological validity and which, because they focus on final form, provide little information about acquisitional processes. If the Natural Order Hypothesis is to be accepted, it must be in a weak form, which postulates that some things are learned before others, but not always. Krashen has provided no theory as to why this is the case, so this hypothesis does not tell us much.

(4) The Input Hypothesis is untestable because no definition is given of the key concept, 'comprehensible input'. The argument that effective input contains structures just beyond the syntactic complexity of those found in the current grammar of the acquirer leads nowhere, because it assumes a non-existent theory of acquisition sequences. The Input Hypothesis also fails to account for the elimination of incorrect intermediate forms, and provides no way of distinguishing between different instructional methods (each of which, if effective, can be argued to provide comprehensible input).

(5) The Affective Filter Hypothesis is also of questionable validity because Krashen has provided no coherent explanation for the development of the affective filter and no basis for relating the affective filter to individual differences in language learning. The hypothesis is incapable of predicting with any precision the course of linguistic development and its outcome.

Furthermore, Krashen has not defined his terms with enough precision, the empirical basis of the theory is weak, and the theory is not clear in its predictions.

Krashen (1985), discussing the Input Hypothesis, has argued that although the theory uses terms that are 'not, at present, completely operationalizable' such as $i + 1$, it would be unwise to wait until more precise measurements were possible before considering application of the Input Hypothesis. According to Krashen, hypothetical constructs such as $i + 1$ are useful at the present stage of our knowledge. Such constructs can be helpful, he argued, in a research area where there are a large number of variables and complex causal relationships, especially if they are supported by theory and research.

As we saw in chapter 1, however, hypothetical constructs have utility in a theory only if they are tied at some level to observables. If this is not the case, it is difficult to evaluate the theory's internal consistency, agreement with data, and testability. The more precisely the terms in a theory are defined, the more possible it becomes for the scientific community to determine the adequacy of the theory. A theory is falsifiable only if its parts are testable and all untestable parts are related to testable ones. But Krashen has not related the $i + 1$ notion to any observable or measurable variables.

> [The use of hypothetical constructs] would not be a problem (a) were the second and only other causal statement in the theory, the (so-called) Affective Filter Hypothesis, related to the first [the Input Hypothesis], and (b) if the Affective Hypothesis did not itself contain a construct. In fact, however, the Affective Filter Hypothesis is not related (except by assertion) to the Input Hypothesis, and further, not only contains a construct but is itself a construct. An affective filter moving up and down, selectively letting input in to penetrate relevant brain areas (see Krashen, 1982, 31) is, after all, a metaphor. Monitor Theory, that is to say, is untestable, and so unfalsifiable, in its current formulation. (Long 1985b, 7–8)

Added to this are three unfortunate tendencies in Krashen's writings: (1) to switch assumptions to suit his purposes (Gregg 1984), (2) to make sweeping statements on the basis of weak empirical data (Taylor 1984), and (3) to brush aside conflicting evidence in footnotes (Takala 1984). The last of these is especially disturbing, as the readers of Krashen's works are unlikely to pore through densely printed footnotes, which in many instances contain the most important arguments against his theory.

This is not to say that Krashen is wrong in his prescriptions about language teaching. Many researchers working in the field agree with him on basic assumptions, such as the need to move from grammar-based to communicatively oriented language instruction, the role of affective factors in language learning, and the importance of acquisitional sequences in second-language development. The issue here is not second-language teaching, but second-language research and whether

Krashen's theory is successful. The answer, obviously, is that it is not.

This has been a critical chapter, and deliberately so. If the field of second-language research is to advance, it cannot, at an early stage of its development, be guided by a theory that provides all the answers. Krashen's theory – in my view and in the opinion of many other researchers – is counterproductive. More limited and more specific theories are needed at this stage, not a general, all-inclusive theory.

At the end of such a critical chapter one feels the need to temper criticism with praise. Certainly Krashen deserves praise for developing an extensive and detailed theory. Its inadequacies will doubtless stimulate others to improve on the theory or develop better ones. In this sense his contribution is real.

What is less praiseworthy is Krashen's tendency to make broad and sweeping claims for his theory, claims that would be disputed by most researchers in the field today. For instance, in advocating the Natural Approach to second-language teaching, Krashen and Terrell argued that this approach was the first to base a method of language teaching on a theory of language acquisition. This approach, they wrote,

> is based on an empirically grounded theory of second language acquisition, which has been supported by a large number of scientific studies in a wide variety of language acquisition and learning contexts. (1983, 12)

This is, at best, a controversial statement.

Unfortunately, many teachers and administrators accept the theory as the word of God and preach it to the unenlightened. In their enthusiasm for the Gospel according to Krashen, his disciples do a disservice to a field where there are so many unresolved theoretical and practical issues and where so many research questions are unanswered.

3

Interlanguage theory

In chapter 1 a distinction was made between 'inductive' and 'deductive' theories. An inductive theory starts from the data, and attempts to build up or discover the laws of nature one by one. The components of the theory enter into a network of relations, a set of laws, each of which specifies one of the factors that play a part in what is to be accounted for. Inductive theories are 'bottom-up' theories in the sense that theory arises from empirical observations.

Deductive theories are more 'top-down' in the sense that the component laws are presented as deductions from a small set of basic principles. There are fewer and more general laws at the top of the pyramid, and a greater number of more specific laws at the base. Theory begins with the theorist's best guess as to the reason for a phenomenon. The theory is not restricted to empirical laws, but attempts to go beyond data via a set of causal statements meant to provide an explanation of the phenomenon in question. Thus bottom-up or inductive theories derive from the data and aim at a set of laws that describes the data. Deductive theories aim at understanding the process they purport to explain and employ sets of definitions of theoretical concepts and constructs, which are directly or indirectly tied to operational definitions.

Inductive theory has the advantage of staying close to the data. Such theories build low-level or intermediate-level constructs before jumping to conclusions about the larger picture. The disadvantage is that inductive theories are restricted in range and account only for phenomena where repeated observations show the same behavioural pattern. The advantage of a heavily top-down or deductive theory is that it provides interesting claims about the phenomenon in question. In going beyond the data, such theories stimulate researchers to look at the whole picture. The disadvantage is that to do so means invoking theoretical constructs that are remote from empirical data and only indirectly tied to observations.

As was noted in the first chapter, in practice theories of second language can be placed somewhere along a continuum, from those that are more deductive to those that are more inductive. Krashen's theory, with its appeal to hypothetical constructs, such as *i* + *1*, is more at the deductive end. He has attempted to provide a view of the 'whole picture' of second-language learning. Most other theorists take a more bottom-up approach and provide a more restricted view of part of the picture. This is true of the theories to be discussed in the remaining chapters of this book. Rather than aiming at 'general' theory, these approaches are intermediate-level theories, concerned with describing a restricted range of data. The first of these is interlanguage theory.

Early interlanguage studies

The term 'interlanguage' was coined by Selinker (1969, 1972) to refer to the interim grammars constructed by second-language learners on their way to the target language. The term won favour over similar constructs, such as 'approximative system' (Nemser 1971) and 'transitional competence' (Corder 1967). Since the early 1970s 'interlanguage' has come to characterize a major approach to second-language research and theory.

Unfortunately, the term has taken on various meanings, some authors using it as synonymous with second-language learning generally. The first goal of this chapter is to look at various uses of the term 'interlanguage' and their theoretical implications and then to trace early research related to the interlanguage concept. The second section of this chapter discusses recent issues and developments in Interlanguage theory, and the final section is an evaluation of the contribution and future promise of this approach.

Early formulations

Generally speaking, the term 'interlanguage'means two things: (1) the learner's system *at a single point in time* and (2) the range of interlocking systems that characterizes the development of learners *over time*. The interlanguage is thought to be distinct from both the learner's first language and from the target language. It evolves over time as learners employ various internal strategies to make sense of the input and to control their own output. These strategies were central to Selinker's thinking about interlanguage.

Interlanguage and learning strategies
Selinker (1972) argued that the interlanguage, which he saw to be a separate linguistic system resulting from the learner's attempted pro-

duction of the target language norm, was the product of five central cognitive processes involved in second-language learning:

(1) Language transfer: some items, rules, and subsystems of the interlanguage may result from transfer from the first language.
(2) Transfer of training: some elements of the interlanguage may result from specific features of the training process used to teach the second language.
(3) Strategies of second-language learning: some elements of the interlanguage may result from a specific approach to the material to be learned.
(4) Strategies of second-language communication: some elements of the interlanguage may result from specific ways people learn to communicate with native speakers of the target language.
(5) Overgeneralization of the target language linguistic material: some elements of the interlanguage may be the product of overgeneralization of the rules and semantic features of the target language.

The development of the interlanguage was seen by Selinker as different from the process of first-language development because of the likelihood of *fossilization* in the second language. Fossilization is the state of affairs that exists when the learner ceases to elaborate the interlanguage in some respect, no matter how long there is exposure, new data, or new teaching. Selinker maintained that such fossilization results especially from language transfer (French speakers who retain the uvular /R/ in their English interlanguage, English speakers who use English word order in German sentences, etc.), but fossilization may also be the result of other processes. For example, strategies of communication may dictate to some individuals that they stop learning the language once they have learned enough to communicate. Because fossilization does not occur in first-language development, the acquisition of the interlanguage is thought to be different from the acquisition of a first language.

Although the interlanguage hypothesis was applied principally to adult second-language performance, Selinker and his associates (1975) extended the notion to child second-language performance as well. They argued that under certain circumstances – when the second language was acquired after the first language and when it occurs in the absence of native-speaking peers of the target language – an interlanguage will develop in the speech of the children. These conditions were realized in the subjects studied – 7-year-old children in a French immersion programme in an English-language elementary school in Canada.

The children were 10 boys and 10 girls who had been instructed entirely in French by a native speaker during both kindergarten and the first grade. When studied at the end of the first grade, the children consistently used French to talk to their teacher and among themselves in the classroom setting. They had no trouble understanding French and could express in French what they wanted to say. They did not, however, speak French outside class hours and had little contact with native French speakers their own age.

Selinker *et al.* (1975) argued that an analysis of the children's speech revealed a definite *systematicity* in the interlanguage. This systematicity was not seen to be predictable by grammatical rules but to be evidenced by recognizable strategies. By 'strategy' was meant a cognitive activity at the conscious or unconscious level that involved the processing of second-language data in the attempt to express meaning. They focused on three such strategies: language transfer, overgeneralization of target language rules, and simplification. Table 3.1 presents examples of errors resulting from these various strategies.

Thus for Selinker interlanguage referred to an interim grammar that is a single system composed of rules that have been developed via different cognitive strategies – for example, transfer, overgeneralization,

Table 3.1 Errors found in the speech of children in an immersion classroom

Type of error	Construction	Example
Language transfer	English transitive meaning given French intransitive verbs.	Elle *marche* les chats. (She's walking the cats.)
	Lexical confusion.	*Des temps* (sometimes)
	English word order.	Je aller le *français camp*. (I'm gonna go to a French camp.)
	Improper pronoun placement.	Le chien *a mangé les*. (The dog ate them.)
Overgeneralization	Overgeneralization of French adjective placement rule.	Une *maison nouvelle* (A new house)
	Past tense form modelled on most common conjugation.	Il a *couré*. (He ran.)
	Use of subject form where object form is required.	Je lis des histoires *a il* en français. (I read stories to him in French.)
Simplification	Use of one form (infinitive) for all tenses.	Le fille *mettre* du confiture sur le pain. (The girl put some jam on the bread.)
	Avoidance of French post-position of adjective.	Un *jour qui chaud* (A hot day.)

simplification, and the correct understanding of the target language. At any given time, the interlanguage grammar is some combination of these types of rules.

Interlanguage as rule-governed behaviour

In contrast to Selinker's cognitive emphasis, Adjemian (1976) argued that the systematicity of the interlanguage should be analysed *linguistically* as rule-governed behaviour. In this view, the internal organization of the interlanguage can be idealized linguistically, just like any natural language. Like any language system, interlanguage grammars are seen to obey universal linguistic constraints and evidence internal consistency. We may not be able to generate the interlanguage – or any language – through linguistic constructs, but we can learn something about the second-language learner's speech by making a series of descriptions of the learner's interlanguage.

Adjemian cited Corder's (1973) suggestion that research be directed at the learner's 'transitional competence' – that is, the set of grammatical intuitions about the interlanguage that the learner possesses at a given point in time. Once knowledge is obtained about transitional competence, Adjemian saw the researcher to be in a much better position to infer the psychological mechanisms at play. For this reason Adjemian argued that analysis of the systematicity of the interlanguage should begin with the regularities observed in a large body of data and should be directed at determining the properties of the learner's grammar.

Whereas Selinker's use of interlanguage stressed the structurally intermediate nature of the learner's system between the first and the target language, Adjemian focused on the dynamic character of interlanguage systems, their *permeability*. Interlanguage systems are thought to be by their nature incomplete and in a state of flux. In this view, the individual's first-language system is seen to be relatively stable, but the interlanguage is not. The structures of the interlanguage may be 'invaded' by the first language: when placed in a situation that cannot be avoided, the second-language learner may use rules or items from the first language. Similarly, the learner may stretch, distort, or overgeneralize a rule from the target language in an effort to produce the intended meaning. Both processes Adjemian saw to reflect the basic permeability of the interlanguage.

Interlanguage as a set of styles

A third approach to the interlanguage notion has been taken by Tarone (1979) who maintained that the interlanguage could be seen as analysable into a set of styles that are dependent on the context of use. Tarone cited evidence from the research literature indicating that learner utterances are systematically variable in at least two senses:

(1) linguistic context may have a variable effect on the learner's use of related phonological and syntactic structures, and (2) the task used for the elicitation of data from learners may have a variable effect on the learner's production of related phonological and syntactic structures. Tarone maintained that the evidence shows that interlanguage speech production varies systematically with context and elicitation task.

To account for this finding, Tarone proposed a *capability continuum*, which includes a set of styles ranging from a stable subordinate style virtually free of first-language influence to a characteristically superordinate style where the speaker pays a great deal of attention to form and where the influence of the first language is, paradoxically, more likely to be felt. Tarone compared the spontaneous subordinate interlanguage style to natural spontaneous unmonitored speech; the more careful superordinate style shows the intervention of a consciously learned rule system.

More specifically, Tarone (1983) proposed that variability in the interlanguage can be accounted for by a system of variable and categorical rules based on particular contexts of use. The contexts range along a continuum of styles from formal to vernacular. In some contexts, the linguistic feature can be described by a categorical rule that is supplied 100 per cent of the time in that context. In other contexts, the linguistic feature is best described by a variable rule that is supplied, say, 50 per cent of the time in that context. As the learner style shifts as a result of paying more attention to language form, some categorical rules may become more variable and some variable rules become more categorical, as they are increasingly influenced by the target language.

Like Adjemian, Tarone assumed that the interlanguage is a natural language, obeying the constraints of the same language universals and subject to analysis by means of standard linguistic techniques. She went beyond Adjemian in claiming that language productions show systematic variability, similar to that demonstrated to exist in the speech of native speakers. Thus she added to Adjemian's linguistic perspective a sociolinguistic point of view. For Tarone, interlanguage is not a single system, but a set of styles that can be used in different social contexts.

The difference between these three basic models of interlanguage can be seen in Figure 3.1. The figure is based on a discussion by Bialystok and Sharwood Smith (1985), who depicted Tarone's learner as possessing a set of grammars defining the various styles used in different contexts. However, because she did not directly address this point, it may be just as legitimate to see her learner as possessing a flexible system of rules (and hence more akin to Selinker's thinking than to Adjemian's on this point).

To summarize, the views of interlanguage that guided early research saw second-language learners as possessing a set of rules or interme-

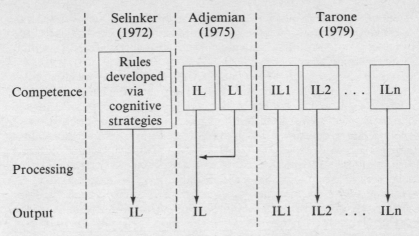

Figure 3.1. Three basic models of interlanguage (based on Bialystok and Sharwood Smith 1985).

diate grammars. Two of these formulations (Selinker and Adjemian) stressed the influence of the first-language on the emerging interlanguage. These authors differed, however, in that Selinker hypothesized that interlanguages are the product of different psychological mechanisms than native languages and hence are not natural languages (though they may evolve into natural languages for some learners). Adjemian and Tarone viewed interlanguages as operating on the same principles as natural languages, but Tarone differed from Adjemian in that she stressed the notion of variability in use and the pragmatic constraints that determine how language is used in context.

Descriptive studies

When the interlanguage notion was introduced in the early 1970s, it was in large part a reaction to the then prevalent views of second-language learning: neo-behaviourist learning theory and contrastive analysis. Second-language research of the early 1970s was to a great extent reactive research: investigators were iconoclasts, their findings heretical. They challenged prevailing behaviourist dogma and made a strong case for internal, possibly language-specific processes in language development. This contrasted sharply with the behaviourists' emphasis on external factors.

The reaction to behaviourism began when investigators discovered that their findings suggested that second-language acquisition was quite different from what was traditionally believed to be the case. The traditional doctrine stressed the role of transfer from the first language. The language learner, like any other learner, was thought to build up habits – old habits interfering with the acquisition of new ones. This, however, was not what investigators were finding. Instead, the evidence seemed to suggest that interference played a minor role in second-language acquisition.

Specifically, researchers reported that contrastive analysis did not predict what errors learners made in acquiring a second language. Contrastive analysis, based on linguistic comparisons of languages, both overpredicted and underpredicted the difficulties of second-language learners. It overpredicted because it identified difficulties that in fact did not arise, and it underpredicted because learners made errors that could not be explained on the basis of transfer between languages (McLaughlin 1984). Instead, learners from different backgrounds seemed to go through similar developmental processes in second-language acquisition. These conclusions derived from two lines of research: the 'morpheme' studies and error analysis.

The morpheme studies
As was mentioned in the previous chapter, this research was based on the work of Brown (1973) who had found that children learning English as a first language follow a common 'invariant' sequence in the acquisition of 14 functor words – such as noun and verb inflections, articles, auxiliaries, copulas, and prepositions. In a number of studies of child second-language learners, Dulay and Burt (1973, 1974b) reported that second-language learners, regardless of their first language, followed a similar developmental sequence.

For example, Dulay and Burt (1973) used the Bilingual Syntax Measure to elicit speech samples from 151 Spanish-speaking children living in Tijuana, Mexico, California, and New York. Even though the three groups differed in their exposure to English, they showed roughly the same pattern in their use of the functors in obligatory contexts. This pattern was similar, but somewhat different from the pattern Brown had observed in monolingual children. Dulay and Burt attributed this variation to the difference in cognitive abilities of children at different stages of their development.

Research with adult subjects (Bailey *et al.* 1974; Larsen-Freeman 1975) indicated that the pattern obtained in cross-sectional studies of children was found in adults as well. Although there were differences due to the subjects' first language and the types of task they were engaged in (Larsen-Freeman 1975), the differences were generally not marked enough to obscure the common pattern in the accuracy order. Statistical correlations were found between learners from various first-language backgrounds, suggesting a common ('natural order') developmental sequence.

Error analysis

The main evidence against contrastive analysis came from the analysis of learners' errors. In their research, Dulay and Burt (1972, 1974a) reported that cross-sectional analysis revealed that the majority of errors that children make reflect the influence of the target second language more than the influence of the child's first language. For example, data from Spanish-speaking children who were learning English were seen to indicate that the majority of errors were developmental in nature – that is, most errors were seen to be of the type that monolingual children make when they are acquiring English (Dulay and Burt 1972). Even errors that presumably reflect the child's first language could, Dulay and Burt argued, just as well reflect overgeneralizations, which, though not found in the speech of monolingual children, do correspond to strategies used by monolingual children. For instance, errors such as *Now she's putting hers clothes on* are not found in the speech of native speakers of English, but could be overgeneralizations by the second-language learners of the English possessive *'s*. In contrast, overgeneralizations reflecting Spanish constructions such as *bigs houses* and *talls boys* were not found in the data.

In a subsequent study, Dulay and Burt (1974a) examined speech samples from Spanish-, Chinese-, Japanese-, and Norwegian-speaking children acquiring English as a second language. The types of mistakes these children made were strikingly similar. Authors studying adult subjects (e.g., George 1972; Lance 1969) also reported that errors based on first-language constructions were relatively infrequent and that many errors were like those made by children acquiring the target language ('developmental' errors).

In short, the similarities observed in the 'morpheme' studies across learners from different language backgrounds, and the predominance of developmental errors over interference errors led to the view that second-language learning was like first-language acquisition in that both processes involved possibly universal linguistic operations. It was not long, however, before this conclusion was challenged. A number of investigators, working with the same research paradigms, found evidence that the first language did make a difference and that the data from second-language learners diverged sharply from patterns found in first-language learners. Furthermore, there appeared to be serious methodological flaws in the research showing similar developmental sequences in first- and second-language acquisition.

The critique

The morpheme studies have come under attack from a number of directions. The findings may be instrument-specific. Porter (1977) gave the Bilingual Syntax Measure to monolingual English-speaking children and found that they displayed an acquisition order more resembling the order found in second-language learners than the order Brown (1973) had found in first-language learners of English. Since the Bilingual Syntax Measure was the instrument used in most of the morpheme research, the findings might be an artifact of the use of this instrument.

Furthermore, as was noted in the previous chapter, the findings of the morpheme studies are not, strictly speaking, related to *acquisition sequence*, but rather to *accuracy of use*, because the studies are cross-sectional in nature and measure the percent of times subjects supply morphemes correctly in obligatory contexts. Several longitudinal studies have yielded orders of acquisition that did not correlate with the orders of accuracy of use obtained in cross-sectional research (Hakuta 1976; Huebner 1979; Rosansky 1976).

Error analysis research has also come under fire. Schachter and Celce-Murcia (1977) have pointed out that it is difficult to be certain precisely what type of error a second-language learner is making or why the learner makes it. One and the same error can frequently be attributed to intralingual (reflecting developmental mistakes found in monolingual speakers) and interlingual factors (reflecting the influence of the learner's first language). Indeed, this may not be an either–or proposition: there is evidence that some errors are the result of the interaction of both factors (Andersen 1978).

Hakuta and Cancino (1977) argued that error analysis rests on the questionable assumption that an error is an appropriate unit of analysis. Research that indicates that a predominance of errors in a second-language learner's corpus are developmental usually involves coding the omission of high frequency morphemes – such as nouns and verb inflections and the verb *to be* – as developmental errors. Since transfer errors often involve large constituents or changes in word order, Hakuta and Cancino maintained that the relative opportunity of occurrence of the two types is not equivalent. Furthermore, it may well be that second-language learners simply avoid certain linguistic structures in which they would be likely to make errors (Schachter 1974). It is conceivable that such avoidance tendencies reflect structural differences between their first language and the target language.

Another problem with the error analysis research is that it is typically based on cross-sectional samples, in which data are gathered at a single point in time from many subjects with different degrees of proficiency. This contrasts with longitudinal research, in which data are gathered at many points in time from one subject or a small group of subjects. There are relatively few longitudinal studies that examine whether specific errors are prevalent at specific points in time or whether certain errors persist longer than others. There is some evidence that interlingual errors appear primarily at the early stages of development

(Taylor 1975) and that they occur when learners are faced with particularly intransigent problems (Wode 1981).

To summarize, the first wave of systematic research on child second-language learning, the research of the early 1970s, suggested that the acquisition of grammatical constructions followed the same developmental sequences for first- and second-language learners. The second wave of research suggested that this was not always the case and that some of the early studies were methodologically suspect.

The emerging interlanguage paradigm suggested that those who would stress the differences between first- and second-language acquisition and those who would stress the similarities were equally misguided. There were common patterns of development found in second-language learners' speech and common errors, but they owed much to factors other than the shape of the first language or the target language. Rather than focusing on the first or the target language, researchers working in the interlanguage framework began to develop data-analytic procedures that would yield information about the dynamic qualities of language change that made the interlanguage a unique system, both similar to and different from the first and target languages. Such approaches represented a reaction to the 'product' orientation of the morpheme studies and error analysis, and the feeling that a more 'process' oriented approach was needed. This process orientation became more pronounced as Interlanguage theory developed in the late 1970s and 1980s.

Recent developments in Interlanguage theory

Interest in more dynamic, process-oriented accounts of the interlanguage was the result of concern with several major issues facing interlanguage theory:

(1) How systematic and how variable is the interlanguage?
(2) How are interlanguages acquired?
(3) What is the role of the first language?

Attention to these issues has provided the context for recent developments in Interlanguage theory.

Systematicity and variability

We saw earlier in this chapter that early interlanguage theorists differed in their view of how dynamic and changeable the interlanguage is. Adjemian, especially, stressed the notion that interlanguage systems are changeable and in a state of flux. Most analyses of interlanguage, however, tended to focus on the product – what it is that the interlanguage demonstrates at a given point in time. Variability and change were given short shrift in the morpheme studies and error analysis. As disenchantment with these techniques grew, linguistically-orientated researchers began to direct their attention to the developmental process and to how one could account for both systematicity and variability in the development of the interlanguage.

Variation within systematicity

This approach is represented in the work of Andersen (1978) and Hyltenstam (1977), both of whom used *implicational scaling techniques* to examine individual variability within uniformity. This procedure, often used in sociolinguistic research, involves the analysis of attributes of language use such that the presence of a particular attribute in the speech of individuals being studied implies the presence of other attributes in their speech. The presence or absence of attributes in individual speakers or groups of speakers is displayed by an implicational table from which one can derive a 'coefficient of reproducibility' (Guttman 1944). If the coefficient is high, it means that there is a great deal of systematicity in the data – certain attributes of language must be present before others are acquired. If the coefficient is low, it means that there is not a regular pattern in the data – behaviour is essentially random.

Andersen (1978) and Hyltenstam (1977) found that their subjects showed systematicity in their second-language acquisition. Subjects from different first-language backgrounds showed a single implicational order, although there was evidence in both studies of individual variation. For example, subjects learning Swedish in Hyltenstam's study could be placed along a continuum according to the parts of the negative they had acquired. Although there was variability in their responses, the general tendency was to follow a definite order: first putting negatives after auxiliary forms and then putting them after main verbs.

Both Andersen and Hyltenstam stressed the uniformity and systematicity in their data, but they were also careful to note the variability that the implicational orders revealed. The coefficients of reproducibility were not perfect; there was variation between and within learners at various points along the road. There was also backsliding, as new forms were learned and forgotten.

Functional variation

Additional evidence for variation comes from the research of Huebner (1979, 1983) who looked at the acquisition of the English article by a Hmong speaker. In examining speech samples from 17 one-hour taping sessions over the course of a year, Huebner found little systematicity in the use of the article until he examined *how* it was used. The learner initially used /da/ (for English *the*) to mark nouns as specific and known

Table 3.2 The development of a system of articles in the speech of a Hmong speaker

	+ Specific + Known to hearer	+ Specific − Known to hearer	Other
Time 1	89%	3%	8%
Time 2	78%	19%	3%
Time 3	85%	14%	1%
Time 4	90%	7%	3%

Based on Huebner 1979.

to the hearer, but not the topic of the sentence. There followed a period in which /da/ was more widely used in all noun phrase environments. At a later stage, toward the end of the year, the speaker's usage began to approximate standard English and /da/ was dropped from noun phrases where the information was not known to the hearer. Table 3.2 shows this progression. At Time 1 there was little use of /da/ when the referent was not known to the hearer, but this usage increased at Times 2 and 3. In the final phase, Time 4, /da/ was once again becoming limited to situations where the nouns were specific and known to the hearer.

Huebner maintained that the learner's interlanguage was systematic beneath its superficial chaos, and that variability was due to the subject changing his hypotheses about the target language. Huebner argued that over the course of the year his subject was shifting from a topic-prominent (Hmong-like) system to a subject-prominent (English-like) system. In a topic-prominent system, the topic (a discourse category) is taken to be basic and hence occurs first in a sentence, as in *That tree* (topic), *the leaves are big*. In a subject-prominent system, the subject (a syntactic category) is taken to be basic and occurs first. As evidence for the shift, Huebner noted that at Time 1 his subject had relatively few pronouns and only topics appeared in sentence initial positions. These topics were, however, not marked with /da/. By Time 4, he had a full set of definite and indefinite pronouns and there were apparently no restrictions on noun phrases occurring in sentence initial position. At this point, /da/ was used to mark topics.

Huebner noted that an order-of-acquisition approach to his subject's acquisition of the article morpheme would have made it appear that learning with respect to this morpheme had stopped, when in fact the learner's hypotheses about the target language were under continual revision. Huebner's research demonstrates the importance of examining not simply linguistic forms, but the way in which these forms assume in a target language the range of meanings and functions they have in the learner's first language. Such a 'dynamic' paradigm for interlanguage research focuses on the evolution of grammatical encodings of a particular functional domain, beginning with a form and tracing its functional distribution in the data over time. This approach requires examining the possible functional variation of a form and the way in which other forms in the learner's interlanguage are used to cover roughly the same functional domain as the form in question.

Systematic variability

It has become increasingly apparent that, although they are systematic and internally consistent, interlanguages may contain alternate rules for performing the same functions. On some occasions one rule is used; on other occasions – and at the same stage in development – another rule may be used. Thus, despite the evidence for uniformity in the developmental profile of different learners from different first-language backgrounds, there are variations in the overall course of development that learners follow. As Tarone (1983) put it, the evidence indicates that interlanguage, like any other natural language, is systematically variable.

Tarone's explanation for this systematic variability, as we have seen earlier, is based on the notion of a 'capability continuum', which assumes that the learner's competence is made up of a continuum of styles, ranging from the careful to the vernacular. The style used in a particular situation is determined by the degree of attention paid to language form, which in turn is a reflection of social factors and personal style. Tarone argued that, in spite of this variability, the interlanguage is systematic because it can be described through a set of variable and categorical rules and because it has internal consistency.

Non-systematic variability

Ellis (1985a), however, has argued that in addition to systematic variability, there is non-systematic variability in the interlanguage. Ellis took Huebner's view that learners acquire forms that are used to realize existing functions, which later are mapped onto the exact functions they serve in the target language. In the early stages of second-language acquisition, new forms are used that have not yet been integrated into the learner's form-function system. Two or more forms may be used in free variation. This process Ellis saw to involve non-systematic variability in the interlanguage. Systematic variability occurs only when the new forms have been accommodated by a restructuring of the existing form–function system to one that more closely approximates that of the target language.

Ellis gave the example of a learner who used two different negative rules (*no* + *verb* and *don't* + *verb*) to perform the same illocutionary meaning in the same situational context, in the same linguistic context, and in the same discourse context. Nor was there evidence for any difference in the amount of attention paid to the form of the utterance. Ellis argued that the two forms were in free variation and that such variability in use is non-systematic until a reorganization phase begins when the forms are distinguished in terms of situational, linguistic, and discourse use. Non-systematic variability was seen by Ellis to be a necessary part of the acquisition process as the learner extends a new form to cover a range of functions and then attempts to discover which of these functions can be served by the form.

As Rutherford put it, interlanguages are 'fluid, malleable, sporadic, permeable, amorphous, pervasive, and dynamic' (1984, 137). Ellis's distinction between systematic and non-systematic variability is an attempt to allow for the basic instability and unpredictability of interlanguages. It is his view that this instability is basic to the acquisition process.

The acquisition of the interlanguage

The shift from a product to a process orientation has led to increasing interest in how it is that the interlanguage develops. Rather than appealing to vaguely defined 'universal linguistic processes' that guide acquisition, researchers working within the interlanguage framework have begun to look at how learners map form–function relationships. Ellis's argument that second-language acquisition involves the sorting out of form–function relationships assumes that the learner begins with forms. Another view is that the learner begins with functions.

The functional approach
Specifically, a number of authors have argued that second-language data shows evidence of the acquisition of function without the acquisition of form. For example, researchers working with 'guestworkers' in Europe have noted that their subjects often mark temporality via other means than verb morphology (Dittmar 1981; Meisel 1982). Rather than using past endings and auxiliary forms, some subjects use temporal adverbs such as 'yesterday' and 'in a month' with the infinitive to mark past or future time. Other subjects use other devices, such as those itemized in Table 3.3. Sato's (1984) analysis of conversational units indicated that second-language learners relied on implicit inferences and context to mark temporality. Thus in the last two examples in Table 3.3, the learner is using the narrative or the descriptive context to express past time: *The referee* was *unfair* and *She* walked *across.*

These researchers looked at how their subjects established past time reference because the interlanguage data did not indicate that they were using morphological markers. Past tense verb forms simply did not occur in the learners' speech. But closer analysis revealed that the learners did have techniques for expressing temporality. This is another

Table 3.3   Some linguistic devices used to express temporality in the interlanguage of second-language learners

---

(1) Temporal adverbials: 'yesterday', 'last night'
(2) Locative adverbials: 'in Vietnam', 'at work'
(3) Calendar expressions: 'January', 'Tuesday'
(4) Clause sequencing: 'I go to school Vietnam. I come US'
(5) Interlocutor scaffolding:
    Native speaker: Yeah, tell me about your goal. How did you
                 make it?
    Learner: Left foot. I shoot left foot.
(6) Implicit reference in narrative context:
    Learner: I don't know what he (imitates whistle blowing).
    Native speaker: The referee? The referee.
    Learner: He unfair.
(7) Implicit reference in descriptive context:
    Learner: She walk across. (describing snapshots)

Based on Sato 1984.

example of the advantage of a process over a product orientation. By
simply focusing on the product (what the learner is saying), one is in
danger of losing sight of the process (what the learner is trying to
say).

It seems clear that both form-to-function and function-to-form analyses are needed to understand the process of second-language acquisition (Long and Sato 1984). That is, researchers need to look at how
forms are mapped onto functions, and how functions are mapped onto
forms. The functional approach has the advantage of indicating how
it is that beginning second-language learners express functions they
can express in their native language – such as temporality, gender,
modality – in a language in which they have limited syntactic and lexical devices. At the same time, Ellis was correct in noting that analyses
are needed that examine in detail how forms acquire new functions and
lose old ones as they are mapped onto the exact functions they serve in
the target language.

The role of discourse
Huebner's (1983) work is a good example of how it is possible to attend
to both form and function in the acquisition process. One of the
features he examined in his Hmong learner was the use of the form *isa*
in the English interlanguage. This form derived from the standard
English and was used initially to mark topic–comment boundaries. For
example, the subject said, *What I do everyday isa water the plants* and
What I eat for breakfast isa Love's (bread) *and butter.* This initial usage
served a specific function and acted as a discourse marker rather than a

copular verb. That is, the form identified a discourse boundary. Only later did the learner begin to use the form in its copular verb function in various syntactic structures.

Huebner's emphasis on discourse functions is consistent with the view of many interlanguage researchers who give critical importance to the role of 'collaborative discourse' in the acquisition process. Rather than looking at isolated utterances for instances of particular grammatical forms, researchers have begun to examine how linguistic functions are marked across utterances in a conversation. Thus in the research on temporality mentioned above it was found that speakers use temporal 'anchor points' previously established either by themselves or by their conversational partners, rather than morphological markers (Meisel 1982; Sato 1984):

Native speaker: 'What did you do yesterday?'
Learner: 'Yesterday, I play ball.'

Native speaker: 'When did you come to this country?'
Learner: 'I come by boat.'

Conversational analysis
As Long and Sato (1984) have pointed out, many researchers regard such conversational 'scaffolding' as the crucible of language acquisition. Hatch (1978), for example, has argued that language learning evolves out of learning how to carry on a conversation and that syntactic constructions develop out of conversations. Rather than assuming that the learner first learns a form and then uses that form in discourse, Hatch assumed that the learner first learns how to do conversation, how to interact verbally, and out of this interaction syntactic forms develop. Although careful not to claim a causal relationship, the argument is made that conversation precedes syntax. Specifically, in building a conversation with a partner ('vertical construction'), the child establishes the prototypes for later syntactic development ('horizontal construction').

To do conversation the child has to learn to call the partner's attention to very concrete objects and to on-going actions. Once a child nominates a topic, the partner has a limited number of possible replies. Hatch (1978) gave the example of the child pointing to a fish in a fish tank. The adult conversational partner can say:

'What's this? It's a fish.'
'Where's the fish?'
'Whose fish is that?'
'Is that yours?'
'How many fish are there?'
'What colour is the fish?'

'What's the fish doing? He's swimming.'
'Can he swim?'
'No, it's not a fish.'

By questioning and responding in this way, the adult is prompting the use by the child of specific syntactic constructions – precisely those that are found early developmentally.

The process is seen to be the same in first- and second-language learning. When the adult asks a question, he or she is in essence asking for constituents to fill in slots. By filling in these grammatical slots, the learner gets practice in applying the rules of the language. Hatch's argument is that the learner's initial need is to interact through language, and that by learning how to interact in conversation first- and second-language learners acquire vertical then horizontal – i.e., syntactic – constructions.

In short, interlanguage research has developed from the product orientation of the morpheme studies and error analysis to a more process orientation that focuses on form–function mappings and on the role of discourse in language acquisition. Whether functional analyses and examinations of conversational scaffolding can explain language acquisition is at this point debatable. Nonetheless, such approaches represent important methodological advances over the static techniques of the morpheme studies and error analyses.

The role of the first language

The final topic to be discussed here is the role of the first language in the acquisition of the interlanguage. We have seen that a consensus arose in response to the morpheme studies and error analysis research that it was more important to explore the dynamic qualities of interlanguage development than to argue over similarities and differences between first- and second-language acquisition. The evidence indicated that there was enough regularity in development to talk about systematicity in the interlanguage. But there was also evidence for variability within subjects (as correct and incorrect forms shift back and forth while the learner sorts out form – function mappings) and between subjects (because of differences in the first language).

To this point the discussion has focused on the within-subject variability and on how what appear to be irregularities in the developmental process may in fact be quite revealing of how functions are mapped onto target-like forms or how forms come to express target-like functions. Now I would like to discuss briefly the issue of between-subject variability, meaning by this the question of how a learner's first language influences the interlanguage.

Studies operating at the product level of analysis have, as we have seen, yielded no clear-cut information about the relative occurrence of transfer and non-transfer errors in the speech of second-language learners. There was the serious methodological problem of the non-equivalence of the opportunity of occurrence of transfer and non-transfer errors (Hakuta and Cancino 1977). Furthermore, as Meisel (1983b) has noted, the mere fact that a form occurs in both the first language and in the interlanguage does not prove the existence of the process of transfer.

Transfer as process
As researchers have begun to examine transfer as a process, the inadequacies of a product orientation have become increasingly clear. For example, Keller-Cohen (1979) found that a Japanese, a Finnish, and a German child acquired the English interrogative in roughly the same developmental sequence, but that the Finnish child acquired the use of yes/no questions much slower than the other two children, presumably because of the lack of correspondence between first- and second-language structures. The end result was the same, but the processes differed because of differences in first language.

Similarly, Zobl (1982) noted that two case studies involving the acquisition of the English article – in one instance by a Chinese-speaking child and in the other by a Spanish-speaking child – indicated that the children had taken different paths to acquisition. Chinese has no formal category of articles and the Chinese child initially used a deictic determiner (*this airplane, this paper school*) to approximate English language usage. Spanish does have articles and the Spanish child did not use the deictic determiner.

Another difference in the developmental process that is due to first-language influence is the observation that speakers of some languages take longer to learn certain forms than do speakers of other languages because their own first languages have similar forms. Thus Schumann (1982) reported that *no + verb* forms are more difficult to eliminate from the interlanguage of Spanish-speakers than they are from the interlanguage of other speakers learning English because of the existence of this pattern in Spanish.

Other transfer phenomena
In addition to showing that transfer results in learners taking different developmental paths to target-language mastery or makes it more difficult to learn certain constructions, recent work on transfer has looked at the following phenomena (Gass 1984):

> (1) Transfer of typological organization. Wode (1981) has argued that before transfer can occur there must be a certain degree of typological similarity between first- and second-language structures. Without this syntactic congruity, Wode maintained, there will be little confusion and first-language

forms will not appear in the interlanguage. Zobl (1979) has made a similar argument.

(2) Avoidance. Schachter (1974) argued that Japanese and Chinese students produced far fewer relative clauses than did Persian and Arabic students because of transfer from first-language constructions. Japanese and Chinese are not right-branching languages and so relative constructions in English are more difficult for students from this background than they are for Persian and Arabic speakers (which are right-branching languages). This difficulty, however, did not show itself in errors, but in avoidance of use of the English relative.

(3) Overproduction of certain elements. Schachter and Rutherford (1979) found that Japanese and Chinese students overproduced certain target-language forms, such as 'It is fortunate that . . .' and 'There is a . . .'. They speculated that this is because these languages are topic prominent and that first-language discourse functions are retained through second-language syntactic forms.

(4) Language facilitation. Transfer may also be facilitative of learning. There is some evidence from research on vocabulary development (Ard and Homburg 1983) that there is a response facilitation effect that generalizes beyond items that show overt similarity. Thus Spanish learners did well on vocabulary items where there was a direct similarity in form and meaning between Spanish and English items. In addition, they did well on items where there was no such similarity. No such facilitation was reported for Arabic learners.

(5) Modification of hypotheses. Schachter (1983) argued that the learner's previous knowledge constrains the hypotheses that are possible about the new language. Thus transfer should not be thought of simply in terms of its direct effect on the learner, but also in terms of the more indirect, higher-order influence it has on hypothesis formation. In addition, Schachter noted that previous knowledge of language includes the new information the learner has gained about the target language, which may be incomplete and inaccurate. Hence learners may make mistaken generalizations based on their faulty hypotheses about the target language.

Transfer as decision-making

It can be seen from these examples that the concept of transfer has taken on a number of different meanings for researchers and that in much of this research the influence of the first language would have gone unobserved were the traditional, product-oriented definition of transfer used (Gass 1984). Kellerman (1979, 1983) has argued that transfer should be looked on as a cognitive process in which decisions are made on the basis of (1) the learner's perception of the similarity between first- and second-language structures, and (2) the degree of markedness of the first-language structure. More marked structures are those that the person thinks of as irregular, infrequent, and semantically opaque. Transfer is predicted to occur when the perceived similarity between the two languages is great and when the structures involved are marked. A number of studies (Gass 1979; Jordens 1977; Rutherford 1982) support these predictions.

For example, Kellerman (1979) applied the markedness concept to the domain of semantics. He argued that second-language learners show preferences for particular meanings of words, such that sentences like *I broke the glass* are more acceptable than *He broke his promise*. The first case, Kellerman argued, reflects the core meaning of *break* and is therefore more basic than the second case. Similarly, Dutch learners of English were found to reject as unacceptable sentences such as 'He kicked the bucket', which is acceptable in Dutch but which is viewed as more irregular and language-specific than *He kicked the ball*. More regular (unmarked) forms are viewed by learners as transferable to the target language, assuming that the two languages are thought to be similar (as is true for Dutch and English).

One consequence of these new ways of looking at the notion of transfer is a renewal of interest in contrastive analysis. The rejection of contrastive analysis by researchers such as Dulay and Burt now appears to have been premature. Research on transfer has led to a richer and more sophisticated view of the goal of contrastive analysis (Zobl 1983, 1984a). Emphasis on the notion of markedness, in particular, has led to contrastive statements about predicted learning difficulty (Hyltenstam 1982; Kellerman 1983; Rutherford 1982).

To conclude, the shift from a product to a process orientation has drawn attention to the more subtle and non-obvious effects of the first language on interlanguage development. It has become apparent that the first language does affect the course of interlanguage development, but this influence is not always predictable. The work of Kellerman and others has resulted in some testable hypotheses about when transfer from the first language affects the interlanguage, although the fluid and amorphous nature of the interlanguage and the inadequacy of our testing procedures leave much to be discovered about the role of first-language transfer.

Evaluation

This chapter has traced some developments in Interlanguage theory; other developments will be discussed in subsequent chapters. It is impossible at this time to separate Interlanguage theory from developments in Universal Grammar theory or in Creolization theory. As was mentioned at the beginning of this chapter, some authors use 'interlanguage' as equivalent to second-language generally. Hence it is difficult to demarcate where Interlanguage theory ends and other theories begin.

For example, we have seen that Kellerman used the notion of 'markedness' as one component in his scheme for predicting when first-language transfer occurs in the interlanguage. This concept is also used in a somewhat different sense by Universal Grammar theory and will be discussed more fully in the following chapter. Similarly, Andersen (1983) and Schumann (1978) have argued that the interlanguage forms that characterize early second-language acquisition are the same as those observed in pidgin languages, and that in later stages interlanguage rules become more complex in much the same way as pidgin languages do when required to serve a wide range of functions. This analogy will be discussed in chapter 5.

Interlanguage theory, as was noted in the beginning of this chapter, is an intermediate-level theory, concerned with describing a limited range of second-language phenomena. These include the question of systematicity and variability in the performance of language learners, the question of how the emerging system develops and the role of transfer from the first language in this process. In contrast to Krashen's theory, Interlanguage theory has had a relatively minor impact on pedagogy. Researchers have been primarily interested in describing learners' systems and little attention has been given to pedagogical concerns.

The emphasis in Interlanguage theory on description stems from a conviction that it is important to know well what one is describing before attempting to move into the explanatory realm. There is a sense that as descriptions of learners' interlanguages accumulate, answers will emerge to the larger questions about second-language acquisition. This 'bottom-up' strategy requires careful attention to the limitations of one's data base. This has not always been the case, and the early research in particular produced generalizations and *post hoc* explanations that were premature. As more data accumulated, the claims derived from the morpheme studies and error analysis had to be revised and qualified. Subsequent research has stayed closer to the data.

As was noted in chapter 1, however, researchers do not select their procedures for collecting and analysing data in a vacuum. Their choices are determined by their theoretical orientation and by theoretical views. Methodological choices reflect considerations about theory. As Long and Sato (1984) have argued, recent research indicates a need to focus on the process of interlanguage development, a conviction that function is as important as form, and an awareness that there is an interaction between different levels of analysis – phonological, morphological, syntactic, semantic, and discourse – such that each needs to be simultaneously examined. These methodological insights reflect a theoretical stance: that static, single-level approaches do not do justice to the changing and complex nature of second-language acquisition.

These theoretical considerations have not been clearly spelled out, however. Like the phenomenon it seeks to describe, Interlanguage theory has been fluid and amorphous, constantly changing and incorporating new ideas. In terms of the criteria established in chapter 1, Interlanguage theory has been only partially successful. It was argued there that good theory fits the data well, is consistent with related formulations, is clear in its predictions, and is heuristically rich. Interlanguage theory has scored well on the last of these criteria, in that the theory has generated a great deal of significant research and thinking about second language. It is more difficult to say how well the theory does on the other criteria.

Interlanguage theory has made us think differently about a number of second-language phenomena. Error analysis made clear the inadequacies of a rigid behaviourist–structuralist position. More recent work on transfer has made apparent the folly of denying first-language influence any role in interlanguage development. The work of Kellerman, Zobl, and others has led to predictions about when the influence of the first language will be greatest. Close analyses of the interlanguage development of individual learners, as represented in the work of Huebner, Andersen, Hyltenstam, and others, has led to better understanding of how the process occurs. Thus the theory realizes the goals of any good theory: transformation of thinking, prediction, and understanding.

Without clear and testable predictions, however, it is not clear that Interlanguage theory will provide richer insights into the process of second-language acquisition. What seems to be happening is that 'interlanguage' is a term used by people of various theoretical persuasions and that the more interesting and testable hypotheses are being generated by these theories rather than by Interlanguage theory *per se*. Thus researchers have begun to look at the linguistic, sociolinguistic, and psychological processes that underlie interlanguage development. The next three chapters discuss theoretical developments from each of these perspectives.

4

Linguistic universals

One of the persistent problems in research on second-language acquisition has been to determine to what extent the learner is influenced by the input (system-external factors) and to what extent the learner is influenced by cognitive and linguistic processes (system-internal factors). The theory to be discussed in this chapter focuses on system-internal factors, and, specifically, on the role of linguistic universals in second-language acquisition. Proponents of this approach take the position that the input alone or the input interacting with non-linguistic cognitive principles cannot account for the ultimate attainment of child and adult language learners. The claim is that in order to explain the acquisition of the formal properties of language it is necessary to assume an innate, and universal, linguistic component.

There have been a number of different approaches taken to the study of linguistic universals in second-language research (Gass 1984). In this chapter I will focus on two: (1) work that follows the approach taken by Joseph H. Greenberg, and (2) work that derives from the writings of Noam Chomsky. The Greenbergian approach is *data-driven* and derives from an examination of the surface features of a wide range of human languages in an effort to determine how languages vary and what constraints and principles underlie this variation. In contrast, the Chomskyan approach is *theory-driven*, and derives from an in-depth analysis of the properties of language in an effort to determine the highly abstract principles of grammar that constrain the class of possible human languages. The 'Universal Grammar' consists not of particular rules of a particular language, but a set of general principles that applies to all languages.

The distinction between the two approaches should be a familiar one by this time. It corresponds roughly to the continuum that divides more 'inductive' approaches to theory from more 'deductive' ones. As we shall see, however, this distinction is not entirely unambiguous, as the

Chomskyan approach has tended to assimilate the Greenbergian, so that for some the result is a single theoretical orientation. The first section of this chapter treats work in the Greenbergian tradition; the second section deals with research in the Chomskyan tradition.

Typological universals

The approach taken by Greenberg and his followers begins by analysing data from a representative sample of the world's languages in order to extract universal patternings. There is general agreement among linguists that language universals exist; the question is to what extent different languages are structured according to universal principles. The approach is tedious and subject to constant refinement. Only by sampling from a wide range of languages do the common patterns emerge.

The term 'language typology' refers to a field of study in which patterns that exist among the languages of the world are researched and the possible variation found in human languages is described. The specification of language universals is based on discerned patterns in this variation, the limits of variation defining the universals. Thus the study of language universals and the study of language typology are complementary to each other: the study of universals focuses on what is common to all languages and the study of typology focuses on the variation that exists between languages.

Language universals and language typology

The complementarity between the study of language universals and the study of language typology can be illustrated by an example. In developing a typology, researchers examine actual representations of a particular parameter to determine whether the various logical possibilities are found across languages. If one considers, for instance, Greenberg's (1974) universal that languages with verb-subject-object (VSO) basic word order have prepositions, there are four logical

	Prepositions	
VSO	Present	Absent
	(1)	(2)
Present	Welsh	–
	(3)	(4)
Not present	English	Japanese

Figure 4.1. The four logical possibilities of languages involving the presence or absence of VSO word order and the presence or absence of prepositions (based on Comrie 1981).

possibilities: (1) VSO with prepositions, (2) VSO without prepositions, (3) non-VSO with prepositions, and (4) non-VSO without prepositions. As is seen in Figure 4.1, there are languages falling in the first, third, and fourth categories. Indeed, there are many languages falling in each of these categories. But there are no languages in the second category (Comrie 1981). Thus, the typological endeavour – aimed at assigning languages to different types – leads to the establishment of a universal.

Classification of universals

Researchers working on language universals and language typology distinguish between those properties of language that can be said to be present or absent in natural languages without reference to any other properties of the given language (*non-implicational universals*), and those that relate the presence of one property to the presence of some other property (*implicational universals*). An example of a non-implicational universal is the statement that languages have vowels. No reference is made to any other properties that must or must not be present. In contrast, the example mentioned above – that if a language has a VSO basic word order, it has prepositions – is an example of an implicational universal. To be established, such a universal requires that the implicational statement 'if p, then q' be true – that is, if the language has VSO, it has prepositions. The logical possibilities, (1), (3), and (4) in Figure 4.1 are allowed, but (2) is not. Instances of the disallowed logical possibility would constitute counter-examples to the implicational universal.

Another way in which universals are classified distinguishes between those that are without exceptions (*absolute universals*) and those that have exceptions (*tendencies*) (Comrie 1981). Non-implicational and implicational universals may be absolute universals or tendencies. That all languages have vowels is an absolute non-implicational universal: there do not seem to be exceptions. That all languages have nasal consonants is a non-implicational tendency, because some Salishan languages have no nasal consonants. Similarly, the statement that 'if a language has VSO as its basic word order, it has prepositions' is an absolute implicational universal. In contrast, the statement 'if a language has SOV basic word order, it will have postpositions' is an implicational tendency, because Persian is SOV with prepositions rather than postpositions.

Within this framework, *markedness conditions* are arrived at through an observation of the implicational relationship between categories. Whenever the existence of a category A in a language implies the existence of category B, A is considered more marked than B. For many linguistic phenomena, however, it is not possible to define typological markedness on the basis of implicational relationships, because there are no two categories, A and B, that co-exist in the language and have an implicational relationship. In such cases, markedness is based on frequency, with the categories that occur more frequently among languages identified as unmarked, and those that occur less frequently, identified as marked (Hyltenstam 1982).

The Accessibility Hierarchy

Recent work on language universals has uncovered a number of areas where one property can be described as more marked than some other property. One that is particularly relevant to research on second-language learning is the Accessibility Hierarchy for relativization proposed by Keenan and Comrie (1977). They argued on cross-linguistic grounds that the degree of difficulty of relativizing on a particular noun phrase proceeds from top to bottom along the hierarchy shown in Table 4.1. Thus subjects are predicted to be easier to relativize than direct objects, and so on down the hierarchy. The Accessibility Hierarchy is an example of a chain of implicational universals: if a language can relativize on position *n*, then necessarily it can also relativize on position *n – 1*.

In this analysis to 'relativize on a particular noun phrase' refers to the role of the noun phrase in question within the relative clause, not within the main clause. In the sentence, *I know the man who arrived late*, relativization is on a subject (*the man arrived late*), not on a direct object (*I know the man*). That is, the relevant fact is that *the man* is subject of the subordinate clause, not that it is direct object of the main clause (Comrie 1984).

There are two subparts to the hypothesis. First, if a language can relativize on a given position on the Accessibility Hierarchy, then it must be able to relativize on all positions higher on the hierarchy, because a position lower on the hierarchy cannot be more accessible than one higher. Second, for each position on the Accessibility Hierarchy, there is some possible human language that can relativize on that position but on no lower position, because each position on the hierarchy is thought to define a potential cut-off point.

Note that the postulation of a universal Accessibility Hierarchy for relative clause formation suggests a hierarchy of degrees of markedness (Comrie 1984). That is, it is misleading to say that relativization on indirect objects is marked in any absolute sense. Rather, the hypothesis states that relativization on indirect objects is marked in comparison to relativization on subjects but less marked than relativization on genitives.

Language universals and second-language research

The Accessibility Hierarchy has spawned a number of studies of second-language acquisition, directed at testing predictions concerning

Table 4.1   The Accessibility Hierarchy

Least difficult

      Subject: 'the child that was hit by him'
      Direct object: 'the child that he hit'
      Indirect object: 'the woman to whom he sent the book'
      Object of a preposition: 'the rock under which he put
             the letter'
      Genitive: 'the woman whose child went across the river'
      Object of comparative: 'the amount less than which he
             wanted'

Most difficult

ease of acquisition. This section examines these and other predictions concerning second-language learning derived from typological universals as they relate to acquisitional sequences and to the question of the influence of transfer from the first language.

Acquisitional sequences

Susan Gass (1979; Gass and Ard, 1980) conducted a series of experiments on relative-clause formation in English by learners from various first-language backgrounds. She used three tasks, a grammatical judgement task, a sentence-combining task, and a free composition task, administered six times over a period of four months. The results were seen to indicate that learners of all languages tested followed the constraints of the Accessibility Hierarchy in their English regardless of the positions on which their own languages were able to relativize. Speakers of all languages had more correct responses to subject relative than to direct object relatives and so forth.

Gass also reported that subjects with first languages with pronominal reflexes were more likely to accept sentences with pronominal reflexes in them – e.g., sentences such as *The man that I saw* him *is a professor at the university* – than subjects with first languages without pronominal reflexes. However, this was true only for the first three positions of the hierarchy, suggesting universal difficulty with the processing and production of such structures at the lower end of the hierarchy.

Hyltenstam (1983) used different elicitation methods to examine relative clause formation in learners of Swedish from different first-language backgrounds. Only an oral picture-identification task yielded reliable results. The pattern was consistent with the Accessibility Hierarchy, but there was pronominal-reflex insertion in the interlanguage of all learners, regardless of whether their first language allowed pronominal reflexes (though there was less for speakers from languages without pronominal reflexes). Written compositions, imitation, and judgement tasks did not yield straightforward data.

Indeed, as Kellerman (1984) noted, no entirely satisfactory methodology has yet evolved for studying the role of the first language in the acquisition of relative clauses in a second language. While the bulk of the evidence favours the acquisitional sequences predicted by the Accessibility Hierarchy, there are enough inconsistent findings, especially with judgement tasks (e.g., Muñoz-Liceras 1983), to warrant caution in accepting claims based on the Accessibility Hierarchy. Gass (1979) suggested that there are cases where first-language and target-language factors appear to play a counterbalancing role, resulting in non-hierarchical ordering in some instances.

Kumpf (1982) argued that markedness considerations could lead to the appearance of forms that were not present in either the first or the target language. She reported evidence in the interlanguage of second-language learners that suggested that the tense/aspect system did not correspond to either the first or the target language. For instance, one of her subjects had created a morphological means of marking completed versus uncompleted actions unlike either language. This was seen to reflect the universal tendency found in cross-linguistic research to mark aspect before tense, so that this subject's system was seen to correspond to what would be predicted on the basis of universal principles. Kumpf speculated that in such cases the interlanguage reflects the learner's capacity to create unique forms consistent with universal principles of natural languages. A similar conclusion was reached by Wode (1984).

If we recall the argument of Adjemian (1976), discussed in the previous chapter, that interlanguages are natural languages, then we would expect that whatever universal constraints hold for natural languages would hold true for the interlanguages of second-language learners. That is, the interlanguage should not contain structures that violate language universals, nor should the development of the interlanguage violate predictions of the Accessibility Hierarchy or other predictions based on degree of markedness. There are a number of studies consistent with Adjemian's claim (Anderson 1983; Broselow 1983; Frawley 1981; Schmidt 1980), but there are also examples of putative universals that do not seem to affect the second-language acquisition process (Eckman 1984; Gass and Ard, 1984).

Eckman (1984) noted that language universals have been described and verified on the basis of first-language data rather than second-language data. Hence, he reasoned, if interlanguage development violates language universals, one could argue that the domain over which language universals hold is that of first languages, not second languages. This is the position that Eckman favoured, as opposed to what he saw to be the alternative – to discard the universal as false. There is another possibility, however, not allowed by Eckman, and that is to consider the possibility of universal 'tendencies' (Comrie 1981) that allow of exceptions, both in the developing interlanguage of second-language learners and in the developing interlanguage of child first-language learners (Lord 1984).

Gass and Ard (1984) have proposed that the effect of a particular language universal on second-language acquisition depends on the ontology of that universal. The potential influence of a universal depends on whether it has its basis in perceptual, cognitive, or physical factors (e.g., the shape of the human vocal tract), in which case its influence will be greater than if the universal has arisen out of historical change. The Accessibility Hierarchy is thought by these authors to be based on perceptual/cognitive factors and hence to have direct relevance to second-language acquisitional processes.

The critical question for the theory at this point seems to be determining how characteristics of the universal (e.g., its status as absolute or statistical, its source) affect its role in the process of acquisition. Furthermore, if one allows for the possibility that first- and target-language factors play counterbalancing roles resulting in violations of linguistic universals (Gass 1979), then there is the problem of separating the role of universals from transfer.

Transfer

A way around this difficulty is to reject the search for 'single' etiologies in dealing with the errors made by second-language learners. One reason that it is difficult in particular cases to distinguish between the influence of language transfer and language universals is that both processes can operate at the same time or in complex interaction. That is, the interlanguage can be the product of multiple causation.

This position has been advanced by Zobl (1983, 1984a), who argued that to overcome the inadequacy of the contrastive analysis approach – that is, to explain why some differences between the first and the target language lead to learning difficulty and other differences do not – it is necessary to look at the interaction of transfer forces with other influences on the learner. Specifically, Zobl proposed that one reason for transfer from the first language is that the second-language rule is obscure. There are two main reasons suggested for this obscurity: (1) the second language is typologically inconsistent in that it violates a universal implicational pattern, or (2) the rule is itself typologically variable, so that there are a large number of possibilities. In either of these cases, learners are likely to fall back on their first language and first-language influence will be found in the interlanguage.

The conditions that make for obscurity in the target language imply that the rule is marked in the second language. In such cases, even marked first-language constructions will be preferred (Zobl 1983). However, there may be differences at different stages of interlanguage development in the likelihood that marked features of the first language will be transferred to the second language. Kellerman (1979) reported that learners initially transfer both marked and unmarked features from their first language, but that in the more advanced interlanguage, they resist transferring marked features.

This is not to imply that beginners will necessarily transfer marked features from their first language. Zobl (1984a) noted that, while there are exceptions that violate the constraints of language universals where marked features are transferred, the usual pattern is for second-language learners at all stages of development to avoid transferring marked first-language rules. His example was French speakers learning English. French allows extraction of a noun phrase modified by *combien*: *Combien voulez-vous d'oranges?* is permissible (though marked in comparison with *Combien d'oranges voulez-vous?* which is also permitted). In English *How many do you want oranges* is not permissible. Beginning French learners were found to resist transferring the marked form.

Eckman (1977, 1985) has argued that transfer occurs principally where the first-language feature is unmarked and the second-language feature is marked. According to Eckman's Markedness Differential Hypothesis, those areas of the target language that will be most difficult for second-language learners are those that are both different from the

Table 4.2 The Markedness Differential Hypothesis

The areas of difficulty that a second-language learner will have can be predicted on the basis of a comparison of the first language and the target language such that:

1) Those areas of the target language that are different from the first language and are relatively more marked than in the first language will be difficult.

2) The degree of difficulty associated with those aspects of the target language that are different and more marked than in the native language corresponds to the relative degree of markedness associated with those aspects.

3) Those areas of the target language that are different from the first language but are not relatively more marked than in the first language will not be difficult.

In this conceptualization, markedness is defined in the following terms: 'A phenomenon or structure X in some language is relatively more marked than some other phenomenon or structure Y if cross-linguistically the presence of X in a language implies the presence of Y, but the presence of Y does not imply the presence of X' (Eckman 1985, 290).

Based on Eckman 1977, 1985.

first language and relatively more marked (Table 4.2). An example is the distribution of voice contrast in pairs such as /t/ and /d/ in English and German. Whereas the contrast appears in word-initial, word-medial, and word-final positions in English (*ten/den, betting/bedding*, and *cat/cad*), in German it appears only in word-initial and word-medial positions. Traditional contrastive analysis would predict that English-speakers learning German would have more difficulty than German-speakers learning English, because they have to make a distinction (ignoring the contrast in word-final positions) that does not occur in their first language. Instead, it is German-speakers learning English who experience more difficulty.

This finding can be explained by the Markedness Differential Hypothesis. If it is assumed that voice contrast is marked in final position in comparison to the other two positions, German learners of English have to go from a language that has an unmarked feature to one that has a marked feature. This is predicted by the theory to be more difficult than the situation facing the English learner of German, who is going from a first language where the feature is marked to one where it is unmarked.

The Markedness Differential Hypothesis also differs from the contrastive analysis approach in that it predicts the relative degree of difficulty for various features in a second language. For example, contrastive analysis predicts that voice contrasts in English will be an area of difficulty for a speaker whose first language is Mandarin, a language that has no voice contrasts, but no predictions are made as to relative difficulty associated with learning this contrast in different word positions. The Marked Differential Hypothesis, in contrast, predicts that voice contrasts are an area of difficulty for these learners and that, because final position is the most marked position in which to maintain a voice contrast, this should be the most difficult position in which to acquire this contrast and the one where most transfer from the first language will occur.

Eckman's work suggests that transfer is not always a bidirectional process, as might be inferred from a strict contrastive analysis approach. Instead, this work on linguistic universals indicates that the reason why some first-language structures are transferred and others are not relates to the degree of markedness of the structures in the various languages. The assumption, once again, is that universal constraints interact with the first language and that interlanguage forms result from this multiple causation.

To summarize, Zobl, Gass, Eckman, and others working within this framework assume that second-language learning is restricted by typology and universal constraints on the structure of natural languages. These constraints affect both the overall structural options available to learners and the range of variability found in the learner's interlanguage. The markedness hierarchy and the typological implications inherent in the structures of the target language determine developmental sequences found in the interlanguage. Markedness considerations and transfer operate in close interaction, and a number of fairly specific proposals have been made on the basis of markedness considerations for predicting when transfer from the first language is likely to occur in the interlanguage.

Universal Grammar

The Chomskyan generative grammar approach assumes that the first-language learner comes to the acquisition task with innate, specifically linguistic, knowledge, or Universal Grammar. The claim is that certain principles of the human mind are, to a degree, biologically determined and specialized for language learning. As Chomsky put it:

> Universal grammar is taken to be the set of properties, conditions, or whatever, that constitute the 'initial' state of the language learner, hence the basis on which knowledge of language develops (1980, 69).

These abstract and linguistically significant principles underlie all natural languages and comprise the essential faculty for language with which all individuals are in general uniformly and equally endowed.

Universal Grammar theory does not concern itself with second-language acquisition. The application of the theory to this domain has come about through recent work of a number of second-language researchers. Four considerations motivate interest on the part of these researchers in the Chomskyan position (White, 1985b):

(1) The need for a sufficiently sophisticated linguistic theory to describe the complex structural characteristics of inter-languages. As we have seen in Chapter 3, there is a certain vagueness in Interlanguage theory that derives from an inadequately developed linguistic theory. The same criticism, by the way, has been applied to Krashen's theory (White 1985a). Universal Grammar, its proponents argue, provides a sophisticated and detailed linguistic theory to account for second-language phenomena.

(2) The growing realization that second-language learners face a 'projection problem' – that is, that they, like first-language learners, have to work out a complex grammar on the basis of deficient data. Those working in the Chomskyan tradition argue that the learner's grammatical knowledge cannot be explained by the input data alone. Felix (1984) listed three limitations. First, some structures are so rare and marginal

that it would not be possible for learners to obtain sufficient exposure to them. Second, incorrect hypotheses require negative feedback (correction, identification of errors, etc.) if they are to be discarded, but such feedback usually does not occur. Finally, the rules of any grammar are highly abstract and so do not reflect the surface properties of the language.

(3) The development of parameter theory within generative grammar, which allows for a more precise investigation of language variation – including variation between native and target languages. Thus, as we shall see in more detail shortly, the language properties inherent in the human mind are thought to consist of a set of general principles that apply to all grammars and that leave certain parameters open. Universal Grammar is seen to set the limits within which human languages can vary.

(4) The realization that a rigid critical period hypothesis is open to question, so that one does not have to assume that adult language learning is of a totally different or disadvantaged nature when compared to child acquisition. Researchers interested in second-language acquisition have argued that there is no reason to assume that the language faculty described by Universal Grammar necessarily atrophies with age; instead they maintain that, like first-language learners, adult second-language learners are sensitive to certain structural properties of the language they are acquiring and they use these sensitivities in constructing the grammar of the language they are learning. (Flynn, 1983).

In this section, I will discuss principles of recent Chomskyan thought as they relate to language acquisition and development generally, and then turn to the application of these ideas in second-language research.

Language acquisition and development

The Chomskyan position views Universal Grammar as part of the brain. Consequently, 'learning' is not the correct term to describe how language develops:

A bulb becomes a flower; some cells become a lung. We do not say that the bulb 'learns' to be a flower or the cells 'learn' to be a lung, although in both cases certain aspects of the environment such as water and nourishment are necessary to the process. Instead we say the bulb and the cells 'grow'. Their growth is the realization of their genetic potential in conjunction with 'triggers' from the environment . . . [Similarly] Universal Grammar present in the child's mind grows into the adult's knowledge of

the language so long as certain environmental 'triggers' are provided. . . . Language acquisition is the growth of the mental
organ of language triggered by certain language experiences.
(Cook 1985, 3-4)

Because Chomskyan theory is concerned with grammatical competence, or the speaker's knowledge of the language, 'acquisition'
refers to ideal language learning unaffected by maturation, processing
limitations, memory restrictions, and other cognitive and motivational
factors. The term 'development' is used to refer to the real-time
learning of language by children, whereby the language principles that
are present manifest themselves in accordance with the child's capacity
to process information and other maturational factors.

Developmental sequences
It is generally assumed in Universal Grammar theory that the child
starts with all the principles of Universal Grammar available and that
all human languages conform to these principles. What one sees in
language development is the interaction of the workings of the language faculty with other mental organs. Note, however, that the study
of developmental sequences sheds little light on what Chomsky means
by 'acquisition'. His concern was with the operation of the language
faculty rather than with development. The sequence of development
tells us nothing about acquisition.

If one assumes that the whole of Universal Grammar is available to
the child from the start (White 1981), the language principles that are
present manifest themselves in accordance with the child's 'channel
capacity' – that is, the child's ability to process information, memory
limitations, and other maturational factors. The child does not reveal
all that is known about language at any point in time. Instead, the child
builds the best grammar possible on the basis of what is cognitively
possible at a particular maturational point. What is revealed developmentally, however, tells more about other cognitive systems than about
language acquisition in the Chomskyan sense. Thus, for example, early
in language development the child does not have the channel capacity to
acquire the relative clause in English. That relative clauses appear later
in the child's speech than do simple one-clause structures does not tell
us anything about language 'acquisition' in Chomsky's sense, but tells
us something about the cognitive system and the development of working memory.

Some authors have suggested a different explanation of developmental sequences. Felix (1984), for example, has argued that the
principles of Universal Grammar are themselves subject to an innately
specified developmental process. They lie latent until the moment for
their activation arrives. At that point, the child restructures the

grammar to accommodate a new principle that the existing grammar violates in some way. This argument, however, seems somewhat at odds with Chomsky's view of the language faculty as a mental organ, present from the start but restricted in its operation by non-linguistic factors.

Hypothesis testing

According to Chomsky, Universal Grammar provides the only way of accounting for how children are able to acquire their native language. If one assumes that children form hypotheses about their language that they then test in practice, the question of how they reject incorrect hypotheses needs to be answered. Chomsky and his followers argue that the child does not get enough negative evidence to reject incorrect hypotheses. Nor do children produce enough incorrect sentences to test out hypotheses adequately. Hence it is necessary to assume that children are in some way constrained in the hypotheses they form.

If there are constraints to the range of hypotheses children form, it becomes possible to explain how acquisition occurs. Rather than working from inductive principles alone, the child is restricted by the constraints of Universal Grammar in forming hypotheses about the input. The child's task is to test the options available against input from the environment. Thus the claim is that hypothesis testing is a possible explanation once it is accepted that the child's hypotheses are limited in number and that the environment contributes triggering rather than negative evidence.

As Cook (1985) noted, Chomsky's theory sees the environment to play both a negative and a positive role. Negatively, the theory denies that the environment provides sufficient evidence for learning particular aspects of syntax without the aid of a powerful built-in grammar. Positively, the theory claims that the environment provides positive evidence to help the learner fix the ways in which Universal Grammar is applied to the target language. Consequently, the theory does not deny that external factors influence the course of language acquisition; the right environmental input at the right time furthers the acquisition process.

Parameter setting

According to Universal Grammar theory, the principles of Universal Grammar involve a set of properties with certain parameters. These parameters remain 'open' until they are set by experience with the environment. For Chomsky, language acquisition is not so much a problem of acquiring grammatical rules, but rather a process whereby the learner sets the values of the parameters of the principles of Universal Grammar. The grammar of a language is the set of values it assigns to various parameters. As Chomsky put it, 'Experience is required to set the switches. Once they are set, the system functions' (1984, 25).

An oft-cited example of such a parameter is the pro-drop parameter, which specifies that languages vary with regard to whether they allow the deletion of pronouns in subject positions, together with related phenomena such as inversion of subject and verb. English does not have pro-drop because a subject is required for every sentence and the subject cannot be inverted with the verb in declarative sentences. This is not true of Spanish, however, which, as a pro-drop language, allows empty subjects and subject-verb inversion in declarative sentences.

Another example is the principle of adjacency, according to which noun phrases must be next to the verb or preposition that gives them case. Hence in English an adverb cannot intervene between a verb and its direct object. Sentences such as *Mary ate quickly her dinner* are not allowed, whereas in French such sentences are permitted: *Marie a mangé rapidement le dîner* (White, in press). The French option is assumed to be 'set' for the child learning French as a first language on the basis of positive evidence in the form of such sentences.

As was mentioned in chapter 2, the important question for second-language research is whether the parameters that have been set in the first language need to be reset or readjusted for the second language. This leads, as we shall see, to a reformulation of questions relating to contrastive analysis and language transfer.

Core versus peripheral grammar

Universal Grammar theory maintains a distinction between 'core' and 'peripheral' grammar. Core grammar refers to those parts of the language that have 'grown' in the child through the interaction of the Universal Grammar with the relevant language environment. In addition, however, it is assumed that every language also contains elements that are not constrained by Universal Grammar. These elements comprise the peripheral grammar. Peripheral elements are those that are derived from the history of the language, that have been borrowed from other languages, or that have arisen accidentally. Cook (1985) gave the examples of the expression *the more the merrier*, which comes from Old English and the pronunciation of *police*, which indicates that it is a late borrowing from French. Thus some aspects of the individual's grammar come from Universal Grammar, while others are influenced by other factors.

When children learn a particular language, they form hypotheses within the guidelines set by Universal Grammar. Two children learning different languages make different applications of the same linguistic principles in response to different environments. Although the child's mind is thought to prefer to adopt rules based on Universal Grammar, the child also has to learn aspects of language that are peripheral. These peripheral aspects fall outside the child's pre-programmed instructions and hence are more difficult to acquire.

This is not to say, however, that peripheral aspects of language are learned later developmentally. Chomsky was careful to point out that the order in which structures are learned may be influenced by the child's channel capacity. Aspects of the core grammar may be learned later than peripheral aspects because of processes of maturation or because of frequency effects. Here again sequence of development is an unreliable guide to acquisition (Cook 1985).

To summarize, Universal Grammar theory holds that the ability to acquire a human language is genetically determined. The theory postulates that the child faces a 'projection problem' in that the language-learning task must be accomplished with deficient input data. The only way to explain how children succeed is to assume that they approach the task endowed with a Universal Grammar that comprises a rich set of innate principles that govern the emergence of language. The Universal Grammar constrains the hypotheses that children make and the child's language environment determines which principles of the Universal Grammar will be accessed. Acquisition involves setting the parameters of a particular language in a specific way. Rules of the core grammar are seen to be easier to set than are rules of the peripheral grammar, which are thought to be outside of the child's pre-programmed instructions.

Universal Grammar and second-language acquisition

Chomskyan theory has been concerned almost exclusively with the acquisition by the child of a first language. Indeed, in his early writings Chomsky seemed to believe that second-language learning used other faculties of the mind than did first-language learning and so fell outside the domain of Universal Grammar theory. Early Chomskyan theory endorsed the Critical Period Hypothesis of Lenneberg (1967), which postulated that the limits for first-language acquisition were between the ages of two and puberty. Before this time the child is too immature physically, and after this period the brain is too inflexible.

More recent theory has largely ignored the Critical Period Hypothesis, perhaps because of considerable evidence against it (McLaughlin, 1984), or perhaps because the issue is one that relates more to development than to acquisition as these terms have been defined in current formulations. As was mentioned above, advocates of a Universal Grammar approach working on second-language learning typically argue that there is no reason to assume that the language faculty atrophies with age. Most second-language researchers who adopt the Universal Grammar perspective assume that the principles and parameters of Universal Grammar are still accessible to the adult language learner. This is seen to have important implications for how one views interlanguage development and transfer. Before turning to these topics, however, a few comments are necessary on the critical notion of 'markedness'.

The theory of markedness

The notion of markedness dates back to the Prague school of linguistics. Originally, it was used to refer to two members of a phonological opposition, one of which contained a feature lacking in the other. The phoneme carrying the feature was called marked; the other unmarked (Trubetzkoy 1936). The idea was carried over to inflectional morphology by Jakobson (1941), and was also used by Chomsky and Hallé (1968) in their work on phonology.

We have seen in the previous chapter that Kellerman (1979, 1983) invoked the concept of markedness to predict when transfer is likely to occur from the first language. More marked structures in the learner's first language – those that are perceived to be more irregular, infrequent, and semantically opaque – were predicted to be less transferable than regular and frequent forms. Other authors distinguish marked or unmarked structures according to their degree of complexity. Unmarked forms are thought to be less complex than marked.

In recent Chomskyan thought, the rules of the core grammar are thought to be unmarked and those of the peripheral grammar are marked. The theory predicts that only minimal exposure is needed to learn a core rule, but that peripheral or marked rules need to be learned on the basis of positive evidence of their existence in the grammar. Marked rules cannot be assumed a priori because they represent idiosyncratic features of the language. Hence their instantiation in a grammar takes longer to learn than a related unmarked rule:

> In our idealized theory of language acquisition, we assume that the child approaches the task equipped with Universal Grammar and an associated theory of markedness that serves two functions: It imposes a preference structure on the parameters of Universal Grammar and it permits the extension of core grammar to a marked periphery. (Chomsky 1981, 8)

In the absence of evidence to the contrary, unmarked options are selected.

Second-language researchers have used the concept of markedness to examine various acquisition problems. For example, Irene Mazurkewich (1984a, 1984b) has argued that Chomskyan Universal Grammar theory and the associated theory of markedness can serve as powerful predictors of the acquisition of dative structures by second-language learners. She reported (1984a) that second-language learners were more likely to judge as correct sentences with the unmarked dative prepositional phrase complement (*Give the book to Mary*) than the marked double noun phrase construction (*Give Mary the book*). In another paper (Mazurkewich, 1984b), she found that unmarked passivized direct objects (*A football was thrown to Phillip*) were learned before marked passivized indirect objects (*Phillip was thrown a football*). These findings were seen as evidence for the claim that the determining factor in the acquisition of interlanguage syntax is marked-ness as defined within Universal Grammar theory.

It should be pointed out, as Cook (1985) noted, that present Universal Grammar theory does not assume that markedness is directly reflected in development, even though this is usually assumed by second-language researchers. Unmarked forms should be learned before those that are marked, but the theory allows for features of 'channel capacity' – the way in which information is processed, memory limitations, etc. – to distort the sequence (White 1981). Markedness affects acquisition, but the actual process of development can disguise markedness in many ways.

Interlanguage development
As we saw in the previous chapter, the notion of interlanguage assumes that the second-language learner has a grammar that is systematic in its own right and distinct from both the first and the second languages. Universal Grammar theory assumes that all grammars, interim or final, reflect principles of the Universal Grammar. Thus, according to the theory, second-language grammars must be constrained in the same way as first-language grammars.

Support for this proposition was reported by Schmidt (1980), who found that a group of second-language learners of English produced sentences such as *John sang a song and played a guitar* and *John plays the guitar and Mary the piano*, but not **Sang a song and John plays a guitar* or **John the violin and Mary plays the piano*. Schmidt argued that his learners obeyed the Universal Grammar principle that only the second identical noun or verb may be omitted from the sentence.

Similar results were reported by Ritchie (1978) who found that adult learners of English correctly judged to be grammatical sentences such as *That a boat had sunk that John had built was obvious*. However, sentences such as **That a boat had sunk was obvious that John had built* were judged to be ungrammatical. Ritchie saw this to be evidence that the learners had access to the Universal Grammar principle called the 'right roof constraint', which limits the movement of elements in a sentence across certain types of boundaries.

These studies have been interpreted by advocates of the Universal Grammar approach as evidence that interlanguages reflect the principles of Universal Grammar and that the types of errors that second-language learners make are constrained by universal principles.

However, it is also possible, according to Universal Grammar theory, for errors in the interlanguage to reflect channel capacity, so that apparent violations can be explained away as resulting from development, not acquisition.

We have seen earlier in this chapter that the language learner is thought by Universal Grammar theory to test a limited number of hypotheses – those compatible with the presented input – and to choose from the store of potential grammars a specific one that is appropriate to the data. The learner's internal Universal Grammar severely restricts the range of hypotheses that can be entertained. Thus interlanguage development is thought by the theory to be constrained by the limited number of possibilities provided by Universal Grammar.

Zobl (1984a) has proposed that, in addition, the learner's task is made easier by what he referred to as a 'projection device', whereby implicated rules are activated once one rule in a cluster of rules is acquired. Thus, for example, once a learner discovers that the word order of a target language is verb-subject-object, it may become apparent – through the internal Univeral Grammar – that the language has prepositions.

Contrastive analysis revisited

Besides the application of the theory of markedness and of the principles of Universal Grammar to interlanguage development, researchers have applied Universal Grammar theory to transfer problems. White (1983), for example, has extended the theory to the relative markedness of different settings of a parameter. She maintained that the typical acquisition route proceeding from unmarked to marked forms is sometimes not followed in the interlanguage of second-language learners. Instead, learners at the initial stages of acquisition are likely to show the effect of the first-language parameter and hence marked forms may appear in their interlanguage before unmarked ones. Thus French learners of English were found to have a particular problem with movement rules in English, because their first language has more marked settings than the language they are learning, English, has less marked settings. Muñoz-Liceras (1983) also demonstrated that differences in the parameter settings for relative clause formations in English and Spanish can lead to marked forms appearing before unmarked ones in the interlanguage of second-language learners.

Flynn (1983) argued that the direction of grammatical anaphora accords with the principle branching order of a language. Students of English whose first language is right-branching (e.g., Spanish) were predicted to have less difficulty with the comprehension of anaphora than students whose first language is left-branching (e.g.,Japanese). Flynn had her subjects perform an English imitation task that included

Table 4.3 Examples of imitation errors in adult speakers of Japanese and Spanish

Japanese speaker	
Stimulus:	The man introduced the policeman when he delivered the plans.
Response:	The man introduced the policeman.
Stimulus:	The mayor questioned the president when he entered the room.
Response:	Mayor questioned the president . . . with the diplomat.
Spanish speaker	
Stimulus:	When he prepared the breakfast, the doctor called the professor.
Response:	When he finished the breakfast he called to the professor.

Based on Flynn 1983.

examples of anaphora, and found that the results supported her predictions. Table 4.3 shows some examples of errors made by Flynn's subjects. In contrast to the types of errors made by the Japanese subjects, Spanish subjects were typically able to make some sense of the anaphora.

Flynn noted that her results could not be accounted for by traditional contrastive analysis, which predicts interference in second-language acquisition from the first language where surface features of the first and the second language do not match. According to this analysis, left-branching subordinate *when* clauses ('When the actor finished the book, the woman called the professor') should be easier for Japanese subjects than right-branching *when* clauses. This follows because left-branching sentences match the principal recursive direction of Japanese and right-branching sentences do not. What Flynn found was a general depression in amount correct for Japanese subjects on both types of sentence structures and no significant differences in amount correct between left- and right-branching structures. Taken together Flynn's findings suggest that it is not surface features of the two languages that predict when transfer occurs, but more profound and abstract universal principles of acquisition. She argued that when the value of a parameter is set in the first language it may or may not need to be revised in the second-language acquisition process depending on the correspondence of the two languages.

Thus Universal Grammar theory does not treat transfer as a matter of structural comparison of rules as is done in contrastive analysis, but in terms of how the rules exploit the same underlying principles. As Cook (1985) has pointed out, however, this comparison needs to be supplemented by an account of how first and target grammars deviate from core grammar. For example, English and French can be seen to be similar in terms of the core parameter of sentence order, but their relationship also needs to take in the more peripheral rule that auxiliaries precede the subject in certain types of question.

> At the core, the theory provides a common measuring stick for two grammars; as we move to the periphery, the stick becomes less appropriate and more attention has to be paid to other factors than Universal Grammar (Cook 1985, 14).

To summarize, Universal Grammar theory postulates that second-language learning occurs as learners encounter more evidence from the second language, and fix the parameters of the new grammar. During the initial stages of acquisition the interlanguage is likely to show the effect of the first-language parameter and hence marked forms may appear before unmarked ones. Similarly, at the periphery, when the evidence is not consistent with core grammar, the learner is likely to adopt more marked solutions. Universal Grammar theory offers an alternative to contrastive analysis in that the theory postulates a set of deep principles common to all languages and fundamental to both first- and second-language acquisition.

Evaluation

Research on second-language learning within the Typological or the Universal Grammar framework is a recent development in the field. There have been a limited number of studies, some of which suggest that an approach based on linguistic universals holds a great deal of promise for clarifying our understanding of interlanguage development and transfer. The research has also made more apparent problems with this perspective.

The Typological approach

Methodological issues
The Typological approach stresses the comparison between languages in its search for linguistic universals. This approach, however, requires strict methodological caveats. For one, universal statements require for their validity a representative sample of human languages. Because there are an estimated 4,000 extant languages, it is difficult to know when any one sample is 'representative' of the population of actual languages of the world. How is one to know that the sample is sufficiently large and varied to include examples of all the kinds of structures found in human languages?

Even if the sample could be shown to be representative, there remains the problem of demonstrating the empirical validity of putative linguistic universals. Comrie's distinction between 'absolute' universals and universal 'tendencies' is helpful in this connection. As he pointed out:

> In a representative sample of languages, if no universal were involved, i.e., if the distribution of types along some parameter were purely random, then we would expect each type to have roughly an equal number of representatives. To the extent that the actual distribution departs from this random distribution, the linguist is obliged to state and, if possible to account for, the discrepancy. One way of looking at a universal tendency, perhaps the best way of looking at one, is as a statistically significant deviation from random patterning. An absolute universal, in this sense, is just the extreme case of deviation from random distribution: certain logical possibilities fail to occur at all, rather than just being rare. (1981, 19)

In recent work on language universals, as Comrie noted, the term 'tendency' is usually replaced by the term 'statistical universal', referring to the fact that the universal in question has only a certain statistical, rather than absolute, validity. In such a formulation, the question of whether a language universal has empirical validity is a statistical one that depends on the sampling procedures used.

This approach allows the theory to permit exceptions. One need not set up a classification of universals in terms of the different domains in which they apply. Such a classification scheme was postulated by Eckman (1984), for example, who argued that it is necessary to restrict universal statements either to all language types, to first languages, or to interlanguages, because of evidence he interpreted as indicating that an interlanguage violated a universal statement formulated on the basis of data from first languages. However, once it is accepted that universals need not be exceptionless, there is no need for restricting them to different language domains.

There is another methodological issue that needs to be mentioned here. In his review of cross-linguistic influences on second-language acquisition, Kellerman (1984) noted the limitations of various elicitation techniques in generating reliable and consistent data. Research on the Accessibility Hierarchy has, as we have seen, yielded different results depending on the elicitation method. The predictions with respect to relative-clause patterns have been more extensively studied than have other constructions, so this methodological caution needs to be kept in mind when considering evidence for other constructions, where – as is often the case – a single elicitation method is used.

Markedness

The Typological Universals approach uses the terms 'less marked' and 'unmarked' to refer to what is expected, normal, or natural in human languages. This approach does not necessarily establish the 'marked' form, because many instances involve a series based on a scale of naturalness of some sort. Thus an implicational series is an ordered series in which the existence of a category A in a language implies the existence of category B, and so forth – A being considered more marked than B.

Note that in this approach no single causal explanation is proposed for the phenomenon of markedness:

> Perceptual, articulatory, cognitive, and other factors may be operative singly or in combination to result in the implicational series. From this perspective, markedness is viewed as probabilistic, depending on the interaction of the factors involved. The value of the concept lies in the strong tendencies toward agreement among the various attributes of less or greater markedness (frequency, overtness, complexity, early acquisition, neutralization, etc. . . . and consequent possibilities of prediction. (Ferguson 1984, 249)

We have seen that researchers in the second-language field use various definitions of markedness – from the internal complexity of the structure or structural system to be learned (Wode, 1984) to frequency of occurrence in languages (Hyltenstam 1982). Table 4.4 summarizes some of the predictions made on the basis of this research.

It should be pointed out that some of the most interesting predictions concerning transfer effects based on markedness considerations are

Table 4.4 A summary of markedness predictions based on typological universals

(1) Learners transfer unmarked first-language forms when the corresponding second-language forms are more marked.
(2) The effect of the first language will be observed more strongly in cases that involve marked rules in the second language.
(3) In general, marked forms are not transferred into interlanguage, particularly when the first language possesses both marked and unmarked constructions.
(4) Marked forms may be transferred in the early stages of second-language acquisition.
(5) A first-language pattern that corresponds to an interlanguage universal can accelerate or delay second-language acquisition, depending on whether the correspondence is with an early- or late-occurring developmental pattern.

Based on Ellis 1985.

relatively subtle ones. As Rutherford (1984) noted, there are *indirect* effects from the intersection of first and native languages that are typologically different. In such cases the resulting interlanguage phenomenon may not be a product, but rather a process. That is, there may be an increased sensitivity toward certain solutions, a propensity to view language in a certain way, that influences the course of acquisition.

The problem is that various definitions of markedness can lead researchers to different predictions about the effect on second-language learning. This is clearly an area that needs more research:

> Until reliable and generally accepted means are found for establishing which of two or more forms are marked and unmarked or more or less marked, the whole construct of markedness must be considered of doubtful value for empirical research (Ellis 1985b, 212).

This brings us to the issue of falsifiability.

Testing the theory
Rapidly accumulating information about language typology and language universals offers an empirical handle to the problem of the nature of the constraints and biases with which humans are equipped to acquire and use languages (Hakuta 1984). It should be noted, however, that Comrie (1984) contended that the claims of a literal psychological interpretation of the Accessibility Hierarchy hold only where 'other things are equal' – i.e., where processing strategies or other factors do not override the predictions based on implicational universals.

This, of course, allows one to account for findings that do not fit the predictions of the theory by an appeal to independently motivated processing strategies, the counter-balancing role of first- and target-languages (Gass 1979), or other factors. Because second-language acquisition takes place under an incredible array of different circumstances – e.g., at various ages, with and without formal instruction, in literate and non-literate communities, with varying social functions of the respective languages (Ferguson 1984), such appeals can almost always be made to account for differences in rates or paths of acquisition.

Nonetheless, as Hatch (1984) noted, developmental claims (especially in phonology) have been validated in research testing predictions based on linguistic universals. Hecht and Mulford (1982), for example, compared predictions based on transfer from the first language and developmental factors (derived from universals of phonology and markedness considerations) and were able to show where transfer and developmental factors would predict errors and where each would predict the substitutions used. Eckman's (1984) Markedness Differential Hypothesis makes similar predictions. Other research uses statistical procedures, such as implicational scaling (Hyltenstam 1982) and multidimensional scaling (Kellerman 1978), to discover the dimensions defining universals and to test the psychological reality of language universal claims. The theory clearly has utility. Not enough studies have been carried out in this framework, however, to know whether it can be falsified through empirical research.

The Universal Grammar approach

Universal Grammar theory originally based its case on the analysis 'in depth' of a single language – which happened to be English. In recent years, the theory has been more open to the contribution of the Typological approach and there has been a growing convergence of the two approaches as the notion of parameterization has stimulated Chomskyan interest in cross-linguistic variation. This helps the theory deal with certain problems, but others remain.

The learnability problem

The Chomskyan, Universal Grammar approach to language learning maintains that, in addition to relatively close-to-surface levels of syntactic representation, there are more abstract levels of representation. The theory claims that children cannot induce these abstract principles simply from the data presented to them in adult speech. This is the 'poverty of the stimulus' argument – that input to children is meagre and degenerate and therefore cannot provide an adequate basis for setting the parameters of the language. To solve this projection problem – to work out a complex grammar on the basis of insufficient data – the theory contends that children acquire first language so effortlessly because the crucial abstract principles of Universal Grammar are available to them innately. Children can learn their first language readily because Universal Grammar constrains the hypotheses they make about input.

In recent years, the poverty of the stimulus argument has been under attack as it has become more apparent that parents and caregivers tailor their speech to young children in a way that makes the input more understandable (McLaughlin, 1984, ch. 2). In attempting to communicate with the child, caregivers provide (1) conversational lessons when they help the child to sustain a conversation by means of attention-getters and attention-holders, prompting questions, and expansions, (2) mapping lessons when they provide utterances that can be decoded by use of context, and (3) segmentation lessons when they give clues as to how utterances are divided into words, phrases, or clauses (Clark and Clark 1977). Language used with young children is simpler, slower, related to events and objects in the here-and-now, and contains a more limited vocabulary. As we saw in chapter 2, the effect of these features of the input language on children's language acquisition is in debate, but there is general agreement that the input is better suited to the child's needs than Chomsky saw it to be. At least in the early stages, environmental influences may be important in language acquisition.

Furthermore, another argument for the need of an innate mechanism has been criticized. This is the notion that children do not receive enough negative input to explain how they form correct hypotheses about the language. Schachter (1984) has pointed out that phenomena such as confirmation checks, clarification requests, and failures to understand qualify as negative input. Consider these conversations:

Child: Read to me a book.
Adult: What?
Child: Read a book to me.

Non-native speaker: Um in Harvard, what you study?
Native speaker: What?
Non-native speaker: What you es study?
Native speaker: What am I studying?
Non-native speaker: Yeah.

Such examples indicate that language learners can be led to appropriate speech in other ways than through explicit corrections. Once one accepts a broader reading for negative input, the learnability problem becomes less intractable than Universal Grammar theory supposes. This does not mean that the problem is solved; it is not entirely clear whether negative feedback leads to the kind of corrections that are called for. Nonetheless, environmental factors may play more of a role than is allowed by the poverty of the stimulus argument.

Core vs. periphery grammars and markedness
As we have seen, the rules of the core grammar are those that are thought to be unmarked and those on the periphery are marked. In essence, then, the notions of core grammar and peripheral grammar are simply reformulations of the theory of markedness. The prediction is that as soon as the linguistic input triggers a learner's awareness of the existence of a core or unmarked rule in the grammar, the rule not only would be learned easily, but it would be learned on the basis of minimal exposure to that language because it is predicated on a principle of Universal Grammar. In the case of peripheral or marked rules, the prediction is that they would have to be learned on the basis of positive evidence of their existence in that grammar.

So the fundamental question becomes one of determining which rules are marked and which are unmarked. This has not always proved easy. Indeed, Ellis (1985b) cited the example of the pro-drop rule, which was viewed by White (1983) as a marked form, whereas Hyams (1983) regarded it as unmarked. There is also the danger of circularity: an unmarked or core rule is one that is learned early and one that is learned early is unmarked. Without independent means of defining marked and unmarked rules, the predictions of the theory cannot be tested empirically.

Another issue relating to markedness considerations concerns universals such as the Accessibility Hierarchy, which create difficulties for Universal Grammar theory because they imply a continuum from rules that are most accessible and most easily learned, to those that are least accessible and learned with more difficulty. Does this mean that there is a continuum from unmarked core grammar to marked peripheral grammar? If Universal Grammar theory is to incorporate the findings of the Typological approach, it needs to provide some account of implicational statements consistent with the properties of Universal Grammar.

Finally, there is the issue of acquisition versus development. Even if one could show that unmarked forms are learned before marked ones, there remains the possibility that features of channel capacity and maturation (which are thought to be reflected in development) distort the acquisition sequence. How then is the theory to be tested?

The problem of falsifiability

As is well known, Chomsky's is a theory of grammatical competence, not of grammatical performance. The theory is based on abstraction:

> To discover the properties of Universal Grammar and core grammar we must attempt to abstract away from complicating factors of various sorts, a course that has its hazards but is inescapable in serious inquiry. . . . (Chomsky 1981, 39).

The theory separates competence from performance, acquisition from development, and the core from the periphery. Each of these operations takes the inquiry further from actual language as it is used by its speakers.

Chomsky contended that this is the price to be paid for insight into language; others disagree. For his critics, Chomsky's solution is too radical and may in fact be based on a questionable assumption. The theory depends critically on the poverty of the stimulus argument that speakers know things they could not have learned from the language encountered. This argument and its corollary – that learners do not receive sufficient negative input to correct erroneous hypotheses about the language – have, as was noted above, been questioned by recent work on caregiver speech. Furthermore, as Ellis (1985b) has suggested, learners may be able to disconfirm incorrect hypotheses on the basis of positive input if they are prepared to abandon hypotheses after a time when the absence of supporting evidence suggested they were improbable.

This is not to deny the importance of system-internal factors, however. It seems clear that over and beyond what can be explained on the basis of system-external factors, cognitive and linguistic factors constrain the course of language acquisition in children and adult learners. It remains to be determined which aspects of language learning are constrained by Universal Grammar and which by external factors.

The more general issue in this context is how to make the connection from a linguistic theory of language competence to a theory of second-language learning. Chomsky is not concerned in his writings with second-language learning. The burden rests on those who would apply his ideas to second language to show how the connection is to be made. What has happened to this point is that researchers have used Universal Grammar theory as a source of hypotheses about second-language learning. This enterprise has yielded interesting information about interlanguage development, but attention has been restricted to a relatively small set of syntactic phenomena. If this approach is to lead to a more general theory of second-language acquisition, the range of phenomena it can account for needs to be expanded and more attention needs to be given to the question of what methodology should be employed to link a theory of competence to the actual performance of second-language learners.

To conclude, both the Typological approach and the Universal Grammar approach have generated useful predictions about the course of interlanguage and the influence of the first language. The bulk of the evidence to date suggests that language acquisition proceeds by mastering the easier unmarked properties before the more difficult marked ones. There seem to be exceptions, however, in the early stages of acquisition and where both first-language and target-language constructions are marked. Nor is all research consistent. The exceptions and inconsistencies make apparent the need for a clear-cut and generally agreed-upon definition of markedness.

5

Acculturation/ Pidginization theory

In this chapter the perspective shifts from a purely linguistic analysis of the second-language learning process to one that emphasizes sociolinguistic and social psychological factors as well. A number of researchers studying second-language acquisition without formal instructions have been struck by the relationship between social psychological acculturation and degree of success in learning the target language. This line of research has been greatly influenced by Schumann's (1978a) innovative, if controversial, analogy between early second-language acquisition and pidginization.

These researchers have approached interlanguage development from a theoretical framework that stresses linguistic variation and change, a framework based on the sociolinguistic investigations of such authors as Labov (1966, 1969), Bailey (1973), and Bickerton (1971, 1973). Language is viewed by these authors as constantly changing over time. Theirs is a 'dynamic paradigm', which contrasts with the 'static paradigm' of structuralism and the transformational approach (Bailey 1973). The focus on pidgin-creole communities is consistent with this dynamic view, because language change in these contexts is variable and accelerated. Following Schumann's extension of the pidginization process to describe the acquisition of English by a native Spanish speaker, other researchers interested in second-language acquisition have looked, as we shall see, at various aspects of pidginization, depidginization, creolization, and decreolization.

The argument from analogy represents a somewhat different theoretical approach. Researchers working in this framework are at the more inductive end of the inductive–deductive continuum, in that they do not have a well-developed theory that drives their research. Yet they do start with certain assumptions about the phenomena under investigation, assumptions that are based on a body of knowledge about pidgin and creole languages. The hope is to arrive at a fuller understanding of second-language processes by exploring the similarities between pidgin and creole phenomena and second-language acquisition.

Acculturation theory

In his work on the acculturation of American Indian tribes, Linton (1963) described the general process of acculturation as involving modification in attitudes, knowledge, and behaviour. These modifications were seen to require not only the addition of new elements to an individual's cultural background, but also the elimination of certain previous elements and the reorganization of others. Thus the overall process of acculturation demands both social and psychological adaptation. Part of this process involves learning the appropriate linguistic habits to function within the target-language group (Stauble 1980).

Schumann's Social and Psychological Distance Hypothesis

Schumann characterized the relationship between acculturation and second-language acquisition in the following way:

> Second language acquisition is just one aspect of acculturation and the degree to which a learner acculturates to the target-language group will control the degree to which he acquires the second language (1978b).

In this view, acculturation – and hence second-language acquisition – is determined by the degree of social and psychological 'distance' between the learner and the target-language culture. *Social distance* pertains to the individual as a member of a social group that is in contact with another social group whose members speak a different language. It is the result of a number of factors, such as domination versus subordination, assimilation versus adaptation versus preservation, enclosure, size, congruence, and attitude. *Psychological distance* is the result of various affective factors that concern the learner as an individual, such as resolution of language shock, culture shock, and culture stress, integrative versus instrumental motivation, and ego permeability.

It is assumed that the more social and psychological distance there is between the second-language learner and the target-language group, the lower the learner's degree of acculturation will be toward that group. It is then predicted that the degree to which second-language learners succeed in socially and psychologically adapting or acculturating to the target-language group will determine their level of success in learning the target language.

More specifically, social and psychological distance influence second-language acquisition by determining the amount of contact learners have with the target language and the degree to which they are open to the input that is available. Positive (little distance) and negative (greater distance) social and psychological situations are described in Table 5.1. In a negative social situation, the learner will receive little input in the second language. In a negative psychological situation, the learner will fail to utilize available input.

In Schumann's model (1978a), acculturation is the causal variable in the second-language-learning process. He argued that the early stages of second-language acquisition are characterized by the same processes that are responsible for the formation of pidgin languages. When there are hindrances to acculturation – when social and/or psychological

Table 5.1 Factors determining social and psychological distance

Social distance

Positive	Negative
Social equality between target- and second-language groups	No social equality
Both groups desire assimilation	No desire of assimilation
Second-language group is small and not cohesive	Second-language group is large and cohesive
Second-language group's culture is congruent with target-language group	Culture of second-language group not congruent
Both groups have positive attitudes toward each other	Groups do not have positive attitudes toward each other
Both groups expect second-language group to share facilities	No expectation of shared facilities
The second-language group expects to stay in the target-language area for an extended period	No expectation by the second-language group that they would stay in the target-language area for an extended period

Psychological distance

Positive	Negative
No language shock	Language shock
No culture shock	Culture shock
High motivation	Low motivation
Low ego boundaries	High ego boundaries

Based on Schumann 1978a.

distance is great – the learner will not progress beyond the early stages and the language will stay pidginized.

Schumann documented this process in a case study of a 33-year-old Costa Rican immigrant, Alberto. As a member of a group of Latin-American working-class immigrants, Alberto was seen as socially and psychologically quite distant from the target-language group. He interacted almost exclusively with a small group of Spanish-speaking friends, and showed no interest in owning a television, which would have exposed him to the English language, because he said he could not understand English. He chose to work at night as well as during the day, rather than attend English classes.

Alberto showed very little linguistic development during the course of a 9-month longitudinal study. His interlanguage was characterized by many simplifications and reductions:

(1) Use of the general preverbal negators: 'no' 'don't'.
(2) No question inversion.
(3) Lack of auxiliary.
(4) No inflection of possessive.
(5) Use of uninflected forms of the verb.

These simplifications and reductions Schumann saw to be a form of pidginization, which leads to fossilization when the learner no longer revises the interlanguage system in the direction of the target language. This process occurred not because of a cognitive deficit – Alberto performed adequately on a Piagetian test of adaptive intelligence – but because of a minimal amount of acculturation to the target language group.

Andersen's Nativization Model

Andersen (1983) extended Schumann's framework by stressing to a greater degree the role of internal processing mechanisms. He distinguished 'nativization' and 'denativization' processes, which are viewed as analogous to the Piagetian notions of assimilation and accommodation. Nativization involves assimilation as the learner makes the input conform to an internalized view of what constitutes the second-language system:

> Creolization, pidginization, and the creation of a unique interlanguage in first and second language acquisition in early stages of acquisition share one attribute – the creation of a linguistic system which is at least partly autonomous from the input used for building that system. The system can then be considered 'native' to the individual in that it is the individual's mental capacity to construct such a linguistic system that makes it possible for a new 'native' language to arise. . . . (1983, 11)

Thus learners simplify the learning task by forming hypotheses based on innate, language-specific knowledge.

Denativization consists of accommodation to the external system. During this process, the learner adjusts the internalized system to make it fit the input:

> When circumstances cause the learner to reconstruct his inter-language to conform more closely to that of the input, he must in effect dismantle parts of his 'native' system (the system that he constructed previously or that he is in the process of cons-tructing). . . . Thus decreolization, depidginization, and later stages of first and second language acquisition constitute types of 'denativization'. (1983, 12)

Nativization and denativization are used in Andersen's model to capture the different directions the learner takes in building the inter-language. In the nativization process there is growth independent of the external norm that is thought to be consistent with natural acquisition processes and with the constraints on perception and production. The denativization process involves growth toward the external norm as pressures to conform to the target language cause learners to override natural acquisitional processes.

In Andersen's framework, nativization comes about because of rela-tively restricted access to target-language input. He is less concerned than Schumann with defining the factors that lead to restricted access, but agrees (Andersen 1981) that a combination of 'negative' social and psychological factors leads to restricted access. With time and increased exposure to the input, Andersen argued that the learner's interlanguage begins to approximate the structure of the input.

The Heidelberg project

Further evidence in support of the importance of access to native language sources of input comes from the Heidelberg Research Project for Pidgin German (1976). In this project 48 Italian and Spanish immi-grant workers were studied as they acquired German without formal instruction. The investigators developed an index of syntactic develop-ment that was in turn related to several social factors – leisure con-tact with Germans, age upon entering Germany, contact with Germans at work, length of education, mother tongue, and sex. Each of these variables except the last two were significantly related to language development, age yielding a negative relationship. Leisure contact with Germans was found to have the highest correlation with syntactic development, suggesting that social proximity is a critical factor.

The individuals who had the highest contact with Germans were those who had German partners. This situation fostered a high level of learning because of the possibility for extensive social proximity and access to input from a native speaker. The investigators also speculated that having a German partner increased the prestige of non-native speakers and thereby enhanced their opportunities to gain access to other Germans. Subjects who had little contact with Germans only exchanged greetings and had brief conversations with Germans in shops. This group consisted mainly of workers who lived in dormitories maintained by companies for industrial workers. In such cases social and psychological distance is greatest.

Two members of the Heidelberg group (Dittmar 1982; Klein 1981) studied the speech of a Spanish immigrant worker who had been living in West Germany for five years but whose knowledge of German had fossilized at a rudimentary level. Like Schumann's Alberto, this learner had very limited social contacts with native speakers. His language had the following characteristics:

(1) Extensive use of the general preverb negator: 'nicht'.
(2) No use of copulas.
(3) No use of auxiliaries with the infinitive.
(4) Active language based mainly on nouns; few function words.
(5) No use of inflection.

These simplifications and reductions are similar to those Schumann found in his subject and were seen by these investigators as evidence of a similar process of pidginization.

The ZISA project

Another German research project with immigrant workers, the *Zweitspracherwerb italienischer und spanisher Arbeiter (ZISA)* project, was perhaps the most ambitious in its efforts to link social-psychological and linguistic aspects of second-language development. These researchers (Meisel 1980: Meisel *et al.* 1981) argued from their data that there was no single path to second-language acquisition. They advocated a multidimensional model in which groups of learners form different paths to the target language.

In this model, the learner's position relative to the target language is defined by two dimensions: the learner's *developmental stage* and the learner's *social-psychological orientation*. The developmental stage is defined on the basis of linguistic criteria, but within a stage learners may differ because of their social-psychological orientation. Meisel (1980) proposed that learners vary along a continuum that ranges from a segregative to an integrative orientation, depending on how favourably they are disposed to speakers of the target language.

Thus a learner whose social-psychological orientation is segregative may have attained the same level of syntactic development as another learner whose social-psychological orientation is integrative. The segregative learner, however, is more likely to fossilize at that level than is the integrative learner, who has a better chance of learning the target language well. The advantage of the integrative learner comes from the use of different learning strategies. Specifically, Meisel (1980) distinguished two strategies of simplification: 'restrictive' simplification and 'elaborative' simplification. Restrictive simplification is an early strategy that involves the omission of elements and morphology and is more likely to be retained by learners with a segregative orientation. Elaborative simplification occurs later in the learning process and involves the formulation of hypotheses about the rules that apply in the target language. Learners with an integrative orientation are seen as using elaborative simplification more and hence making greater progress.

To summarize, the researchers we have discussed to this point are alike in their emphasis on the role of social and psychological factors in second-language development. Fossilization occurs in naturalistic adult second-language acquisition because of a combination of social and psychological factors relating to acculturation. The common theme in this work is that acculturation is a determining variable in that it controls the level of success achieved by second-language learners.

Pidginization, depidginization, creolization and decreolization

As we have seen, Schumann proposed that early second-language acquisition is analogous to pidginization and that learners who do not acculturate remain fossilized in this pidginized stage. The other authors discussed above have expressed similar views. In general, researchers working within this framework have been influenced by work on pidgin and creole languages, so that to understand their account of early and late second-language learning requires an appreciation of the processes involved in pidginization, depidginization, creolization, and decreolization.

It was pointed out earlier in this chapter that because pidgin-creole communities are characterized by multilingual and highly variable sociolinguistic contact, they have served as a source of analogies for second-language acquisition. The argument is that the processes involved in pidgins and creoles are similar to those that occur as second-language learners form hypotheses about the target language. There is, however, as we shall see, some disagreement as to what processes are involved in the development of pidgins and creoles, and how understanding these processes relates to second-language acquisition.

Pidginization

One of the major problems facing researchers who would draw analogies between second-language learning and pidgins is to define exactly what is meant by pidginization. For example, Meisel (1977) objected to the use of the term 'pidgin' by the Heidelberg group with reference to the German of immigrant workers. According to Meisel, one of the traditional criteria of pidgins is that they are linguistically stable, which is not the case for the interlanguage of adult second-language workers. Other authors (e.g., Fox 1983) argued that such a criterion is too restrictive and excludes the early stages of almost all pidgins, which initially show a great deal of variability and instability. One of the classic definitions of a pidgin language is based on a biological model developed by Whinnom (1971). This is a good starting point for a discussion of the issues relating to the pidginization analogy.

Linguistic hybridization

Schumann (1983) noted that his suggestion of an analogy between the early stages of second-language acquisition and the process of pidginization is based on a metaphor formulated by Whinnom (1971), who distinguished between primary, secondary, and tertiary hybridization. The biological use of the term primary hybridization refers to a phenomenon involving the fragmentation of a species into different races. The analogy in language development is the break-up of a species language into dialects. Secondary hybridization refers to the interbreeding of distinct species and is thought to be parallel to the imperfect speech of second-language learners acquired through restricted contact with speakers of the target language.

Tertiary hybridization, which Whinnom considered to be necessary for the development of a true pidgin, is the process by which new breeds of domestic animals or wild plant populations are formed. What occurs here is that secondary hybrids interbreed and are prevented from further breeding with the parent species. The linguistic analogy is to a situation in which a dominant language community is in minimal contact with two or more subordinate communities, and the subordinate communities use the developing contact language to communicate with each other. Thus the interlanguage of immigrant groups qualifies as a pidgin if the speakers are deprived of contact with the target language group and lack the motivation to improve in the target language.

Schumann (1983b) and others (Decamp 1971; Hall 1966) have argued that secondary hybridization (i.e., the interlanguage of second-language learners) constitutes 'pidginization', but that tertiary hybridization is required for the formation of a true pidgin. In other words, this position is that early second-language acquisition involves *the process of pidginization*, but that it does not result in a pidgin language. Alberto did not speak a pidgin, but because the simplifications and reductions in his English were characteristic of pidginization, Schumann maintained that his English showed evidence of pidginization.

What Schumann has done, essentially, is shifted the ground from an argument about what constitutes a pidgin language to what constitutes the process of pidginization. This does not resolve the debate, because there is little consensus as to what is meant by pidginization (Washabaugh and Eckman 1980). Schumann's reaction to this criticism was to go one step further, and rather than argue that early second-language acquisition is *like* pidginization, he maintained (Schumann 1982) that early second-language acquisition *is* pidginization.

The role of transfer
The identification of second-language acquisition and pidginization was first made by Bickerton, who argued:

> Existing theories about the process of pidginization have all either implied or directly stated that it is a process somehow distinct from other processes of language acquisition, whether these involve a first or a second language. . . . However, the present paper will suggest that . . . pidginization is second language learning with restricted input. (1977, 49)

Thus, rather than seeing an analogy between early second-language acquisition and early pidginization, as Schumann (1978) initially did, Bickerton and Schumann (1982) argued for identity of process.

A careful comparison of Bickerton's work based on 24 speakers of Hawaiian Pidgin English (Bickerton and Odo 1976) and Schumann's research on Alberto indicated similarities in the following language characteristics (Andersen 1981):

(1) reliance on word order rather than inflections for expressing grammatical relations
(2) native-language transfer in word order as well as use of English word order
(3) sporadic emergence of preverbal markers which come from lexical verbs promoted to auxiliary status
(4) a basic pidgin negation
(5) lack of inversion in questions
(6) preponderance of uninflected verb forms

There was also one unique feature in Alberto's speech, the frequent use of noun plural -s, which Andersen suggested was due to positive transfer from Spanish.

Andersen concluded that the evidence from the research of Bickerton and Schumann favoured the conclusion that pidginization is characteristic of all early second-language acquisition:

> I have attempted to show that Schumann is correct in characterizing Alberto's speech as being pidginized and early second-language acquisition as pidginization and that Bickerton is correct in characterizing pidginization as second-language acquisition with restricted input. Researchers in pidgin and creole studies and researchers in second-language acquisition are really studying the same phenomenon, each from a different perspective. (1981, 193)

However, Gilbert (1981), who also compared the work of Bickerton with that of Schumann, reached a somewhat different conclusion. He suggested that there is an alternative hypothesis that needs to be discounted before accepting the identity of pidginization and early second-language acquisition. This is the hypothesis that the characteristics Schumann observed in Alberto's speech are due to transfer from Spanish. Indeed, Gilbert argued that because so many of the forms in Alberto's speech can be attributed to positive or negative transfer from Spanish, it would be more appropriate to characterize his English by transfer rather than by pidginization.

Further, Gilbert maintained that the pidginization hypothesis was unnecessary. He quoted Bickerton:

> [Pidginization] is a process that begins by the speaker using his native tongue and relexifying first only a few key words. . . . Even when relexification is complete down to grammatical items, substrate syntax will be partially retained, and will alternate, apparently unpredictably, with structures imported from the superstrate. [This] probably also accords with the way in which speakers naturally acquire second languages that are not pidgins. (1977, 54)

Thus for Bickerton all second-language acquisition, including the formation of pidgins, is a process of piecemeal relexification with gradual modification of surface syntax in the direction of the target language. Gilbert argues that the only strategy necessary in this process is transfer:

> This renders Schumann's pidginization hypothesis unnecessary, since pidginization is now seen to be a subcategory of second-language acquisition generally, with a strategy of transfer being used throughout. (Gilbert 1981, 210)

Essentially, this reduces to a terminological dispute, Gilbert disallowing as pidginized those interlanguages that contain a large proportion of forms that are due to transfer from the first language and

Bickerton arguing that any interlanguage that is pidginized will contain a large percentage of forms that can be accounted for by transfer from the first language. Schumann's position (1981b), like Bickerton's, is that pidginization in no way excludes transfer.

Creolization

As traditionally defined, creolization is the acquisition of a pidgin language by the children of pidgin speakers. Bickerton has taken the position that creolization is in no way like pidginization: 'Pidginization is second-language learning with restricted input and creolization is first-language learning with restricted input' (1977, 49). Not everyone agrees with Bickerton, however, and some authors, as we shall see, have drawn parallels between creolization and second-language learning.

Creolization as distinct from second-language acquisition

Bickerton's position is that pidginization and creolization are as different as 'chalk and cheese' (1983, 236). For Bickerton, pidginization and early second-language acquisition involve reduced non-native versions of the target language; creolization involves a totally new language similar in many ways to other creoles. Table 5.2 lists some differences he identified between early second-language acquisition (pidginization) and creolization. It can be seen from this table that there are, in this view, important differences between the two processes.

Table 5.2 Differences between second-language acquisition and creolization

Second-language acquisition	Creolization
Learned by individuals	Learned by groups
Has a target	Does not have a target
Mainly adult learners	Child learners
Yields a second language	Yields a first language
Learners have 'normal' language background	Learners have 'abnormal' language background

Based on Bickerton 1983.

For Bickerton (1981) the study of creole languages plays a key role in the search for biologically determined underlying principles of language development, or what he calls the 'bioprogram', Bickerton provided evidence that first generation creoles represent cases of substantial structural and functional expansions as compared to the preceding pidgin, and argued that the child learners make use of genetically transmitted principles and mechanisms to 'create' the new language. Bickerton maintained that certain creole innovations cannot be accounted for by pidgin input or by the influence of other languages involved in the creolization process. He concluded that these innovations reflect the children's innate knowledge of what is possible in human language. This conclusion is supported by evidence that similar features appear in otherwise unrelated creoles. Furthermore, Bickerton reviewed the literature on first-language acquisition and presented evidence that the same features appear in 'normal' – i.e., non-creole first-language acquisition.

Bickerton gave the bioprogram little scope in adult second-language acquisition. He cited some evidence that suggested that 'the promptings of the bioprogram are by no means extinguished but rather overlaid by subsequent learning' (1984, 157). Nonetheless, in this view, adult second-language acquisition, because of the levels of intervening subsequent learning, is a different phenomenon from child creolization or first-language learning.

It should be noted that Bickerton (1981) repeatedly stressed that his approach is different from that of Chomsky and his followers. However, he ignored recent developments in Chomskyan theory (Meisel 1983a) which are entirely compatible with his ideas. The notions of 'core' and 'periphery', as well as the theory of markedness, are consistent with the argument that some aspects of language are highly specified at a biologically determined initial state, while others vary considerably from this core. Indeed, more recently, Bickerton has recognized this similarity (Bickerton, cited in Macedo 1986).

Creolization as related to second-language acquisition
In contrast to Bickerton, Valdman (1983) argued that there are parallels between creolization and second-language acquisition. Although creolization is a cross-generational phenomenon and second languages are acquired by individuals, Valdman maintained that 'from a psycholinguistic perspective these two processes do not differ substantially' (1983, 230). Both processes are seen to involve the operation of cognitive and linguistic universals, though they differ because of social circumstances that promote acquisition of the target language. Valdman argued that creolization comes about when social conditions lead learners to develop a language that is at least partially independent of the target language. This language serves as the primary means of communication and of social cohesion for the emerging community. In second-language acquisition, on the other hand, social conditions lead to the development of the target language.

However, Valdman accepted Andersen's (1981) notion of 'nativization' as a process whereby, at least in the initial stages, second-language learners develop form–meaning relations that are independent of the target language. It is this process that underlies the similarities he saw between second-language acquisition and creolization. Valdman argued that substantial differences in form–meaning relations are exhibited by various creoles, and that the development of an autonomous system of form–meaning relations may extend over a period bridging several generations. This led him to agree with Mühlhäusler's contention that adults have access to the cognitive and psycholinguistic mechanisms underlying such development:

> Once a pidgin acquires some stability and begins to expand, the second language speaker's intuitions about naturalness begin to determine the direction of its growth. It would seem that both gradual expansion and sudden creolization obey the same laws. In both the added rules are natural in that they conform with natural developmental hierarchies. (1980, 42)

For Valdman, then, the same laws operate in early second-language acquisition and creolization, differences being due to the amount of nativization that occurs: in second-language acquisition there is little nativization, whereas in creolization there is extensive nativization. These differences are seen to be due to social conditions rather than to qualitative differences in the two processes.

Bickerton disagreed with Valdman (and Andersen) in that he did not feel that adults possess the ability to create parts of language not available in the target language. In Bickerton's scheme of things, children do this (through the bioprogram) in their acquisition of a first language – especially a creole – but, as we have seen, adult second-language acquisition is 'overlaid' by subsequent learning, so that adult second-language acquisition is thought to be a different phenomenon from child creolization or first-language learning.

Decreolization

Andersen (1981), as we have seen, used the term 'nativization' to refer to the process whereby acquisition is directed 'toward an internal norm'. His argument is that nativization is evident in the processes of pidginization, creolization, and in the early phases of first- and second-language acquisition. In each of these situations the emergence of linguistic forms is heavily influenced by the innate system and, as a result, idiosyncratic forms emerge that are different from the target language. Thus nativization is thought to involve the assimilation of linguistic input to existing structures.

'Denativization' is directed 'toward the external norm', and is seen by Andersen to be evidenced in the processes of depidginization, decreolization, and the later phases of first- and second-language acquisition. In each of these processes there is a preponderance of accommodation over assimilation, in that the learner has to accommodate to the norms of the target language. If, as Bickerton (1983) argued, nativization plays an insignificant role is adult second-language acquisition, the analogy to depidginization or decreolization may be helpful in shedding light on second-language phenomena.

Depidginization or decreolization?

Schumann (1981a) has pointed out a confusion in the literature concerning the terms 'depidginization' and 'decreolization'. Bickerton and Odo (1976) argued that pidginization is second-language acquisition with restricted input and implied that as the input becomes less restricted through increased contact, second-language development occurs through the process of depidginization. Andersen (1981) took a similar view and regarded depidginization as denativization towards the external norm brought about by a lack of social, psychological, and physical distance. This process he saw to be analogous to 'normal' successful second-language acquisition toward the target-language norm.

There exists, however, no careful documentation of the depidginization process (Schumann 1981a), and there is no agreement on what the term means. Andersen and Bickerton saw depidginization to refer to the second-language development that takes place as the learner gains increasingly greater access to the target-language input. Other authors, however, understand the term as referring to the elaboration a pidgin language undergoes when it is used in a wide range of communicative contexts without access to target-language input (e.g., Ferguson and DeBose 1977).

As Schumann (1981a) noted, the use of depidginization in the sense that Andersen and Bickerton employ does not distinguish it from decreolization, at least at the process level. If one understands decreolization to refer to continued development of creole language speakers toward a target-language norm, both depidginization and decreolization can be seen to result from increased access to the target language causing speakers to replace and restructure elements of their language. Perhaps, as Schumann suggested, depidginization and decreolization involve the same processes but have different starting points – a pidginized second language in one case and a creole in another.

Indeed, many authors seem to make no distinction between depidginization and decreolization. Bickerton used both terms as analogous to the later stages of second-language acquisition. In Bickerton and Odo (1976) late second-language acquisition was seen as a depidginization process and in Bickerton (1977) it was suggested that late second-language acquisition is like decreolization in that second-language learners can be placed on a continuum between the native language and the target language in much the same way that speakers can be placed on a post-creole continuum between the creole and the standard language. Stauble (1978) provided evidence for this argument by using data on the acquisition of English negation, which she saw to indicate that second-language learners' development beyond the early stages is similar to decreolization because both are motivated by acculturation and accomplished by the processes of replacement and restructuring.

In her work, Stauble used the terms 'basilang', 'mesolang', 'acrolang' to refer to different stages of the second-language acquisition process. Basilang is the early stage of second-language acquisition, mesolang is the middle stage, and acrolang the later stage. These terms parallel the terms Bickerton (1977) used to describe decreolization as progressing from the 'basilect' (the lect closest to the creole) to the 'mesolect', to the 'acrolect' (the lect closest to the target language). By replacement Stauble referred to the substitution of morphemes of non-standard appearance by others modelled on the standard target language. Restructuring referred to the reformulation of underlying grammatical rules in conformity with the input from the target language.

Decreolization and late second-language acquisition
The notions of replacement and restructuring were used by Schumann and Stauble (1983) to draw parallels between studies of English negation in second-language acquisition, depidginization in Hawaiian pidgin English, and the decreolization of Guyanese Creole. In each case they saw evidence of 'replacement of surface forms and much later restructuring of underlying units in order to eventually replace auxiliary negation' (1983, 266). Thus negative forms such as *don't* or *don* are not analysed into *do-auxiliary* + *not*, but are introduced into the negative system as monomorphemic chunks which simply replace *na* in creole and *no* in pidgin and in the speech of second-language learners. Later, restructuring occurs as these monomorphemic negators begin to function as carriers of tense as well as negation. Table 5.3 lists examples of these developmental processes. Schumann and Stauble concluded that depidginization, decreolization, and second-language acquisition are manifestations of the same kind of linguistic phenomenon. Each of them was seen to produce a continuum of developmental stages through which individual learners pass in the acquisition of the target language.

Thus the analogy between late second-language acquisition and depidginization or decreolization rests on similarity of process. To return to Andersen's notions, the concepts of pidginization and creolization exemplify the nativization process whereby learners move away from the target language and are driven by internal linguistic universals and cognitive constraints on perceiving, processing, remembering, and using linguistic material to convey meaning. Depidginization and decreolization exemplify the denativization

Table 5.3 Development of negation in depidginization, decreolization, and second-language acquisition

System	Depidginization	Decreolization	SLA
Preverbal negation	Pidgin negation: *no* + predictive phrase, *don't know*, *no moa* in possessive and existential sentences	Basilect: *na* + predicate phrase, *kyan/mosn*	Basilang: *no* + predictive phrase, variation with *don't/isn't*
Transition phase	Less primitive pidgin negation: *nat* in verbless sentences, *neba* in past contexts, *kaenat* Next: unanalysed *don*	From basilect to mesolect: replacement of *na* by *doon(t)*, *dozn(t)*, *didn(t)*, *en*, use of *izn(t)/wazn(t)*	From basilang to mesolang: dominant use of unanalysed *don't*, cop/aux + neg. constructions
Postauxiliary negation	Next: *won, izn* Much later: reanalysis/ restructuring of *don*	From mesolect to acrolect: restructuring of unanalysed neg. forms and establishment of present/past distinctions of neg. forms	From mesolang to acrolang: restructuring of unanalysed *don't* forms, elimination of nontarget forms, establishment of present/past distinction among neg. forms

Based on Schumann and Stauble 1983.

process whereby the learner is driven toward the target language by access to native speakers. Schumann and Stauble were able to show how the data on negation in second-language acquisition, depidginization in Hawaiian pidgin English, and the decreolization of Guyanese Creole indicate that each of these language phenomena involves the same processes – specifically, replacement and restructuring.

Evaluation

Acculturation/Pidginization theory is concerned with the question of why second-language learners, unlike first-language learners, often fail to achieve mastery of the target language. The explanation given is in terms of 'distance': the second-language learner may be cut off from access to native speakers (and hence to the necessary input) because of social distance and/or because of psychological distance. In such a case, the learner's development fossilizes and there is no further development of the interlanguage.

A second question that concerns the theory is why second-language learners use certain strategies to deal with the input they receive. To shed light on this question, researchers have drawn analogies to other language phenomena – i.e., pidgins and creoles – in attempting to identify strategy shifts. Thus Andersen's notions of 'internal' and 'external' norms are employed to account for why early and late second-language acquisition are so different. Pidginization is seen to be analogous to early second-language acquisition, where attention is on the internal norm and learners rely on strategies of simplification and reduction. Depidginization and decreolization are seen to be analogous to late second-language acquisition, where attention is on the external norm and learners turn to various elaborative strategies – especially replacement and restructuring – to bring their interlanguage into conformity with the target-language norm.

The analogy of second-language acquisition to pidginization, depidginization, and decreolization places emphasis upon the dynamic nature of interlanguage change. The theory is concerned with such changing and variable factors as access to the target-language norm, the availability of a peer group whose language deviates from the target-language norm, and individual attitude and motivation.

Acculturation theory

The acculturation notion provides the theory with an account of how long and in what direction a learner will refine hypotheses about the target language. Such social-psychological factors as attitude toward the target language, motivation to learn, and social distance are seen to underlie the impetus toward acculturation. The theory has successfully integrated research on the social psychology of second-language acquisition, though there are two questions that require elaboration.

The question of variability
In spite of the 'dynamic' orientation of Acculturation/Pidginization theory, relatively little attention has been given to the possibility of changes in individual motivation and attitude as they relate to second-language acquisition. The connection of the theory to social-psychological factors is made, but the changing nature of these factors is not emphasized. A dynamic theory could profit from a more elaborate account of how intergroup uses of language reflect variable social

and psychological attitudes in intergroup relations (e.g., Gardner 1980; Gardner and Lambert 1972).

Specifically, a more dynamic account needs to take into consideration the manner in which social and psychological factors are subject to constant negotiation. Giles and his associates (Giles *et al*. 1979; Giles and Byrne 1982) have stressed this point in their analyses of the social-psychological factors that affect second-language acquisition. How the ingroup defines itself relative to the outgroup may change constantly in accordance with shifting views of identity and the boundaries of group membership.

Schumann assumed that such factors as degree of social equality, desire to assimilate, cohesiveness of the second-language group, cultural congruity, attitudinal factors and expectations (see Table 5.1) determine in some objective fashion the amount of social distance between second-language and target-language groups. But it is unclear how these variables are to be measured (Brown 1980), and, in any event, it is not objective conditions but what the learner perceives that forms the learner's reality (Acton 1979). This reality is constantly shifting as the individual's perceptions change. In this sense, considerations of social distance reduce to questions of psychological distance.

The question of causality
The acculturation hypothesis, as reflected in Schumann's notions of social and psychological distance, Meisel's integrative or segregative orientation, or Andersen's nativization and denativization, assumes a causal model in which attitude affects access to input which in turn affects second-language acquisition. Attitude, or the perception of distance between the learner and the target group, is seen to control behaviour. Learners who see little distance between themselves and the target group are more likely to avail themselves of opportunities for informal acquisition than are learners who perceive great distance between themselves and the target group.

It is possible, however, that the line of causality, rather than going from attitude to second-language acquisition, goes in the opposite direction. Successful learners may be more positively disposed toward the target-language group because of their positive experience with the language. Their success may be more a function of intelligence, social skills, and language-learning ability than of perceived distance from the target-language group. There is evidence from research on children (Hermann 1980; Strong 1984) that suggests that learners who are already fluent in a language show more positive attitudes and a significantly greater desire to associate with members of the target-language group than do less fluent speakers.

Most likely, the line of causality is bi-directional. Perceived distance affects second-language acquisition and is affected by success in second-language acquisition. Furthermore, other factors, such as intelligence and language-learning skills, can be presumed to play an important role in second-language acquisition. A uni-directional and uni-factorial model fails to reflect the complexity of the process.

Pidginization, depidginization, creolization, and decreolization

The theoretical approach discussed in this chapter is, as was noted, a significant departure from other theories treated in this book, because it uses a somewhat different style of thinking and is based on reasoning by analogy. To what extent has the analogy of second-language acquisition to such processes as pidginization, depidginization, creolization, and decreolization led to a greater understanding of how adults learn second languages in untutored situations? Three topics deserve consideration: (1) the relationship of these processes, in general, to the mechanisms of second-language learning, (2) the comparison of early second-language acquisition and pidginization, and (3) the comparison of late second-language acquisition and decreolization.

The mechanisms of language learning

The model of second-language learning provided by the Acculturation/Pidginization theory has been criticized by Ellis (1985b) because he saw it to provide little information about how second-language knowledge is internalized and used:

> Andersen's 'internal' and 'external norms' suggest that the internal mechanisms play a crucial part, but this is not elaborated upon. And neither Andersen nor Schumann pays attention to the potentially facilitating effects of input/interaction. . . . In short, what is missing from these models is an account of the role of interaction between situation and learner. (1985b,255)

In fact, however, Schumann and Stauble (1983) and Andersen (1981) have provided fairly detailed accounts of the formation and elaboration of second languages. The analogy to pidginization and decreolization has been helpful in illuminating the transition from an internal to an external norm as learners switch from reliance on simplification and reduction to replacement and restructuring strategies.

Perhaps the most interesting aspect of Acculturation/Pidginization theory as it relates to the mechanisms of learning is Andersen's concept of nativization. As Slobin (1983) pointed out, this is something of a misnomer, in that 'nativization' calls 'native language' to mind. In fact, as we have seen, Andersen used the term to refer to an inherent capacity of the learner to structure language along certain lines. Andersen agreed with Bickerton that creolization, because of the lack in the input language, requires that learners rely on internal mental capacities to construct the language.

As Bickerton noted, first-generation creole languages represent cases of substantial structural and functional expansions as compared to the preceding pidgin. If, as Bickerton claimed, certain creole innovations cannot be accounted for by the pidgin input available or by the influence of other languages, then these innovations may be seen to reflect the children's innate knowledge of what is a possible human language (especially if similar features appear in other unrelated creoles).

It may, however, be unnecessary to call on the process of 'nativization' or to postulate a 'bioprogram' to account for the linguistic innovations that occur in creolization. There are, in all probability, constraints on what possible human languages might be, constraints on learnability, and constraints on expressibility. These constraints limit the form of possible languages and indicate where learners are to look to find a device in the target language to encode a particular concept (Meisel 1983a). It is impossible at present to disentangle the contributions to language learning of innate linguistic constraints, general learning strategies, problem-solving routines, and social factors.

As Schumann (1983b) noted, it is probably premature at this stage of our knowledge about second-language acquisition to make commitments to various accounts of language learning. Schumann preferred to remain neutral about the role of innate mechanisms in adult second-language learning. He also regarded the theory as open with respect to the relationship between first- and second-language acquisition, the role of transfer from the first language in second-language acquisition, and to the possibility of variant, or invariant, acquisitional sequences.

Furthermore, speculations about the contributions of innate vs. cognitive structures and processes do not enlighten our understanding about the mechanisms of adult second-language acquisition. What creolization research does underscore is a tendency that Slobin (1983) saw to run through the course of individual language development: the tension between demands for explicitness and demands for economy. This competition leads to different solutions at different stages of the language-learning process.

Early second-language acquisition and pidginization
If the argument from analogy is to help understanding, there is a need to go beyond description to explanatory accounts of how language learning takes place. Here advocates of this approach do not always agree. In his analysis of the relationship of early second-language acquisition and pidginization, Andersen (1981) compared Bickerton's work with Hawaiian Pidgin English speakers and Schumann's data from Alberto. As we have seen, he concluded that Schumann and

Bickerton were correct in maintaining that pidginization is characteristic of all early second-language acquisition. Gilbert (1981), however, argued that the way in which Schumann and Bickerton accounted for language learning at this stage was quite different.

One of Gilbert's points was that, whereas Schumann saw the pidginization/early second-language acquisition process to be characterized by simplification and regression to a more primitive state of language, Bickerton ruled out simplification:

> [Pidgin] speakers arrive at a common system through . . . the progressive and quite strictly constrained process of replacing parts of their original grammar with rules drawn from their perceptions of the superstrate or of the grammars of other language groups. . . . This replacement process, rather than any kind of 'simplification', whether conscious or otherwise, appears to be the dominant factor in early pidginization; the notion that the pidgin speaker has any kind of direct access to universals (rather than merely, like all speakers, being constrained by what they will permit) would appear to be incorrect. (Bickerton and Odo 1976, 306-7)

Note that Bickerton also rejected Andersen's notion of nativization - i.e., that early second-language acquisition involves the creation of an autonomous system based on innate linguistic knowledge.

This disagreement as to the processes involved in early second-language acquisition and pidginization is also apparent in Meisel's (1983b) discussion of the notion of simplification. As we have seen, Meisel pointed out that simplification can serve different functions for different learners, even though the output is the same.

> Different functions may produce similar surface linguistic results - a learner can simplify a structure to avoid accumulation of complexity in a way that may be interpreted as a learning aid preparing the next step towards the target grammar. In other instances, observed changes do not serve such a purpose; they merely seem to facilitate the use of the internalized linguistic competence without necessarily contributing to its further elaboration. Both kinds of simplification, however, may be structurally identical, for 'simplicity' is defined as structural change resulting in cognitively less complex outputs. (1983b,122)

Thus, in Meisel's analysis, any account of the language-learning process needs to take the learner's 'orientation' into consideration, which is determined by social-psychological factors (e.g., 'integrative' vs. 'segregative' orientations).

Meisel did not disagree with Schumann's emphasis on simplification in pidginization/early second-language acquisition, but rather

attempted to clarify the processes involved, arguing that structural properties, functions, and motivation for simplification must be kept
separate. He did, however, differ from Schumann in the role assigned
to transfer in early second-language acquisition. Whereas Schumann
(1983) was neutral as to the role of transfer in second-language acquisition, Meisel gave transfer a minimal role in pidginization/second-
language acquisition. Meisel disagreed most sharply with Bickerton on
this point. In contrast to Bickerton's relexification version of first-
language transfer, Meisel contended that there is little evidence for
transfer as a major strategy in early second-language acquisition.

This discussion should serve to indicate the range of disagreement
among researchers working in the pidginization/second-language
acquisition framework. Once one goes beyond the level of description,
it is difficult to be sure that researchers are talking about the same
things. Bickerton rejected simplification and emphasized transfer.
Schumann stressed simplification and was neutral with respect to
transfer. Meisel rejected transfer and emphasized universal strategies,
though he (Meisel 1983a) was uncomfortable with innate mechanisms,
which Andersen, on the other hand, saw to be central to the process of
nativization. Researchers in this area are comfortable describing *what* it
is that learners learn; they are less comfortable accounting for *how* it is
that they do it. Indeed, Meisel and Gilbert have questioned whether the
identification of pidginization and early second-language acquisition is
a useful heuristic.

Late second-language acquisition and decreolization
As we have seen, researchers working in the Acculturation/Pidgin-
ization paradigm have compared late second-language acquisition to
the processes of depidginization and decreolization. Because detailed
documentation of the depidginization process is lacking and because
depidginization and decreolization are often used to refer to similar
processes, most researchers prefer the decreolization analogy. In this
context decreolization refers to continued development toward a
target-language norm as creole speakers replace and restructure elements of their language because of increased access to target-language
language speakers. A similar process is seen to occur in late second-
language acquisition as speakers develop their language toward target-
language norms.

Thus the analogy between late second-language acquisition and
depidginization or decreolization rests on similarity of process. This
argument has been challenged by the creolist, John Rickford, who
maintained that 'decreolization involves *extensions* of one's linguistic
repertoire from an earlier stage while normal second-language acquisition involves *replacements*' (1983, 304). Thus Rickford argued that
whereas second-language learners do not retain the interlanguage

they had at an earlier stage when they go on to another one, creole speakers who have advanced beyond the basilect (or other lower lects) maintain their competence in these lower lects. This suggests a major difference between the processes of second-language development and decreolization.

As Rickford pointed out, creole speakers may not want to jettison their basilect completely when they decreolize, because the language of close friends and relatives may be restricted to the basilect. Thus what happens in decreolization is that learners are expected to control a broad range of interlanguage competence and to have room for stylistic manoeuvre. This is not true of late second-language acquisition, where learners simply replace one interlanguage with another.

As Rickford noted, the parallels drawn between decreolization and second-language acquisition are made on the basis of comparisons of individual data in the case of second-language learners and cross-sectional data in the case of decreolization. The kinds of changes observed in second-language acquisition occur over generations in decreolization. Unfortunately, not enough comparisons of the two processes have been made over a broad range of linguistic structures. Nor have characterizations of the linguistic processes involved been specific enough (Sankoff 1983).

In chapter 1, I argued that scientific progress is achieved as we come to illuminate our knowledge progressively by taking different perspectives and by utilizing diverse methods of research. In this respect, Acculturation/Pidginization theory has provided second-language researchers with a different perspective to the phenomena they are trying to understand. The analogy to pidginization, depidginization, creolization, and decreolization has introduced to second-language research a new way of viewing linguistic processes. Unfortunately, the introduction of new terms to the field has not always been illuminating. As we have seen, authors disagree on the meaning of such terms as 'pidginization', 'depidginization', and 'creolization', and the introduction of other terms such as 'tertiary hybridization', 'basilang-mesolang–acrolang', and 'nativization' tends to lead to a level of abstraction that is confusing (Sankoff 1983).

A second criterion for good theories is that they fit the data well, are clear in their predictions, and are heuristically rich. Here Acculturation/Pidginization theory receives mixed grades. There are not enough data, and it is not always clear what the theory predicts. More detailed comparisons of pidginization and early second-language acquisition and of decreolization and late second-language acquisition are needed if insight is to be gained into the mechanisms of second-language acquisition. But does the comparison of pidginization and decreolization yield more information than careful study of second-language acquisition in and of itself?

I would argue that the work of researchers working in the framework of Acculturation/Pidginization theory has enriched second-language research. In particular, as we have seen, the analogy to pidginization and decreolization have been helpful in illuminating the transition from an internal to an external norm as second-language learners switch from reliance on simplification and reduction to replacement and restructuring strategies. More detailed research is needed on these processes and on different linguistic structures, but work on pidgin and creole languages, such as Mülhäusler's and Rickford's, provides valuable sources of hypotheses for second-language researchers.

Acculturation/Pidginization theory is addressed to naturalistic adult second-language acquisition, where learners have more or less contact with the target-language community. The model says nothing about classroom second-language learning, where learners do not have contact with native speakers other than the teacher. The factors responsible for social distance are not relevant for foreign language learning in the classroom, although the factors that generate psychological distance – individual attitude and motivation – presumably operate in this context (Ellis 1985b).

Finally, good theory is falsifiable. At the acculturation end the theory is false if it can be shown that second-language acquisition is not affected by social and psychological distance. The difficulty here is that, as we have seen, social distance reduces effectively to psychological distance, and psychological distance is not easy to measure. Furthermore, there is the chicken/egg problem of the relationship between second-language acquisition and one's perception of oneself *vis-à-vis* the target-language community. The theory also assumes some analogy or identity between pidginization and second-language acquisition, and presumably is falsified if this analogy is incorrect. As more detailed research on the development of various linguistic structures in pidginization and in second-language acquisition appears, the characteristics of the two processes may become clarified and the theory validated. Presently, there simply is not enough information.

6

Cognitive theory

In chapter 4 we saw that Universal Grammar theory focused on system-internal factors, and, specifically, on the role of linguistic universals in second-language acquisition. This chapter deals with the work of investigators who also focus on system-internal factors, specifically on the role of cognitive processes in second-language acquisition. My colleagues and I (McLaughlin *et al.* 1983; McLeod and McLaughlin 1986) and other authors (e.g., Hulstijn and Hulstijn (1984); Levelt 1978; Segalowitz 1986) have argued that such a perspective raises new questions that are empirically testable, and sheds light on findings from a number of areas of second-language research.

Cognitive theory is based on the work of psychologists and psycholinguists. Individuals working within this framework apply the principles and findings of contemporary cognitive psychology to the domain of second-language learning. The theory is, in this sense, derivative. It represents the application of a broader framework to the domain of second-language research. The intent is to determine whether such a perspective casts light on second-language phenomena.

Learning as a cognitive process

Within this framework, second-language learning is viewed as the acquisition of a complex cognitive skill. To learn a second language is to learn a *skill*, because various aspects of the task must be practised and integrated into fluent performance. This requires the automatization of component sub-skills. Learning is a *cognitive* process, because it is thought to involve internal representations that regulate and guide performance. In the case of language acquisition, these representations are based on the language system and include procedures for selecting appropriate vocabulary, grammatical rules, and pragmatic conventions governing language use. As performance improves, there is constant restructuring as learners simplify, unify, and gain increasing control over their internal representations (Karmiloff-Smith 1986). These two notions – automatization and restructuring – are central to Cognitive theory.

The routinization of skills: automaticity

The acquisition of the skills involved in any communication task requires the assessment and coordination of information from a multitude of perceptual, cognitive, and social domains. The speaker must communicate the intended message unambiguously and must learn to obey a large number of conversational conventions. Because humans are limited-capacity processors, such a task requires the integration of a number of different skills, each of which has been practised and made routine.

Controlled and automatic processing

Several researchers (Hasher and Zacks 1979; LaBerge and Samuels 1974; Posner and Snyder 1975; Schneider and Shiffrin, 1977; Shiffrin and Schneider 1977) have conceived of the differences in the processing capacity necessary for various mental operations in a dichotomous way: either a task requires a relatively large amount of processing capacity, or it proceeds automatically and demands little processing energy. Furthermore, a task that once taxed processing capacity may become, through practice, so automatic that it demands relatively little processing energy.

In their discussion of human information processing, Shiffrin and Schneider conceived of memory as a large collection of nodes that become 'complexly interassociated' through learning. Each node is a grouping or set of informational elements. Most of the nodes are inactive and passive and, when in this state, the interconnected system of nodes is called long-term store. When, because of some kind of external stimulus, a small number of these nodes are activated, the activated nodes constitute short-term store.

There are two ways in which these nodes become activated: Shiffrin and Schneider called these the automatic and the controlled modes of information processing. *Automatic processing* involves the activation of certain nodes in memory every time the appropriate inputs are present. This activation is a learned response that has been built up through the consistent mapping of the same input to the same pattern of activation over many trials. Since an automatic process utilizes a relatively permanent set of associative connections in long-term storage, most automatic processes require an appreciable amount of training to develop fully. Once learned, an automatic process occurs rapidly and is difficult to suppress or alter.

The second mode of information processing, *controlled processing*, is not a learned response, but a temporary activation of nodes in a sequence. This activation is under attentional control of the subject and, since attention is required, only one such sequence can normally be controlled at a time without interference. Controlled processes are thus tightly capacity-limited, and require more time for their activation. But controlled processes have the advantage of being relatively easy to set up, alter, and apply to novel situations.

Automaticity and learning
In this framework, learning involves the transfer of information to long-term memory and is regulated by controlled processes. That is, skills are learned and routinized (i.e., become automatic) only after the earlier use of controlled processes. It is controlled processes that regulate the flow of information from short-term to long-term memory. Learning involves time, but once automatic processes are set up at one stage in the development of a complex information-processing skill, controlled processes are free to be allocated to higher levels of processing. Thus controlled processing can be said to lay down the 'stepping stones' for automatic processing as the learner moves to more and more difficult levels (Shiffrin and Schneider 1977).

In this conceptualization, complex tasks are characterized by a hierarchical structure. That is, such tasks consist of sub tasks and their components. The execution of one part of the task requires the completion of various smaller components. As Levelt (1978) noted, speaking is an excellent example of a hierarchical task structure (Table 6.1). The first-order goal is to express a particular intention. To do this, the speaker must decide on a topic and select a certain syntactic schema. In turn, the realization of this schema requires sub-activities, such as formulating a series of phrases to express different aspects of the intention. But to utter the phrases there is the need for lexical retrieval, the activation of articulatory patterns, utilization of appropriate syntactic rules, etc. Each of these component skills needs to be executed before the

Table 6.1 The hierarchical task structure of speaking

First-order goal:	to express particular intention
Second-order goal:	to decide on topic
Third-order goal:	to formulate a series of phrases
Lower-order goals:	to retrieve lexicon needed
	to activate articulatory patterns
	to utilize appropriate syntactic rules
	to meet pragmatic conventions

Based on Levelt 1978.

higher-order goal can be realized, although there may be some parallel processing in real time.

In order to function effectively humans develop ways of organizing information. Some tasks require more attention; others that have been well practised require less. The development of any complex cognitive skill involves building up a set of well-learned, automatic procedures so that controlled processes will be freed for new tasks. In this way limited resources can be spread to cover a wide range of task demands. The notion of a capacity-free (automatic) process provides an explanation for improvement in performance. Because human learners are limited in their information-processing abilities, only so much attention can be given at one time to the various components of complex tasks. When a component of the task becomes automatized, attention can be devoted to other components of the task and a previously difficult or impossible task becomes possible.

Restructuring

The integration of hierarchically ordered skills requires practice. Repeated performance of the components of the task through controlled processing leads to the availability of automatized routines. But there is more to learning a complex cognitive skill than automatizing sub-skills. The learner needs to impose organization and to structure the information that has been acquired. As more learning occurs, internalized, cognitive representations change and are restructured. This restructuring process involves operations that are different from, but complementary to, those involved in gaining automaticity.

Restructuring and cognitive organization

In acquiring complex skills, such as second languages, learners devise new structures for interpreting new information and for imposing a new organization on information already stored. Cheng (1985) described this process as the result of a restructuring of the components of a task so that they are coordinated, integrated, or reorganized into new units, thereby allowing the procedure involving old components to be replaced by a more efficient procedure involving new components.

Cheng gave the example of two alternative procedures for solving arithmetic problems, such as finding the sum of ten twos. One can solve this problem by nine addition operations; or one can learn the multiplication table and solve the problem by looking up the entry 2×10. A single multiplication operation would thus be equivalent to nine addition operations. Cheng argued that the gain in efficiency thus achieved is not the result of performing nine additions operations in an automatic manner. Nor is the gain in efficiency the result of an automatic multiplication operation. Rather the limitations in performance have been overcome by restructuring the task procedure.

Another example Cheng gave is piano-playing. Why is it that learners have difficulty in coordinating two tasks, each of which has been automatized – such as coordinating the two hands in playing the piano? For players with some experience, combining four even notes to a measure with eight even notes to a measure is relatively easy, as is combining three even notes to a measure with six or nine even notes. But although these tasks are automatic, combining three even notes against four even notes is extremely difficult. That this task is learnable indicated for Cheng that the difficulty does not stem from any physiological incompatibility, but rather from lack of a suitably structured skill.

A more detailed treatment of the restructuring process has been provided by Karmiloff-Smith (1986), who argued that children and adults attack new problems by going through the same recurrent phases. Phase one is data-driven; components of the task are mastered, but there is no attempt at overall organization. Organization is imposed at phase two, when behaviour is dominated by 'organization-oriented procedures', which result from the learner's attempts to simplify, unify, and gain control over the internal representation. Phase three involves the integration of the data-driven, bottom-up processes that guide phase one and the internally-generated, top-down processes that guide phase two. This integration results from the restructuring at work in phase two, which, once consolidated, can take environmental feedback into account without jeopardizing the overall organization (see Table 6.2).

Restructuring occurs because learners go beyond the success of phase one and attempt to control and link previously isolated procedures into a unified representational framework:

> my argument has been that the human organism (both linguistic and cognitive) incorporates a drive to have control not only over

Table 6.2 The phases of learning

	Phase 1	Phase 2	Phase 3
Source of output	Environmental stimuli	Internal representation	Both
Negative feedback	Utilized	Under-utilized	Utilized
Controlling mechanism	Bottom-up	Top-down	Both
Organization	Isolated procedures	Unified representational framework	Unified representational framework

Based on Karmiloff–Smith 1986.

the external environment (the input stimuli) but also, and impor-
tantly, over its own internal representations and finally over the
intricate interaction between the two. (Karmiloff-Smith 1986,
175)

Thus, in this view, once the procedures at any phase become automatized, consolidated, and function efficiently, learners step up to a
'metaprocedural' level, which generates representational change and
restructuring.

Restructuring and learning
Karmiloff-Smith's analysis implies that learning inevitably goes
beyond mere automaticity. Learning involves a constant modification
of organizational structures. Her approach is similar in many respects
to that of Rumelhart and Norman (1978), who identified restructuring
as a process that occurs 'when new structures are devised for interpreting new information and imposing a new organization on that already
stored' (39). They contrasted this process of learning with (a) accretion, whereby information is incremented by a new piece of data or a
new set of facts, and (b) tuning, whereby there is a change in the categories used for interpreting new information. In tuning, categories, or
schemata, are modified; in restructuring, new structures are added that
allow for new interpretation of facts.

In contrast to Karmiloff-Smith, who saw automaticity and restructuring as different phases in a single process, Rumelhart and Norman
argued that learning is not a unitary process, but that there are different
kinds of learning, one of which is restructuring. Whereas some learning
is seen to occur continuously by accretion, as is true of the development
of automaticity through practice, other learning is thought to occur in a
discontinuous fashion, by restructuring. This discontinuity would
account for a second-language learner's perceptions of sudden
moments of insight or 'clicks of comprehension'. At such moments,
presumably, the learner can be said to understand the material in a new
way, to be looking at it differently. Often learners report that this experience is followed by rapid progress, as old linguistic information and
skills are fitted into this new way of understanding.

Whether it is necessary to postulate different *kinds* of learning, as
Rumelhart and Norman suggested, or whether automaticity and
restructuring can be seen as different *phases* of a single learning process, as Karmiloff-Smith would have it, these authors agree that there is
more to learning a complex cognitive skill than developing automaticity
through practice. As Kolers and Roediger (1984) put it, learning
involves a reassembly and refinement of procedures of the mind.
Acquisition of cognitive skills involves consolidation, refinement, and
restructuring, as the learner gains increasing control.

Second-language learning

According to Cognitive theory, second-language learning, like any other complex cognitive skill, involves the gradual integration of sub-skills as controlled processes initially predominate and then become automatic. Thus the initial stages of learning involve the slow development of skills and the gradual elimination of errors as the learner attempts to automatize aspects of performance. In later phases, there is continual restructuring as learners shift their internal representations.

Automaticity and second-language acquisition

Some researchers have applied this perspective to second-language-learning phenomena. For example, Tarone (1982) argued that data gathered in informal settings reveal the most systematic interlanguage style and the style least subject to interference. The informal or 'vernacular' speech style is a product of language skills that have become automatic. Tarone maintained that when the learner directs attention to speech, controlled processes come into play and performance is likely to be interfered with – just as driving or typing are likely to be interfered with, or at least slowed down, when these automatic skills are given too much attention. When skills are not completely automatic, however, performance can be improved by giving the learner more time to apply controlled processes. Thus learners in test situations sometimes do better when given more time because the test items are not automatized and require the application of controlled processes. A similar explanation for differential performance under various test conditions was given by Hulstijn and Hulstijn (1984).

Automaticity in lexical retrieval

Much recent psycholinguistic research has focused on the relevance of the automatic/controlled dichotomy to the manner in which the strength of association between a word and its meaning is established (e.g., Posner and Snyder 1975). One experimental paradigm is the lexical decision task, in which subjects are required to make a decision about a target stimulus for which they have been given either a prime signal that is the same or different from the target stimulus, or a simple warning signal that is neutral with respect to the target. By varying the amount of time between the onset of the prime or warning signal and the onset of the target, it is possible to discriminate between kinds of processing operations. When little time is given, all processes that require subjects to commit significant amounts of processing capacity are excluded, and only the automatic processing of the prime is possible. When more time is given, some controlled processes can operate.

Favreau (1981) used this paradigm to investigate the extent to which there is a semantic facilitation effect (i.e., where a prime that is semantically related to a target word increases the speed with which the target word is processed) for both balanced bilinguals and dominant bilinguals highly skilled in their second language. Subjects were shown a prime that was either semantically related or unrelated to the target, having been told to expect such a relation or not. The time between the prime and the target was manipulated and the subjects' task was to decide as rapidly as possible whether the target formed a word. Because only automatic processing can occur if the time interval between the prime and the target is short, subjects who show semantic facilitation in this condition can be assumed to have highly efficient (i.e., highly automatized) lexical processing.

Favreau found that both balanced and dominant bilinguals showed evidence of semantic facilitation in their first language and in the long time interval condition in their second language, but only balanced bilinguals showed the same semantic facilitation in the short time interval condition in their second language. This was interpreted as evidence that the dominant bilinguals, who were judged to be fluent in their second language, nonetheless do not process lexical items as efficiently as balanced bilinguals. This lack of automatized lexical processes was thought to be the reason why the dominant bilinguals were found to read more slowly in their second than in their first language, while this was not the case for the balanced bilinguals.

More proficient second-language learners also differ from less proficient learners in that they use different techniques for encoding lexical items in memory. Henning (1973) found that after reading a passage, adult second-language learners made more or less use of acoustic encoding in a vocabulary recognition task as a function of their degree of proficiency in the second language. More advanced learners and native speakers tended to make vocabulary recognition errors that indicated semantic clustering for lexical items, whereas less advanced learners showed evidence of a predominance of acoustic clustering rather than semantic clustering. The less advanced learners have not yet automatized formal – in this case acoustic and orthographic – aspects of the language, and so have less cognitive energy available for semantic aspects. More advanced learners bypass the acoustic and orthographic aspects of the task, having already achieved automaticity with respect to these sub-components.

Dornic (1979) conducted a series of studies dealing with automaticity of processing in bilingual subjects. Using speed of processing as a measure of automaticity, Dornic found that speed increased as a function of experience with language. This was true both with respect to decoding and encoding efficiency. Even when a bilingual had had many years of experience with a second language, performance in that language lagged behind performance in the first language. The semantic content of words tended to be decoded more slowly in the second language and the subject's ability to encode information in the second language (as measured by naming latencies) tended to be inferior to performance in the first language. Presumably the second language did not attain the degree of automaticity that characterizes the first, even in the case of subjects who are overtly balanced bilinguals. Dornic (1979) also reported that high information load enhanced the dominance of the bilingual's stronger language system. Noise and other stressors interfered significantly with the weaker language – speech in that language becoming slowed down, rendered less precise, or even entirely blocked.

In a study of judgements of acceptability of deviant and non-deviant English sentences, Lehtonen and Sajavaara (1983) found that non-native speakers required more time in making such judgements than did native speakers, presumably because speech recognition and interpretation skills in a second language are less automatic. Lehtonen and Sajavaara postulated that native speakers' decisions as to acceptability are automatically 'primed' by lexical, semantic, syntactic, and pragmatic constraints.

Automaticity in syntactic processing
Hatch *et al.* (1970) asked native and non-native speakers of different levels of proficiency to cross out all instances of certain letters (e.g., all *e*s) occurring in a text. They reported that while the least proficient non-native speakers found the instances of occurrence of the letters with equal frequency for both content and function words, native speakers ignored the letters more often in the function words than in the content words. Such an advantage for non-native speakers can be explained in terms of the amount of cognitive work required by the non-native speaker to process the language. Non-native speakers expended equal cognitive effort in processing both syntactic (as represented by the function words) and semantic (as represented by the content words) aspects of language. Native speakers, on the other hand, more frequently missed the target letters found in function words, suggesting that they generally did not focus their attention on such words. Instead, native speakers focused their attention on meaning (on content words), processing syntactic elements automatically when scanning a text.

Psycholinguistic evidence for differential processing of semantics and syntax in native speakers comes from Sachs' (1967) classic finding that recognition memory for semantic features of an utterance was superior to recognition memory for syntax. Rossman (1981) hypothesized that this would not be the case for non-native speakers, who have not yet achieved the degree of automaticity in processing syntax that characterizes native speakers. Rossman compared the performance of native speakers with two groups of non-native speakers of

English on a reading recognition test. Native speakers showed better recognition for semantic rather than for syntactic changes. Non-native speakers, however, showed a greater ability to recognize whether the form of the sentence was changed than to recognize that its meaning was altered.

In a similar study, Wolfe (1981) tested 55 English-speaking children learning French as a second language in California schools. The children read a paragraph and were shown a target sentence that they were to identify as 'the same' or 'different' from a sentence in the paragraph. The paragraphs were either entirely in English or entirely in French or mixed with sentences in both languages. The target sentences were either the same or in a different language and had either the same or a different meaning. Children who were more proficient in the second language identified more 'different' sentences correctly when only the meaning was changed than was true of the less proficient children. On the other hand, the less proficient children had higher scores for target sentences when the language changed and the meaning stayed the same. This suggests that the less proficient children had not yet achieved the degree of automaticity with respect to processing form (in this case the specific language of the sentence) that the more proficient children had attained.

Nation and McLaughlin (1986) found that multilingual subjects performed better than did monolingual or bilingual subjects in learning a miniature linguistic system under 'implicit' (no instruction) conditions. One explanation of these findings is that multilingual subjects are superior to other language learners in organizing linguistic stimuli because of superior automatic processing skills. Thus in the implicit-learning condition, these subjects may have excelled because they were able to employ automatic letter- and pattern-recognition skills, while at the same time being flexible enough to tolerate disruptions of automatic processing required by more controlled processing.

Automaticity in reading

One aspect of second-language performance where the automatic/controlled processing distinction is especially relevant in reading. As we have seen, Shiffrin and Schneider (1977) argued that in learning to read children utilize controlled processing to lay down 'stepping stones' of automatic processing as they move on to more and more difficult levels of learning. The transition from controlled to automatic processing at each stage results in reduced discrimination time, more attention to higher-order features, and ignoring irrelevant information.

If the reading process can be viewed as a sequence of transitions from controlled to automatic processing, one would expect second-language learners to differ from native speakers in processing text. Cziko (1980) compared French oral reading errors of two groups of 12-year-old English-speaking students with those committed by native French-speaking students. Students who were less proficient in French made a significantly higher proportion of substitution errors that graphically resembled the text than did advanced second-language speakers or native speakers. Moreover, the less proficient group also made a significantly lower proportion of deletion and insertion errors than did the other two groups. That is, the least proficient group, when reading a sentence such as *She shook the piggy bank and out came some money*, would be likely to substitute *many* for *money* (relying on graphic information), whereas more advanced second-language learners and native speakers were more likely to insert *dimes* or *dollars* for *money* (relying on contextual and semantic information). This lends support to the notion that a sequence of stages is involved in the reading process and that less proficient second-language learners have not yet automatized skills that more advanced learners possess.

Segalowitz (1986) found reduced automaticity in word recognition and slowed second-language reading in otherwise fluent bilinguals. He also reported data that provided evidence that single words in the second language of fluent bilingual subjects activated semantic representations less deeply and for shorter duration than do translation equivalents in the first language. Segalowitz argued that the data suggest that these basic processing operations, rather than the strategic use made of linguistic knowledge, may be responsible for the relatively slow second-language reading of many bilinguals.

Restructuring and second-language learning

We have seen that in Cognitive theory learning involves both gain in automaticity through repeated practice and restructuring. Although both processes occur throughout the learning of any complex cognitive skill, gains in automaticity are thought to be more characteristic of early stages of learning and restructuring of later stages. For the most part, second-language researchers have been more concerned with the development of automaticity than with restructuring, though there has been some recognition of the role restructuring plays in second-language acquisition.

Restructuring and the development of the second language

A number of authors have commented on discontinuities in the second-language learning process (e.g., Pike 1960; Selinker 1972). Lightbown (1985) pointed out that second-language acquisition is not simply linear and cumulative, but is characterized by backsliding and loss of forms that seemingly were mastered. She attributed this decline in performance to a process whereby learners have mastered some forms and then encounter new ones that cause a restructuring of the whole system.

[Restructuring] occurs because language is a complex hierarchical system whose components interact in non-linear ways. Seen in these terms, an increase in error rate in one area may reflect an increase in complexity or accuracy in another, followed by over-generalization of a newly acquired structure, or simply by a sort of overload of complexity which forces a restructuring, or at least a simplification, in another part of the system (1985, 177).

Ellis (1985a) described a similar phenomenon in his discussion of systematic and non-systematic variability in the interlanguage. As we saw in chapter 3, Ellis argued that the interlanguage is characterized by both systematic and non-systematic variability. According to this analysis, in the early stages of second-language acquisition, new forms are used that have not yet been integrated into the learner's form–function system. Two or more forms may be used in free variation. This process Ellis saw to involve non-systematic variability in the interlanguage. Systematic variability occurs only when the new forms have been accommodated by a restructuring of the existing form–function system to one that more closely approximates that of the target language. In this sense, restructuring is part of the 'denativization' process (Andersen 1981), whereby learners adjust the internalized system to make it fit the input.

Once second-language learners choose a feature that is not part of their interlanguage, the new form becomes accommodated only if it acquires the meaning, function, and distribution it has in the target language. Bickerton (1975) has described this restructuring in his analysis of the process of decreolization. A new form acquired from the acrolect is used first with the meaning, function, and distribution of the form it is replacing in the basilect. Subsequently, the interlanguage system is restructured to incorporate the meaning, function, and distribution of the form in the target language.

Stauble (1978) provided a detailed analysis of the process of restructuring in adult second-language acquisition. A longitudinal investigation of the acquisition of English negation by two second-language learners indicated that they passed through a series of transitional grammars which gradually approximated the target language. The developmental stages in negation exhibited by these learners was seen to parallel in many ways the decreolization process observed by Bickerton.

As we have seen, Karmiloff-Smith (1986) saw restructuring to be the result of a 'drive' to control and link previously isolated procedures into a unified representational framework. From the perspective of Universal Grammar theory, it results from a general tendency to activate innate principles (Felix 1984). What makes the learner restructure the interlanguage, according to this theory, is the emergence of a new principle that the existing interlanguage violates in some way. A more cognitive perspective stresses the role of procedural strategies aimed at achieving fluency and clarity in communication.

Restructuring and learner strategies

Faerch and Kasper (1983) applied the distinction between declarative and procedural knowledge to second-language processes. Internalized rules and memorized chunks of the language constitute the 'what' of the learner's system, or *declarative knowledge*. In contrast, *procedural knowledge* consists of knowing 'how' to employ strategies and procedures to process second-language data for acquisition and use. Procedural knowledge accounts for how learners accumulate and automatize rules and how they restructure their internal representations to match the target language.

Ellis (1985b), drawing on the work of Faerch and Kasper, categorized the processes involved in using second-language knowledge into learning, production, and communication strategies (Table 6.3). Learning strategies relate to the acquisition of procedural knowledge rather than its use; production and communication strategies refer to language use. Production strategies refer to those strategies used by learners to realize communicative goals. This assumes a production plan, an articulatory programme, and a motor programme. Communication strategies result from initial failure to implement a production plan. They are employed

Table 6.3 A typology of learner strategies

Type of strategy	Examples

Learning strategies	Simplification
	  (1) Overgeneralization
	  (2) Transfer
	Inferencing
	  (1) Intralingual
	  (2) Extralingual
	Hypothesis-testing strategies
	Practice

Production strategies	Planning strategies
	  (1) Semantic simplification
	  (2) Linguistic simplification
	Correcting strategies

Communication strategies	Reduction strategies
	  (1) Formal
	  (2) Functional
	Achievement strategies
	  (1) Compensatory
	  (2) Retrieval

Based on Ellis 1985b.

when speakers cannot realize the original communicative goal in the way planned, and are forced to modify the goal or to adopt alternative means to reach it.

Learning strategies are sub-divided into simplification strategies (which include overgeneralization and transfer), inferencing (which includes those inferences bases on intralingual factors and those which are based on extralingual features of the physical environment), various hypothesis-testing strategies, and practice. Production strategies include planning strategies (both those involving semantic simplification, or the reduction of propositional elements that are linguistically coded, and linguistic simplification, or the omission of form words and affixes), and correcting strategies or monitoring. Communication strategies include reduction strategies (which can be formal – i.e., the avoidance of certain second-language rules – or functional – i.e., the avoidance of certain speech acts or discourse functions). Other communication strategies relate to achievement strategies: compensatory strategies, which involve replacements or substitutions of forms or functions, and retrieval strategies, which are used when the learner has a problem locating the required item but decides to perseverate rather than use a compensatory strategy. A fuller account of these strategies and their various manifestations can be found in Ellis (1985b).

The procedural strategies involved in restructuring are those that relate to acquisition (learning strategies), rather than to language use (production and communication strategies). In the initial stages of the acquisition process, learners tend to simplify, regularize, overgeneralize, and reduce redundancy. At this point, learners seek to override the evidence of the input by constructing an internal representational system that is more simple than the input and relies on the first language and on universal principles. This corresponds Andersen's 'nativization' process.

At later stages in second-language development, inferencing strategies predominate as learners attend more closely to input data. Hypotheses are tested in a variety of ways (Faerch and Kasper 1983):

(1) Receptive hypothesis testing: the learner attends to the input and compares hypotheses with the data provided by speakers of the target language.
(2) Productive hypothesis testing: the learner produces utterances in the second language and assesses their correctness through feedback received.
(3) Metalingual hypothesis testing: the learner consults a native speaker, teacher, grammar, or dictionary to validate a hypothesis.
(4) Interactional hypothesis testing: the learner elicits a repair from a native speaker.

If learning requires a constant modification of organizational structures, then it is these strategies of inferencing and hypothesis testing that govern the process of restructuring.

Restructuring in reading a second language
McLeod and McLaughlin (1986) analysed the errors of beginning and advanced ESL students reading aloud in English and found that the errors that beginning ESL students made were primarily nonmeaningful, which was seen to be due to these students focusing on the graphic aspects of the text. Their command of the syntax was also not secure enough to allow them to make accurate predictions in reading, as evidenced by a cloze test. Advanced ESL students were significantly better at making predictions on the cloze test and made significantly fewer errors in reading than did the beginning students. However, there were no differences between advanced students and beginning students in the proportion of meaningful errors in their reading.

Successful readers interact actively with the text – adding, deleting, and substituting words where appropriate. They use the cues available to seek the most direct path to meaning, drawing on prior conceptual and linguistic competence to predict what might plausibly come next. A number of authors have made the point that fluent reading requires going beyond the 'mechanics' of the reading process, which involves attention to graphic and orthographic information, to extracting meaning from words (e.g. Gibson and Levin, 1975; Goodman 1968; Smith 1971). Some poor readers apparently have mastered the mechanical aspects of reading, but continue to process the text word by word, not using contextual semantic relations and syntactic information to comprehend meaning (Cromer 1970).

McLeod and McLaughlin argued that this was the problem the advanced ESL students in their study had. Their errors showed that they were not utilizing semantic and syntactic cues as well as they could have. They were not approaching the task as 'a psycholinguistic guessing game', in which graphic cues are used to make predictions about what the printed text means – even though the evidence from the cloze test suggests that they were quite capable of making such predictions. Their increasing syntactic and semantic competence enabled them to make nearly twice as many accurate predictions as the beginners on the cloze test. Yet they had not applied this competence to their reading behaviour.

McLeod and McLaughlin maintained that the advanced subjects had not yet reached the point in their reading performance where restructuring occurs. That is, they were using old strategies aimed at decoding in a situation where their competencies would have allowed them to apply new strategies directed at meaning. Their performance on the cloze test indicated that they had the skills needed for 'going for meaning'.

Presumably they read this way in their first language. But they had not yet made the shift (restructured) in their second language. In this language, they did not make strategic use of the semantic and syntactic knowledge at their disposal.

Evaluation

Cognitive theory stresses the limited information-processing capacities of human learners, the use of various techniques to overcome these limitations, and the role of practice in stretching resources so that component skills that require more mental work become routinized and thereby free controlled processes for other functions. As automaticity develops, controlled search is bypassed and attentional limitations are overcome. The acquisition of a complex cognitive skill, such as learning a second language, is thought to involve the gradual accumulation of automatized subskills and a constant restructuring of internalized representations as the learner achieves increasing degrees of mastery.

How successful are the notions advanced in this chapter in providing a theoretical framework for second-language learning? Obviously, the present author is not an unbiased observer; this critique needs to be supplemented by those of others less favourably disposed to the cognitive approach. However, a number of the limitations of this approach are quite apparent – even to the partial observer.

Information processing and linguistic systems

Cognitive theory treats the acquisition of linguistic systems as it does the acquisition of any complex cognitive skills. One of the assumptions of many workers in the fields of first- and second-language acquisition is that the development of language to a greater or lesser extent follows its own course. According to this view, in acquiring a language the learner builds up a series of internal representations of the language system. This occurs as a result of 'natural' processing strategies that lead the speaker in predictable stages toward target-language competence. If there are indeed natural acquisitional sequences in first- and second-language acquisition, how are they to be treated in Cognitive theory? More generally, how does this approach treat linguistic data?

Natural acquisitional processes
There is general agreement in the second-language field that there are predictable sequences in acquisition such that certain structures have to be acquired before others can be integrated (Lightbown 1985). Unfortunately, as we have seen, only a few acquisitional sequences have been described in detail – e.g., the English negative, subject-auxiliary inversion in English questions, word order rules in German. Even when we

know something about acquisitional stages in the development of a particular construction in a particular target language, we do not have sufficient data from a variety of speakers with different first languages acquiring the target language. That is, we may know something about how Turkish speakers learn German word order, but we have no information about, say, Hungarian speakers.

Furthermore, as we saw in chapter 3, there is evidence from some research that indicates that the first language of the learner has an effect on acquisitional sequences, either slowing their development or modifying it. In addition, there seems to be considerable individual variation in how learners acquire second languages due to different learning, performance, and communication strategies. These individual differences may obscure the acquisitional sequences for certain constructions.

Nonetheless, it should be apparent from previous chapters that many authors in the field are convinced that learners follow acquisitional sequences and that these sequences are determined by the nature of the internal linguistic system. The second-language learner's utterances are seen to be a natural outcome of the internal system. Thus Acculturation/Pidginization theory holds that in the early stages of acquisition learners revert to the internal system to build an autonomous interlanguage, free in part from the constraints of the input. Universal Grammar theory also stresses the regularity in learner's acquisitional processes and postulates that language learners approach the task endowed with innate, specifically linguistic, knowledge that is biologically determined and specialized for language learning. The predication of natural developmental sequences is also central to Krashen's theory.

Rather than stressing internal, predetermined linguistic processes, Cognitive theory emphasizes the cognitive processes involved in the internalization of procedural knowledge that accounts for how learners accumulate and automatize rules and how they restructure their internal representations to match the target language. The acquisition of a cognitive skill is seen to result from the automatization of routines or units of activity. Initially the execution of these routines requires the allocation of large amounts of mental effort (controlled processing), but repeated performance of the activity leads to the availability of automatized routines in long-term memory. The result of this process is that less and less effort is required for automated routines and the learner can devote more effort to acquiring other sub-skills that are not yet automated.

Within this framework, it is possible to incorporate natural acquisitional sequences if one assumes that some acquisition involves the development, in predictable sequences, of routines that are already automatized when they emerge (Sajavaara 1978). Thus there are assumed to be two acquisitional routes: (1) a route that is highly determined by linguistic constraints, that is predetermined and automatic, and that follows natural acquisitional sequences, and (2) a route that is not determined but that requires automatization through controlled processing. Although, as we shall see, there are problems with such an assumption, it does provide a way for Cognitive theory to deal with the constraints of linguistic phenomena.

Dealing with the linguistic facts

In general, Cognitive theory needs to be linked to linguistic theories of second-language acquisition. By itself, for example, the cognitive perspective cannot explain such linguistic constraints as are implied in markedness theory or that may result from linguistic universals. These specifically linguistic considerations are not addressed by an approach that sees learning a second-language merely in terms of the acquisition of a complex cognitive skill.

Learning a second language does involve the acquisition of a complex cognitive skill, but it involves the acquisition of a complex linguistic skill as well. Thus, as has been pointed out (McLaughlin *et al*. 1983), the cognitive perspective to second-language learning is not a complete one. Such a perspective is only one way of looking at language learning. It becomes more powerful if it is complemented by linguistic research.

For example, understanding the process of restructuring is a central concern of the cognitive approach, but a more thorough understanding of restructuring in second-language acquisition requires the analysis of linguistic data. Thus the work of Bickerton, Schumann, Stauble, and others on restructuring in decreolization and late second-language learning enriches our understanding of the linguistic details of the restructuring process.

Similarly, an account of transfer phenomena requires linguistic considerations. According to Cognitive theory, transfer occurs because the speaker has incorrectly activated an automatic routine based on the first language. Such errors occur because learners lack the necessary information in the second language or the attentional capacity to activate the appropriate second-language routine. But such an account says little about why certain linguistic forms transfer and others do not. Here a theory of markedness may generate detailed predictions that are more specific than the Cognitive theory account, which does not make predictions that are as explicit about when transfer will occur.

Testing the theory

Cognitive theory does not represent a highly articulated theoretical position. There have been relatively few attempts to spell out with any degree of precision what the predictions of such a theory would be for second-language learning. Nonetheless, the writings of Faerch and

Kasper (1980, 1984), in particular, have clarified conceptual and theoretical issues, and a number of researchers, as we have seen in this chapter, have used this approach to examine second-language phenomena. The theory has gone beyond the 'proto-theoretical' stage, in that it represents more than a loose connection of generalizations about second-language phenomena, and attempts to get at explanatory statements.

The theory is at the more inductive end of the inductive-deductive continuum. There is an attempt to build up a picture of more complex phenomena out of specific research findings. However, because the range of phenomena the theory accommodates is relatively restricted, Cognitive theory is a more 'micro' theoretical enterprise than Interlanguage theory, Universal Grammar theory, or Acculturation/Pidginization theory. The specific focus of Cognitive theory is the learning process, viewed as the acquisition of a complex cognitive skill, whereas these other theories deal with a broader range of issues that have traditionally concerned second-language researchers: transfer, developmental sequences, motivational factors in learning, and so forth.

This does not mean that understanding the learning process from a cognitive-psychological perspective is any less important than these other concerns. From a practical point of view, a fuller appreciation of the central processes of automaticity and restructuring has important implications for second-language teaching. Consequently, a theory of language processing that uses such notions to provide testable hypotheses can make important contributions to an understanding of second-language acquisition.

Falsifiability
In chapter 1 the argument was made that good theories fit the data well, are consistent with related formulations, are clear in their predictions, and are heuristically rich. Are the predictions based on Cognitive theory specific enough to allow researchers to test the theory? Is research within this framework capable of disconfirmation?

The central premises of Cognitive theory are: (1) learning a complex cognitive skill involves the use of various information-handling techniques to overcome capacity limitations, (2) through practice component skills become automatized and controlled processes are freed for other functions, and (3) there is a constant restructuring of internalized representations as the learner achieves increasing degrees of mastery. How would each of these propositions be falsified?

In general, the procedural approach to information processing that has been taken in this chapter can be criticized for imprecision of many key statements and rather loose definition of terms, including such critical concepts as 'capacity-limitations', 'skill', and its 'components'. In reply, advocates of such an approach argue that theoretical precision is premature at the present stage of our knowledge and that more precision would only inhibit research (e.g., Kolers and Roediger 1984). Cognitive theory, it is argued, has been heuristically rich and deserves to be pursued.

The notion that skill acquisition involves the accumulation of automatic processing through initial controlled operations that require more workload and attention is one that has been accepted by psychologists since William James, though it is not without its critics (Cheng 1985). Whether language is such a skill is more debatable. One of the claims of many researchers studying first- and second-language acquisition is that there are natural acquisitional sequences. As we have seen, Sajavaara (1978) has suggested that such predictable acquisitional sequences constitute routines that are already automatized when they emerge. Thus one acquisitional route would not involve the gradual accumulation of automaticity through practice, but would be highly determined by linguistic constraints and the linguistic structures acquired in this manner would be fully automatized upon their appearance. Such an assumption provides a way for Cognitive theory to deal with the constraints of certain linguistic phenomena, but does not leave the theory open to refutation. If it is possible to have it both ways, the theory is not testable (unless there is some way of predetermining which structures are to follow 'natural' developmental sequences and which ones will not).

Furthermore, the restructuring concept opens up the possibility of discontinuities in the learning process, so that the notion that practice leads to improvement in performance as sub-skills become automated allows of exceptions wherein practice produces decrements in performance as learners reorganize their internal representational framework. It seems that the effects of practice do not accrue directly or automatically to a skilled action, but rather accumulate as learners develop more efficient procedures (Kolers and Duchnicky 1985). Performance may follow a U-shaped curve, declining as more complex internal representations replace less complex ones, and increasing again as skill becomes expertise. At this point, however, the theory is not precise enough about when and how restructuring occurs.

The issue of consciousness
One misconception quite prevalent in the second-language literature is that controlled processes require conscious effort for their execution. Zobl (1984), for example, compared predictions based on Krashen's model with those based on a model that assumes that there is a transfer of knowledge from the explicit, conscious domain to the implicit, unconscious domain. This second model was associated with the Cognitive theory notion of automatization. It is assumed in such a reading that controlled processing is explicit and conscious, whereas auto-

matic processing is implicit and unconscious.

Such an interpretation was specifically discounted:

The distinction between controlled and automatic processing is not based on conscious experience. Both controlled and automatic processes can in principle be either conscious or not. Since most automatic processes occur with great speed, their constituent elements are usually, but not necessarily, hidden from conscious perception. Some controlled processes also occur with great speed, so that they may not be available to conscious experience. Shiffrin and Schneider (1977) called these controlled processes 'veiled'. Other controlled processes, those they referred to as 'accessible', are easily perceived by the learner. (McLaughlin *et al.* 1983)

Recourse to conscious or unconscious experience is notoriously unreliable and hence cannot be a source of testable hypotheses about the learning process (see chapter 2 for a critique of Krashen's theory on these grounds).

The advantage of Cognitive theory over more subjective accounts of the learning process is that various empirical techniques have been developed for assessing the contribution of controlled and automatic processing. Thus reaction time measures can be used, as in Dornic's (1979) research, to determine under what conditions the shifts in speed and attention occur that are the hallmarks of automatic processing. Similarly, semantic facilitation effects (Favreau 1981) or Stroop effects (Preston and Lambert 1969) can be seen as evidence for automaticity. Production tasks of various sorts can be used to determine when and under which conditions automaticity in language processing breaks down (Bock 1982).

As more investigators in second-language research take advantage of such empirical procedures, it will become possible to assess more adequately the utility of Cognitive theory. As research accumulates, definitional precision should improve. At present, there has not been enough research on second-language acquisition from this perspective to determine the theory's worth.

7

Conclusion

In chapter 1, I argued that theories serve three functions. First, they allow us to *understand* and organize the data of experience. Theories summarize relatively large amounts of information via a relatively short list of propositions. Second, theories *transform* our thinking about phenomena and enable researchers to use empirical data to draw conclusions that are not evident from the data taken in isolation. They allow us to go beyond the information given. Third, theories guide *prediction* and stimulate research.

I have attempted, in evaluating the theories treated in this book, to assess the extent to which they have realized the goals of understanding, conceptual transformation, and prediction. In this final chapter, I will try to summarize and integrate the discussion in the context of three general issues relating to theory. The first issue concerns what the theory must explain – the current state of our knowledge of adult second-language learning. This leads to an examination of the various analytic frameworks that have influenced second-language research and their associated research methods. Finally, the chapter concludes with a consideration of how theory relates to practice.

Theory and second-language phenomena

Some generalizations
To appreciate what theory must explain, I have listed in Table 7.1 a number of generalizations based on recent 'state of the art' summaries by leading second-language researchers. These generalizations should perhaps be expressed as *hypotheses*, as there is not universal agreement as to their status.

The first four generalizations refer to system-internal factors in language learning. Although developmental sequences have been satisfactorily documented for a relatively small number of constructions

Table 7.1 Some generalizations based on second-language research

(1) There are predictable sequences in the acquisition of a second language such that certain structures have to be acquired before others can be integrated (Lightbown 1985).

(2) The learner creates a systematic interlanguage, which is often characterized by the same errors as are made by children learning the same language as the first language, as well as others which appear to be based on the learner's own native language (transfer) (Lightbown 1985).

(3) Interlanguage development occurs as the product of the learner's Universal Grammar, which makes some rules easier to learn than others (Ellis 1985b).

(4) Second-language learning is an active process in which learners discover how the input is segmented, how the segments are used to represent meanings, how units are assembled structurally, and what principles speakers use to achieve communicative goals and intentions. This active process requires a host of cognitive strategies and skills, as well as social knowledge (Wong Fillmore 1985).

(5) At any one stage of development the learner's interlanguage comprises a system of variable rules (Ellis 1985b).

(6) Knowing a language rule does not mean that one will be able to use it in communicative interactions (Lightbown 1985).

(7) Situational factors are the primary causes of variability in the interlanguage and are indirect determinants of the rate of learning and the level of proficiency achieved (Ellis 1985b).

(8) Good input to second-language learners has their social needs in mind. It is selected for content and modified in form and presentation. It tends to be structurally simpler, more redundant and repetitive, and is characterized by greater structural regularity than is found in normal usage (Wong Fillmore 1985).

(9) Learners have to realize they need to learn the target language and must be motivated to do so (Wong Fillmore 1985).

(10) Some personality or cognitive style characteristics that affect second-language learning include: the willingness to take risks, pattern recognition abilities, tolerance of ambiguity, skill in social interactions, attitude toward the target language, and motivation (Wong Fillmore 1985).

(Lightbown 1985), there is widespread belief in a natural learning sequence in second-language acquisition, which parallels first-language developmental sequences. Krashen and others see this natural development to be the product of the Language Acquisition Device, assumed to operate in adulthood, allowing child-like internalizations of the rules underlying the target language. Other authors stress the role of Universal Grammar in constraining the developmental sequence.

The third and fourth generalizations are not mutually exclusive, because, as we saw in the last chapter, it is possible to argue for the existence of universal innate linguistic properties of language and, at the same time, to argue that the language-learning process involves the utilization of problem-solving and general cognitive skills, as well as social skills, to achieve communicative goals and intentions. In fact, consistent with the argument in chapter 6, a number of researchers have recently advocated a 'modular' approach to second-language acquisition that recognizes the contribution of various systems – linguistic, cognitive, and social (Faerch and Kasper 1986; Felix 1985; Sharwood-Smith 1985).

The next three generalizations are concerned with fluctuations and variability in second-language use. As we saw in chapter 3, Interlanguage theory addresses the issue of variability and its situational and sociolinguistic determinants. Other theories have little to say on this score, although Acculturation/Pidginization theory does address the question of why learners differ in the level of ultimate proficiency they achieve.

The eighth generalization concerns input and the relationship between input and language learning. None of the theories discussed in this book adequately treats the problem of how input becomes intake and how what is taken into the system is integrated into the existing interlanguage. One issue is whether the eighth generalization is correct, or whether what is taken in is controlled by the structure of the internal processing mechanism. That is, does the nature of the input matter, or are learners more influenced by the constraints of the internal system? Universal Grammar theory downplays the role of input, whereas Krashen features it prominently in his theory. However, as we saw in chapter 2, Krashen's account of the role of 'comprehensible input' is tautological and based on a non-existent theory of acquisitional sequences.

The last two generalizations are directed at features of the learner. Acculturation/Pidginization theory has given most attention to this factor in second-language learning. Krashen's theory also incorporates learner variables through the Affective Filter Hypothesis, but here again, the theory is vague and imprecise in its predictions.

In general, Krashen's theory is broadest in the range of second-language phenomena it purports to encompass. Krashen (1985) claimed that his theory accounted for the acquisition of sociolinguistic rules, syntactic rules, discourse rules, phonological rules – indeed, the whole of language acquisition. This allowed him to cite putative evidence for his theory indiscriminately, disregarding the actual domain of that evidence (Gregg, in press). Thus in arguing for the 'younger-is-better' principle of language acquisition, Krashen lumped together studies of syntax and of accent, as though they comprised a global language proficiency factor.

Other authors are more scrupulous about the domain of evidence to which their theories apply. As we have seen, Interlanguage theory and Universal Grammar theory have been concerned primarily with the issues of acquisitional sequences and transfer. These issues have also been central to research on pidginization and creolization, although Acculturation/Pidginization theory had also highlighted the social and psychological factors involved in adult language acquisition. Cognitive theory, discussed in the previous chapter, is concerned exclusively with the cognitive processes operative in second-language learning and says little about most of the linguistic issues that have been the focus of much second-language research.

The role of theory in second-language research
Should a theory attempt to account for the entire range of second-language phenomena? A general theory has the appeal of providing a total picture, but there is the danger – which I have stressed in discussing Krashen's theory – that the details get blurred. As we have seen, the tendency in second-language research is to move away from general theory to theories of more limited scope.

A related question is whether progress in the field of second-language research will come about through what Long (1985a) called a 'theory-then-research' strategy or through a 'research-then-theory' strategy. As was pointed out in chapter 1, no research is entirely a-theoretical, but some research is more theory-driven than other research. Long noted that there are advantages and disadvantages to both the theory-then-research and the research-then-theory orientations.

The theory-then-research strategy has the advantage of providing an approximate answer until the 'final truth' is known. Such theories serve a useful heuristic, assuming that they generate testable hypotheses that can confirm or disconfirm the theory. The disadvantage of a theory-driven approach is what social psychologists call 'confirmation bias' (Greenwald *et al.* 1986): one's preliminary hypotheses have a decided advantage in the judgement process.

The advantages of the research-then-theory approach are that one is closer to the empirical evidence at hand, and it makes only limited claims. The likelihood of a confirmation bias is not ruled out because all research tests implicit theory, but there is less investment in a theoretical point of view. The disadvantage is that such an approach may be too limited and lacks the heuristic power of a more developed theoretical approach.

Long (1985a) argued that the theory-then-research strategy allows for more efficient research. He maintained that the theory governing the research at any point in time tells the investigator what the relevant data are and what is the critical experiment to run. Such a research strategy leads to explanatory accounts of the processes at work in a given domain. In contrast, Greenwald and his associates (1986) have argued that the researcher who sets out to test a theory is likely to become ego-involved with a theoretical prediction, to select procedures that lead eventually to prediction-confirming data, and thereby produce over-generalized conclusions.

The debate has a long history in the philosophy of science. Kuhn (1970) favoured the theory-then-research strategy, and argued that ordinary scientific activity thrives on theory confirmation – solving puzzles within the existing paradigm. He pointed out, however, that theory confirmation does not succeed indefinitely. Anomalous results accumulate until only a major theoretical reorganization (scientific revolution) can accommodate them. Popper (1959), on the other hand, regarded exclusive use of confirmation-seeking methods as non-scientific. In his view empirical knowledge in a scientific domain grows only by the use of critical, falsification-seeking methods.

The difficulty is that falsification-seeking is given more lip-service than practised. If, as I have argued, all research has an implicit theory, it is impossible to escape confirmation bias. Even researchers who stay within a limited domain and deal with only certain issues are likely to have definite expectations about their data.

In second-language research, many investigators are currently working with a research-then-theory strategy, looking first at what the data tell us descriptively and then moving upward toward theoretical claims. Thus there were numerous empirical studies of acquisitional sequences in second-language learning before theoretical arguments were made about 'natural' developmental sequences. Similarly, the data from transfer studies has only begun to be incorporated theoretically as the predictions of markedness theory are tested.

But much research on second-language learning remains at the descriptive (and implicit) level and has not been incorporated into theoretical perspectives. For example, as Long (1985a) pointed out, this is the case for the research on input. None of our current theories provides an adequate account of how and why input affects language learning. This is also true of much research on communicative strategies, which has not been given adequate theoretical treatment. The elaboration of implicit theory into explicit theory will be an indication of progress in these domains.

Theory and research methods

In this book we have seen that researchers seeking to develop a scientific theory of second-language learning come from various disciplines. Most theories – Krashen's Monitor model, Interlanguage theory, Universal Grammar theory – are primarily linguistic in their approach. Acculturation/Pidginization theory is concerned with the course of linguistic development, but also addresses social and psychological factors. Cognitive theory derives from developments in contemporary psychology. There are, as we shall see, other contributions as well.

The faces of second-language research
Lightbown (1984) distinguished five disciplines from which second-language researchers draw theoretical hypotheses. The first is *linguistic* theory. This has been the most fruitful line of inquiry and has generated the most research. The attempt has been to relate second-language acquisition to theories about adult linguistic competence and language universals. This approach focuses less on the language-learning situation and individual differences than upon universal characteristics of language and the human capacity for language learning. As we have seen in chapter 4, recent developments in Chomskyan theory have stimulated research on the constraints that limit the hypotheses a learner makes about specific structures of the language to be acquired. The assumption is made that the Language Acquisition Device functions both in first- and second-language acquisition.

Linguistic research has employed a variety of methods: error analysis, morpheme analyses, grammaticality judgements, and comprehension tasks. In addition, as we saw in chapter 5, researchers have examined the evidence for parallels and analogies to pidginization and creolization processes. Unfortunately, different methods do not always yield comparable data (Kellerman 1984) and Ellis (1985b) has noted that different data collection instruments may have differential effects according to the individual characteristics of the learner being investigated. The same procedure can tap different things in adults and children. Consequently, care needs to be taken in generalizing the results of a study based on one specific data type. Tarone's work, discussed in chapter 3, indicates that second-language learning is not a monolithic process and that there are various types of language use (e.g., a vernacular style and a careful style), no one of which is inherently more important than any other type.

The study of types of second-language use brings us to the domain of *sociolinguistics*. Researchers have examined systematic variation within the interlanguage as a function of different learning and observational contexts. The sociolinguistic approach is also reflected in research that suggests that second-language acquisition is analogous or identical with processes involved in pidginization and creolization. In addition, many second-language researchers have been concerned with discourse analysis and with the way in which language is negotiated in conversation. This research has been more descriptive than theoretical, but has provided insights into how the process of constructing discourse contributes to the development of the interlanguage (e.g., Hatch 1980).

One contribution of the sociolinguistic approach is concern with the functions of language. The linguistic preoccupation with syntactic development has caused researchers to lose sight of the way in which language functions in communication. As Long and Sato (1984) pointed out, one needs to examine how forms take on new functions and how language functions are expressed formally. This requires a multi-level analysis that considers the entire repertoire of strategies and devices used by the learner. These concerns have been given relatively little theoretical attention.

Another approach to second-language research comes from *social psychology*. The focus here is on the situational factors that influence second-language proficiency and on individual difference variables. We saw in chapter 5 that a number of researchers have been concerned with why it is that different learners acquire second languages faster and attain higher levels of proficiency than others. The explanations related to social and psychological distance (Schumann 1978) and to integrative versus segregative orientations (Meisel 1980). It was also pointed out in that chapter that other social-psychological accounts exist (e.g., Gardner and Lambert 1972; Giles *et al.* 1979) that need to be incorporated into a more developed theory.

In contrast to linguistic or sociolinguistic research, most social-psychological studies use large numbers of subjects so as to determine which of several variables contributes most to the variance in learner performance. Because of the concern with rate and level of language proficiency, various paper and pencil tests are used to measure language ability (although more detailed linguistic analyses were used in Schumann and Meisel's studies). Work on the 'good language learner' problem and on personality and learning style variables fits within this tradition.

Another strategy of researchers is to look at second-language learning from a *neurolinguistic* perspective. The focus in this case is on the brain and its role in language acquisition. Lamendella (1977) has developed a neurolinguistic model for second-language acquisition, but because this approach has generated relatively little research, the theory has not been discussed in detail in this book. Moreover, there is considerable uncertainty regarding the identification of neurolinguistic correlates of language performance (Genesee 1982).

The data come from dichotic listening tests, tachistoscopic tests, and various more exotic procedures such as finger tapping and eye movement observations. The study of aphasia has provided insight into the neurolinguistic basis of language acquisition (Paradis 1983). Because much neurolinguistic research depends on opportunities to investigate linguistic phenomena in individuals whose neurolinguistic health has been somehow impaired, progress will likely be slow and generalizations to normal populations uncertain (Lightbown 1984). Nonetheless, this line of research is important for theoretical progress: an ultimate theoretical goal is to link linguistic and psychological constructs with neurolinguistic correlates.

The final discipline mentioned by Lightbown is *cognitive psychology*. The contribution of this approach was outlined in chapter 6. Lightbown noted that this type of research is not generally seen as part of the mainstream of second-language research. In part, this is because much of the research on memory and information processing in bilingual subjects is reported in psychology journals, and also because there has been little direct application of this research to language teaching. There is also a suspicion of psychological approaches that dates back to the days when behaviouristic psychology influenced audio-lingual techniques of language teaching.

A more fundamental issue is the role of psychological theory as a source of knowledge regarding language learning. Theoretical linguists, especially those working within Chomsky's framework, are more concerned with discovering what the language learner knows that makes language possible in the context of limited input data. The emphasis is on innate, language-specific sources of knowledge rather than on cognitive processes. I have argued in chapter 6 that both the linguistic and the psychological approaches are valid and can contribute to understanding second-language learning.

One of the assumptions underlying scientific research discussed in chapter 1 is that there is no one scientific truth. There can be multiple accounts of complex phenomena and these multiple accounts result in multiple truths. Each of the theoretical approaches discussed here has its own metaphorical system (Schumann 1983a) and each is valid to the extent that it increases understanding.

Methods
A multitheoretical approach implies a multimethod approach. Different research questions arise from different theoretical orientations and require different methodological procedures. The procedures are tied to theoretical assumptions in some cases, and care has to be taken not to conclude on the basis of one's method what has been assumed on the basis of one's theory. Lightbown (1984) gave the example of researchers working within the current version of Chomsky's linguistic theory, who use methods that focus on the details of language itself and ignore, as much as possible, external factors that differentiate learners from each other. Prior knowledge of other languages, input variation, and personality and social factors are downplayed in this approach. Thus evidence from a number of studies is taken to indicate that the acquisition of some linguistic structures is not influenced by external variables but seems instead to follow universal patterns of development.

The issue is how generalizable this research is. As Lightbown noted, there is considerable evidence from other research that indicates the influence of the first language on second-language learning, and the importance of variation in input and degree of social integration. Lightbown concluded that the counter-evidence indicates the need, in linguistically-oriented research, to control for and manipulate – rather than ignore – the role of external variables. If this is done, it will be possible to expand generalizability and to demonstrate the validity of certain assumptions, rather than to leave them as just that – assumptions.

Another strategy to avoid overgeneralizing research findings is deliberately to reduce the generalizability of an existing finding. That is, one can seek to determine under precisely which conditions a finding obtains. This is the method of 'condition-seeking' (Greenwald *et al.* 1986), which, in statistical terms, means looking for interaction effects. In second-language research these interaction effects often take the form of interactions between person and situational variables (McLaughlin 1980). Thus Tarone's (1979) work on style shifting in the interlanguage indicates the importance of situational context. Other research shows how different instructional methods are more effective with students with some personality characteristics than with others (e.g. Genesee and Hamayan 1980).

Condition-seeking research initially leads to a more complex picture as results become more and more qualified. The goal, however, is increasing precision and, ultimately, more general theoretical statements. To a certain extent, this is what has happened in research on first-language transfer. As researchers have become aware of the conditions under which transfer does or does not occur, it becomes possible to make more powerful theoretical statements. Developments in markedness theory promise to provide greater generality than traditional contrastive analysis.

Theory and practice

The social psychologist, Kurt Lewin, once wrote that there is nothing as practical as a good theory. Of all the theories we have discussed in this book, none has had greater impact on the practice of language teaching than Krashen's Monitor Model. In discussing Krashen's theory in chapter 2, I argued that one of the reasons for Krashen's popularity among language teachers is that he has been able to package his ideas in a manner that is accessible to practitioners. Moreover, he has captured the *Zeitgeist* – the movement in the field away from grammar-based to communicatively oriented language instruction. His ideas on the role of affective factors in language learning and on the importance of acquisitional sequences in second-language development also appeal to practitioners.

Krashen's strong advocacy of exposure to comprehensible input led him to denigrate the role of formal instruction, although he acknowledged that consciously learning a rule could help make input comprehensible and thus help acquisition. Being taught a rule that is not at i + 1 will not, according to Krashen, lead to acquisition of the rule, but it may make the context more understandable and hence lead to acquisition of other forms that are at i + 1. The difficulty with this position, as was noted in chapter 2, is that if studies show that grammar-based or drill-based instruction is effective, Krashen can argue that it is because such methods indirectly provide comprehensible input. There is no way to distinguish between the effectiveness of grammar-based and communication-based instruction without a more objective definition of comprehensible input.

A more common opinion than Krashen's is that correction and grammar teaching can provide a shortcut for learners. Although there is resistance to the traditional heavy reliance on grammar teaching in second-language instruction, many researchers view conscious instruction in the rules of a grammar as helpful to language learning. Indeed, research indicates that formal instruction in a second language can be effective (Long 1983).

Krashen made reference to internal processes in language acquisition and appears to believe that the LAD is constrained by an innate universal grammar. As was pointed out in chapter 2, however, his notions do not fit well with contemporary Universal Grammar theory, which views language acquisition as a process of setting the parameters of universal principles, not as a problem of acquiring grammatical rules.

The pedagogical implications of the Universal Grammar approach are not fully articulated at this point. Researchers working in this framework tend to focus on very narrowly-defined research questions, which have little direct bearing on teaching practices. However, in the long run the research of this group, and of researchers concerned with Interlanguage theory generally, may have a definite impact on language teaching. The concern with developmental sequences and the sources of transfer from the first language is shared by theorists and teachers. There is general agreement among researchers that it is premature to look to research on developmental sequences for information about how constructions should be presented in the classroom (Gadalla 1981). Rather than using the data from research as a basis for the grading of grammatical materials, the research on interlanguage suggests another approach:

> The progressive elaboration of the interlanguage system of the learner is a response to his developing need to handle even more complex communicative tasks. If we can control the level of these correctly, the grammar will look after itself. Instead, then, of

grading the linguistic material that we expose the learner to, we should consider grading the communicative demands we make on him, thereby gently leading him to elaborate his approximative system. (Corder 1981, 78)

Researchers working in the context of Acculturation/Pidginization theory derive their data from untutored adult learners. Nonetheless, this research may have something to say to teaching practitioners. As we saw in chapter 5, early second-language acquisition is seen to involve simplification and regression and late second-language acquisition replacement and restructuring. The initial phases are thought to be more 'creative' and to rely to a greater extent on some internal universal linguistic base; the later phases are more conditioned by the demands of the target language. Some researchers in this tradition have advocated tolerance for the creative constructions of learners and de-emphasis on error correction in the early stages of learning.

In general, researchers and theorists who approach second-language learning from a linguistic perspective tend to stress the creative construction process. Most teachers, however, follow a more psychological model. The difference between these approaches can be see in Table 7.2. Most teaching approaches are based on the assumption that if we require learners to produce predetermined pieces of language (through drills or questions-and-answers), this productive activity will lead them to internalize the system underlying the language, to the point where the system operates without conscious reflection (Littlewood 1984).

The model followed by most teachers is closest to the cognitive-psychological perspective outlined in chapter 6. In this view, the use of a second language is a cognitive skill and, like other cognitive skills, involves the internalization, through practice, of various information-handling techniques to overcome capacity limitations. Skill acquisition is seen to involve the accumulation of automatic processing through initial controlled operations that require more workload and attention. Internalized rules are restructured as learners adjust their internal representations to match the target language. This restructuring process involves the use of learning, production, and communication strategies.

Table 7.2   Two models of the teaching process

Creative construction model	Model underlying most teaching
Input from exposure	Input from instruction
Internal processing	Productive activity
System constructed by learners	System adopted by learners
Spontaneity and fluency	Spontaneity and fluency

Based on Littlewood 1984.

The difficulty with a skill model of language learning is that teaching can easily lapse into drill-and-practice exercises. The critique of the traditional approach to language teaching made by Krashen and others is that such an approach leaves little room for creative construction and places too great an emphasis on the conscious learning of rules. I have argued that this is not necessarily the case (McLaughlin *et al.* 1983), and it was noted in chapter 6 that there are ways of accommodating acquisitional sequences based on innate, universal linguistic processes within a cognitive perspective.

What is needed is an intergrated approach that incorporates both the more creative aspects of language learning and the more cognitive aspects that are susceptible to guidance and training. Such a model is outlined in Table 7.3. In this model, instruction, exposure, practice and internal processing all interact to lead to the assimilation and accommodation necessary for spontaneity and fluency in a second language. Learners assimilate as they use their knowledge of language to make sense out of the input. This process dominates in the early stage as learners simplify and transfer forms from their first language. Accommodation dominates in the later stages as learners reorganize their internal system to match the target language.

Table 7.3 An integrated model of second-language teaching

Input from instruction and exposure	Practice and internal processing	Assimilation and accommodation	Spontaneity and fluency

At this point, research and theory cannot act as a sources of prescriptions about teaching procedures. There are still too many gaps in our knowledge, especially of individual difference variables and social factors that play important roles in classroom practice. This is not to deny the potential relevance of theory and research for second-language teaching. Ultimately, teaching benefits by sound understandting of the processes involved in second-language learning.

References

ACTON, W. 1979: *Second language learning and perception of differences in attitude*. Unpublished dissertation, University of Michigan.

ADJEMIAN, C. 1976: On the nature of interlanguage systems. *Language Learning* 26, 297–320.

ANDERSEN, R. 1978: An implicational model for second language research. *Language Learning* 28, 221–82.

——1981: Two perspectives on pidginization as second language acquisition. In Andersen, R.W. (ed.), *New dimensions in second language acquisition research* (Rowley, MA: Newbury House).

——1983: Introduction: a language acquisition interpretation of pidginization and creolization. In Andersen, R.W. (ed.), *Pidginization and creolization as language acquisition* (Rowley, MA: Newbury House).

ANDERSON, J. 1983: Syllable simplification in the speech of second language learners. *Interlanguage Studies Bulletin* 7, 4–36.

ARD, J. and HOMBURG. T. 1983: Verification of language transfer. In Gass, S. and Selinker, L. (eds.), *Language transfer in language learning* (Rowley, MA: Newbury House).

BAILEY, J.-J. 1973: *Variation and linguistic theory*. Washington, DC: Center for Applied Linguistics.

BAILEY, N., MADDEN, C., and KRASHEN, S. 1974: Is there a 'natural sequence' in adult second language learning. *Language Learning* 24, 235–43.

BIALYSTOK, E. 1981: Some evidence for the integrity and interaction of two knowledge sources. In Andersen, R.W. (ed.), *New dimensions in second language acquisition research* (Rowley, MA: Newbury House).

BIALYSTOK, E., and SHARWOOD SMITH, M. 1985: Interlanguage is not a state of mind: an evaluation of the construct for second-language acquisition. *Applied Linguistics* 6, 101–17.

BICKERTON, D. 1971: Inherent variability and variables rules. *Foundations of Language* 7, 457–92.

——1973: On the nature of a creole continuum. *Language* 49, 640–9.

——1975: *Dynamics of a creole system*. Cambridge: Cambridge University Press.

——1977: Pidginization and creolization: language acquisition and lan-

guage universals. In Valdman, A. (ed.), *Pidgin and creole linguistics* (Bloomington: Indiana University Press).
——1981: *Roots of language*. Ann Arbor, MI: Karoma.
——1983: Comments on Valdman's 'Creolization and second language acquisition'. In Andersen, R. (ed.) *Pidginization and creolization as language acquisition* (Rowley, MA: Newbury House).
——1984: The language bioprogram hypothesis and second language acquisition. In Rutherford, W.E. (ed.), *Language universals and second language acquisition* (Amsterdam: John Benjamins).
BICKERTON, D., and ODO, C. 1976: *General phonology and pidgin syntax*. Vol. 1 of Final report on National Science Foundation Grant No. GS-39748 (unpublished).
BOCK, J.K. 1982: Toward a cognitive psychology of syntax: information processing contributions to sentence formation. *Psychological Review* 89, 1–47.
BROSELOW, E. 1983: Non-obvious transfer: On predicting epenthesis errors. In Gass, S. and Selinker, L. (eds.), *Language transfer in language learning* (Rowley, MA: Newbury House).
BROWN, H.D. 1980: *Principles of language learning and teaching*. Englewood Cliffs, NJ: Prentice-Hall.
BROWN, R. 1973: *A first language: the early stages*. Cambridge, MA: Harvard University Press.
BURKE, S.J. 1974: Language acquisition, language learning, and language teaching. *International Review of Applied Linguistics* 12, 53–68.
BURT, M.K., and DULAY, H.C. 1980: On acquisition orders. In Felix, S. (ed.), *Second language development* (Tübingen: Narr).
BURT, M.K., DULAY, H.C., and HERNANDEZ-CHAVEZ, E. 1975: *Bilingual syntax measure*. New York: Harcourt Brace Jovanovitch.
CAMPBELL, D.T., and STANLEY, J.C. 1963: *Experimental and quasi-experimental designs for research*. Chicago: Rand-McNally.
CHENG, P.W. 1985: Restructuring versus automaticity: alternative accounts of skill acquisition. *Psychological Review* 92, 214–23.
CHOMSKY, N. 1968: Noam Chomsky and Stuart Hampshire discuss the study of language. *The Listener* 79, no. 2044.
——1975: *Reflections on language*. New York: Pantheon.
——1980: *Rules and explanations*. New York: Columbia University Press.
——1981: *Lectures on government and binding*. Dordrecht: Foris.
——1984: Changing perspectives on knowledge and use of language. Unpublished manuscript, Massachussetts Institute of Technology. Cited in Flynn, 1985.
CHOMSKY, N. and HALLÉ, M. 1968: *The sound pattern of English*. New York: Harper and Row.
CLARK, H. and CLARK, E. 1977: *The psychology and language: an introduction to psycholinguistics*. New York: Harcourt Brace and Jonanovich.
CLARK, R. 1974: Performing without competence. *Journal of Child Language* 1, 1–10.
COMRIE, B. 1981: *Language universals and linguistic typology*. Chicago: University of Chicago.
——1984: Why linguists need language acquirers. In Rutherford, W.E. (ed.), *Language universals and second language acquisition* (Amsterdam: John Benjamins).

168   *References*

COOK, V.J. 1985: Universal grammar and second language learning. *Journal of Applied Linguistics* 6, 2-18.

CORDER, S.P. 1967: The significance of learners' errors. *International Review of Applied Linguistics* 4, 161-9.

——1973: The elicitation of interlanguage. In Svartik, J. (ed.), *Errata: papers on error analysis* (Lund: EWK Gleerup).

——1981: *Error analysis and interlanguage.* Oxford: Oxford University Press.

CROMER, W. 1970: The difference model: a new explanation for some reading difficulties. *Journal of Educational Psychology* 62, 471-83.

CZIKO, G.A. 1980: Language competence and reading strategies: a comparison of first- and second-language oral reading errors. *Language Learning* 30, 101-16.

DECAMP, D. 1971: Introduction: the study of pidgin and creole languages. In Hymes, D. (ed.), *Pidginization and creolization of languages* (Cambridge: Cambridge University Press).

DITTMAR, N. 1981: On the verbal organization of L2 tense marking in an elicited translation task by Spanish immigrants in Germany. *Studies in Second Language Acquisition* 3, 136-64.

——1982: 'Ich fertig arbeite – nicht mehr spreche Deutsch': semantische Eigenschaften pidginisierter Lernervarietaten des Deutschen. *Zeitschrift für Literaturwissenschaft und Linguistik* 45, 9-34.

DORNIC, S. 1979: Information processing in bilinguals: some selected issues. *Psychological Research* 40, 329-48.

DULANY, D.E., CARLSON, R.A., and DEWEY, G.I. 1984: A case of syntactical learning and judgement: how conscious and how abstract? *Journal of Experimental Psychology: General* 113, 541-55.

DULAY, H.C., and BURT, M.K. 1972: Goofing: an indication of children's second language learning strategies. *Language Learning* 22, 235-52.

——1973: Should we teach children syntax? *Language Learning* 23, 245-258.

——1974a: Errors and strategies in child second language acquisition. *TESOL Quarterly* 8, 129-36.

——1974b: Natural sequences in child second language acquisition. *Language Learning* 24, 37-53.

——1977: Remarks on creativity in language acquisition. In Burt, M., Dulay, H., and Finocchiaro, M. (eds.), *Viewpoints on English as a second language* (New York: Regents).

DULAY, H.C., BURT, M.K., and KRASHEN, S. 1982: *Language two.* New York: Oxford University Press.

ECKMAN, F.R. 1977: Markedness and the contrastive analysis hypothesis. *Language Learning* 27, 315-30.

——1984: Universals, typologies and interlanguage. In Rutherford, W.E. (ed.), *Language universals and second language acquisition* (Amsterdam: John Benjamins).

——1985: Some theoretical and pedagogical implications of the markedness differential hypothesis. *Studies in Second Language Acquisition* 7, 289-307.

EINSTEIN, A. 1934: *Essays in science.* New York: Philosophical Library.

ELKIND, D. 1970: *Children and adolescents: interpretative essays on Jean Piaget.* New York: Oxford University Press.

ELLIS, R. 1985a: Sources of variability in interlanguage. *Applied Linguistics* 6, 118–31.

——1985b: *Understanding second language acquisition.* Oxford: Oxford University Press.

FAERCH, C. and KASPER, G. 1980: Processes in foreign language learning and communication. *Interlanguage Studies Bulletin* 5, 47–118.

——1983: Procedural knowledge as a component of foreign language learners' communicative competence. In Boete, H. and Herrlitz, W. (eds.), *Kommunikation im (Sprach-) Unterricht* (Utrecht: University of Utrecht).

——1984: Two ways of defining communication strategies. *Language Learning* 34, 45–64.

——1986: The role of comprehension in second-language learning. *Applied Linguistics* 7, 257–74.

FALTIS, C. 1984: A commentary on Krashen's Input Hypothesis. *TESOL Quarterly* 18, 352–6.

FATHMAN, A.K. 1975: Language background, age and the order of acquisition of English structures. In Burt, M. and Dulay, H.C. (eds.), *New directions in second language learning, teaching, and bilingual education* (Washington, DC: TESOL).

FAVREAU, M. 1981: *Automatic and conscious attentional processes in first and second languages of fluent bilinguals: implications for reading.* Unpublished dissertation, Concordia University.

FELIX, S. 1984: Two problems of language acquisition: the relevance of grammatical studies to the theory of interlanguage. In Davies, A., Criper, C. and Howatt, A.P.R. (eds.), *Interlanguage* (Edinburgh: Edinburgh University Press).

——1985: More evidence on competing cognitive systems. *Second Language Research* 1, 47–52.

FERGUSON, C.A. 1984: Repertorie universals, markedness, and second language acquisition. In Rutherford, W.E. (ed.), *Language universals and second language acquisition* (Amsterdam: John Benjamins).

FERGUSON, C.A., and DEBOSE, C.E. 1977: Simplified registers, broken language and pidginization. In Valdman, A. (ed.), *Pidgin and creole linguistics* (Bloomington: Indiana University Press).

FLYNN, S. 1983: Similarities and differences between first and second language acquisition: setting the parameters of universal grammar. In Rogers, D.R. and Sloboda, J.A. (eds.), *Acquisition of symbolic skills* (New York: Plenum).

——1985: Principled theories of L2 acquisition. *Studies in Second Language Acquisition* 7, 99–107.

FOX, J.A. 1983: Simplified input and negotiation in Russenorsk. In Andersen, R. (ed.) *Pidginization and creolization as language acquisition* (Rowley, MA: Newbury House).

FRAWLEY, W. 1981: *The complement hierarchy: evidence for language universals from L2.* Paper presented, winter, Linguistic Society of America.

FULLER, S. 1978: *Natural and monitored sequences by adult learners of English as a second language.* Unpublished dissertation, Florida State University.

GADALLA, B.J. 1981: Language acquisition research and the language teacher. *Studies in Second Language Acquisition* 4, 60–9.

GARDNER, R. 1980: On the validity of affective variables in second language acquisition: conceptual, contextual and statistical considerations. *Language Learning* 30, 255-70.

GARDNER, R., and LAMBERT, W. 1972: *Attitudes and motivation in second language learning*. Rowley, MA: Newbury Press.

GASS, S. 1979: Language transfer and universal grammatical relations. *Language Learning* 29, 327-44.

——1984: A review of interlanguage syntax: language transfer and language universals. *Language Learning* 34, 115-32.

GASS, S. and ARD, J. 1980: L2 data: their relevance for language universals. *TESOL Quarterly* 14, 443-52.

——1984: The ontology of language universals. In Rutherford, W.E. (ed.), *Language universals and second language acquisition* (Amsterdam: John Benjamins).

GENESEE, F. 1982: Experimental neuropsychological research on second language processing.*TESOL Quarterly* 16, 315-24.

GENESEE, F. and HAMAYAN, E. 1980: Individual differences in second language learning. *Applied Psycholinguistics* 1, 95-110.

GEORGE, H.V. 1972: *Common errors in language learning*. Rowley, MA: Newbury House.

GIBSON, E., and LEVIN, H. 1975: *The psychology of reading*. Cambridge, MA: MIT Press.

GILBERT, G.G. 1981: Discussion of 'Two perspectives on pidginization as second language acquisition'. In Andersen, R.W. (ed.), *New dimensions in second language acquisition research* (Rowley, MA: Newbury House).

GILES, H., BOURHIS, R., and TAYLOR, D. 1977: Toward a theory of language in ethnic group relations. In Giles, H. (ed.), *Language, ethnicity, and intergroup relations* (New York: Academic Press).

GILES, H., and BYRNE, J. 1982: An intergroup approach to second language acquisition. *Journal of Multilingual and Multicultural Development* 3, 17-40.

GOODMAN, K. (ed.) 1968: *The psycholinguistic nature of the reading process*. Detroit: Wayne State University Press.

GREGG, K.R. 1984: Krashen's Monitor and Occam's razor. *Applied Linguistics* 5, 79-100.

——in press: Krashen's theory, acquisition theory, and theory. In Barasch, R.M. (ed.), *Answers to Krashen* (Berkeley: Sci/Tech).

GREENBERG, J.H. 1966: *Language universals: with special reference to feature hierarchies*. The Hague: Mouton.

——1974: *Language typology: a historical and analytic overview*. The Hague: Mouton.

GREENWALD, A.G., PRATKANIS, A.R., LEIPPE, M.R., and BAUMGARDNER, M.H. 1986: Under what conditions does theory obstruct research progress? *Psychological Review* 93, 216-29.

GUTTMAN, L. 1944: A basis for scaling qualitative data. *American Sociological Review* 9, 139-50.

HAKUTA, K. 1976: Becoming bilingual: a case study of a Japanese child learning English. *Language Learning* 26, 321-51.

——1984: In what ways are language universals psychologically real? In

Rutherford, W.E. (ed.), *Language universals and second language acquisition* (Amsterdam: John Benjamins).

HAKUTA, K., and CANCINO, H. 1977: Trends in second-language acquisition research. *Harvard Educational Review* 47, 294–316.

HALL, R.A. 1966: *Pidgin and creole language*. Ithaca: Cornell University Press.

HASHER, L. and ZACKS, R.T. 1979: Automatic and effortful processes in memory. *Journal of Experimental Psychology: General* 108, 356–88.

HATCH, E. 1978: Discourse analysis and second language acquisition. In Hatch, E. (ed.), *Second language acquisition: a book of readings* (Rowley, MA: Newbury House).

——1980: Second language acquisition – avoiding the question. In Felix, S. (ed.), *Second language development* (Tübingen: Narr).

——1983: *Psycholinguistics: a second language perspective*. Rowley, MA: Newbury House.

——1984: Comments on the paper by Hakuta. In Rutherford W.E. (ed.), *Language universals and second language acquisition* (Amsterdam: John Benjamins).

HATCH, E., POLIN, P., and PART, S. 1970: *Acoustic scanning or syntactic processing*. Paper presented to Western Psychological Association, San Francisco.

HEATH, S.B. 1983: *Ways with words: language, life and work in communities and classrooms*. Cambridge: Cambridge University Press.

HECHT, B.F., and MULFORD, R. 1982: The acquisition of a second language phonology: interaction of transfer and developmental factors. *Applied Psycholinguistics* 3, 313–28.

HEIDELBERGER FORSCHUNGSPROJEKT 'PIDGIN-DEUTSCH' 1976: *Untersuchungen zur Erlernung des Deutschen durch ausländische Arbeiter*. Heidelberg: Germanistisches Seminar der Universität.

HENNING, G.H. 1973: Remembering foreign language vocabulary: acoustic and semantic parameters. *Language Learning* 23, 185–96.

HERMANN, G. 1980: Attitudes and success in children's learning of English as a second language: the motivational versus the resultative hypothesis. *English Language Teaching Journal* 34, 247–54.

HOFF-GINSBERG, E. and SHATZ, M. 1982: Linguistic input and the child's acquisition of language: a critical review. *Psychological Bulletin* 92, 3–26.

HOUCK, N., ROBERTSON, J., and KRASHEN, S. 1978: On the domain of the conscious grammar: morpheme orders for corrected and uncorrected ESL student transcriptions. *TESOL Quarterly* 12, 335–9.

HUEBNER, T. 1979: Order of acquisition vs. dynamic paradigm: a comparison of method in interlanguage research. *TESOL Quarterly* 13, 21–8.

——1983: *A longitudinal analysis of the acquisition of English*. Ann Arbor: Karoma.

HULSTIJN, J. and HULSTIJN, W. 1984: Grammatical errors as a function of processing constraints and explicit knowledge. *Language Learning* 34, 23–43.

HYAMS, N. 1983: The pro-drop parameter in child grammars. In Flickinger, D. (ed.), *Proceedings of WCCFL II* (Stanford, CA: Stanford Linguistics Association).

HYLTENSTAM, K. 1977: Implication patterns in interlanguage syntax variation. *Language Learning* 27, 383–411.

——1982: Language typology, language universals, markedness, and second language acquisition. Paper presented at Second European-North American Workshop on Cross-linguistic Second Language Acquisition Research, Görhde, W. Germany.

——1983: Data types and second language variability. In Ringbom, H. (ed.), *Psycholinguistics and foreign language learning* (Åbo: Åbo Akademi).

IOUP, G. 1984: Testing the relationship of formal instruction to the Input Hypothesis. *TESOL Quarterly* 18, 345–50.

JAKOBSON, R. 1941: *Kindersprache, Aphasie und allgemeine Lautgesetze.* Upsala: Almqvist and Wiksell.

JORDENS, P. 1977: Rules, grammatical intuitions and strategies in foreign language learning. *Interlanguage Studies Bulletin* 2, 5–76.

KAPLAN, A. 1964: *The conduct of inquiry: methodology for the behavioral sciences.* San Francisco: Chandler.

KARMILOFF-SMITH, A. 1986: Stage/structure versus phase/process in modelling linguistic and cognitive development. In Levin, I. (ed.), *Stage and structure: reopening the debate* (Norwood, NJ: Ablex).

KEENAN, E., and COMRIE, B. 1977: Noun phrase accessibility and universal grammar. *Linguistic Inquiry* 8, 63–99.

KELLER-COHEN, D. 1979: Systematicity and variation in the non-native child's acquisition of conversational skills. *Language Learning* 29, 27–44.

KELLERMAN, E. 1978: Giving learners a break: native language intuition as a source of predictions about transferability. *Working Papers in Bilingualism* 15, 59–92.

——1979: Transfer and non-transfer: where we are now. *Studies in Second Language Acquisition* 2, 37–57.

——1983: Now you see it, now you don't. In Gass, S. and Selinker, L. (eds.), *Language transfer in language learning* (Rowley, MA: Newbury House).

——1984: The empirical evidence for the influence of the L1 interlanguage. In Davies, A., Criper, C. and Howatt, A.P.R. (eds.), *Interlanguage* (Edinburgh: Edinburgh University Press).

KLEIN, W. 1981: Some rules of regular ellipsis in German. In Klein, W. and Levelt, W.J.M. (eds.), *Crossing the boundaries in linguistics: studies presented to Manfred Bierwisch* (Dordrecht: Reidel).

KOLERS, P.A. and DUCHNICKY, R.L. 1985: Discontinuity in cognitive skill. *Journal of Experimental Psychology: Learning, Memory, and Cognition* 11, 655–74.

KOLERS, P.A. and ROEDIGER, H.L. 1984: Procedures of mind. *Journal of Verbal Learning and Verbal Behavior* 23, 425–49.

KRAHNKE, K. 1985: Review of *The Natural Approach: Language acquisition in the classroom. TESOL Quarterly* 19, 591–603.

KRASHEN, S. 1977a: The Monitor Model for second language performance. In Burt, M., Dulay, H. and Finocchiaro, M. (eds.), *Viewpoints on English as a second language* (New York: Regents).

——1977b: Some issues related to the Monitor Model. In Brown, H.D., Yorio, C. and Crymes, R. (eds.), *On TESOL '77: teaching and learning English as a second language: trends in research and practice* (Washington: TESOL).

——1978a: Adult second language acquisition and learning: a review of theory and practice. In Gingras, R. (ed.), *Second language acquisition and foreign language teaching* (Washington: Center for Applied Linguistics).

——1978b: Individual variation in the use of the Monitor. In Ritchie, W. (ed.), *Principles of second language learning.* (New York: Academic Press).

——1979: A response to McLaughlin, 'The Monitor model: some methodological considerations'. *Language Learning* 29, 151–67.

——1980: The input hypothesis. In *Georgetown University Roundtable on Language and Linguistics* 1980 (Washington, D.C.: Georgetown University Press).

——1981: *Second language acquisition and second language learning.* Oxford: Pergamon Press.

——1982: *Principles and practices of second language acquisition.* Oxford: Pergamon Press.

——1983: Newmark's ignorance hypothesis and current second language acquisition theory. In Gass, S. and Selinker, L. (eds.), *Language transfer in language learning* (Rowley, MA: Newbury House).

——1985: *The input hypothesis: issues and implications.* London: Longman.

KRASHEN, S., BUTLER, J., BIRNBAUM, R., and ROBERTSON, J. 1978: Two studies in language acquisition and language learning. *ITL: Review of Applied Linguistics* 39–40, 73–92.

KRASHEN, S., and SCARCELLA, R. 1978: On routines and patterns in language acquisition and performance. *Language Learning* 28, 283–300.

KRASHEN, S. and TERRELL, T. 1983: *The natural approach: language acquisition in the classroom.* Hayward, CA: Alemany Press.

KUHN, T.S. 1970: *The structure of scientific revolutions.* Chicago: University of Chicago Press, 2nd edn.

KUMPF, L. 1982: *An analysis of tense, aspect, and modality in interlanguage.* Paper presented at TESOL Meeting, Honolulu.

LABERGE, D., and SAMUELS, S.J. 1974: Towards a theory of automatic information processing in reading. *Cognitive Psychology* 6, 293–323.

LABOV, W. 1966: *The social stratification of English in New York City.* Urban Language Series, I. Washington, DC: Center for Applied Linguistics.

LAMENDELLA, J. 1977: General principles of neurofunctional organization and their manifestations in primary and non-primary language acquisition. *Language Learning* 27, 155–96.

LANCE, D. 1969: *A brief study of Spanish-English bilingualism: final report.* Research Project Orr-Liberal Arts – 15504. College Station, TA: Texas A & M.

LARSEN-FREEMAN, D. 1975: The acquisition of grammatical morphemes by adult ESL students. *TESOL Quarterly* 9, 409–14.

——1976: An explanation for the morpheme acquisition order of second language learners. *Language Learning* 26, 126–34.

LEHTONEN, J., and SAJAVAARA, K. 1983: Acceptability and ambiguity in native and second language message processing. In Ringbom, H. (ed.), *Psycholinguistics and foreign language learning.* (Åbo: Åbo Akademi).

LENNEBERG, E.H. 1967: *Biological foundations of language.* New York: Wiley.

LEVELT, W.J.M. 1978: Skill theory and language teaching. *Studies in Second Language Acquisition* 1, 53–70.

LIGHTBOWN, P.M. 1984: The relationship between theory and method in second-language acquisition research. In Davies, A., Criper, C. and Howatt, A.P.R. (eds.), *Interlanguage* (Edinburgh: Edinburgh University Press).

——1985: Great expectations: second-language acquisition research and classroom teaching. *Applied Linguistics* 6, 173–89.

LIGHTBOWN, P. and WHITE, L. 1986: The influence of linguistic theories on language acquisition research: Description versus explanation. Unpublished paper.

LINTON, E. 1960: *Acculturation in seven American Indian tribes*. Gloucester: Smith.

LITTLEWOOD, W.T. 1984: *Foreign and second language learning: language-acquisition research and its implications for the classroom*. Cambridge: Cambridge University Press.

LONG, M. 1983: Does second language instruction make a difference? A review of research. *TESOL Quarterly* 17, 359–82.

——1985a: Input and second language acquisition theory. In Gass, S.M. and Madden, C.G. (eds.), *Input in second language acquisition* (Rowley, MA: Newbury House).

——1985b: Theory construction in second language acquisition. Paper presented in February at the Second Language Research Forum, University of California, Los Angeles.

LONG, M. and PORTER, P.A. 1985: Group work, interlanguage talk, and second language acquisition. *TESOL Quarterly* 19, 207–28.

LONG, M., and SATO, C.J. 1984: Methodological issues in interlanguage studies: an interactionist perspective. In Davies, A., Criper, C. and Howatt, A.P.R. (eds.), *Interlanguage* (Edinburgh: Edinburgh University Press).

LORD, C. 1984: Comments on the paper by Eckman. In Rutherford, W.E. (ed.), *Language universals and second language acquisition* (Amsterdam: John Benjamins).

MACEDO, D.P. 1986: The role of core grammar in pidgin development. *Language Learning* 36, 65–76.

MAZURKEWICH, I. 1984a: The acquisition of the dative alternation by second language learners and linguistic theory. *Language Learning* 34, 91–109.

——1984b: Dative questions and markedness. In Eckman, F.R., Bell, L.H. and Nelson, D. (eds.), *Universals of second language acquisition* (Rowley, MA: Newbury House).

McLAUGHLIN, B. 1978: The Monitor model: some methodological considerations. *Language Learning* 28, 309–32.

——1980: Theory and research in second-language learning: an emerging paradigm. *Language Learning*, 30, 331–50.

——1984: *Second-language acquisition in childhood. Volume 1: preschool children*. Hillsdale, NJ: Lawrence Erlbaum.

——1985: *Second-language acquisition in childhood. Volume 2: school-age children*. Hillsdale, NJ: Lawrence Erlbaum.

McLAUGHLIN, B., ROSSMAN, T., and McLEOD, B. 1983: Second-language learning: an information-processing perspective. *Language Learning* 33, 135–58.

McLEOD, B. and McLAUGHLIN, B. 1986: Restructuring or automaticity? Reading in a second language. *Language Learning* 36, 109–123.

MEISEL, J. 1977: The language of foreign workers in Germany. In Molony, C., Zobl, H. and Stölting, W. (eds.), *German in contact with other languages*. Kronberg/Ts.: Scriptor.

——1980: Linguistic simplification. In Felix, S. (ed.), *Second language development: trends and issues* (Tübingen: Narr).

——1982: Reference to past events and actions in the development of natural second language acquisition. Paper presented at the 2nd European-North American Cross-linguistic Second Language Acquisition Workshop, Görhde, West Germany.

——1983a: Language development and linguistic theory: review of Derek Bickerton, *Roots of language. Lingua* 61, 231–57.

——1983b: Strategies of second languages acquisition: more than one kind of simplification. In Andersen, R.W. (ed.), *Pidginization and creolization as language acquisition* (Rowley, MA: Newbury House).

MEISEL, J., CLAHSEN, H., and PIENEMANN, M. 1981: On determining developmental stages in natural second language acquisition. *Studies in Second Language Acquisition* 3, 109–35.

MÜHLHÄUSLER, P. 1980: Structural expansion and the concept of creolization. In Valdman, A. and Highfield, A. (eds.), *Theoretical orientations in creole studies* (New York: Academic Press).

MUÑOZ-LICERAS, J. 1983: *Markedness, contrastive analysis, and the acquisition of Spanish syntax by English speakers.* Unpublished dissertation, University of Toronto.

NAGEL, E. 1961: *The structure of science.* New York: Harcount, Brace and World.

NATION, R. and McLAUGHLIN, B. 1986: Experts and novices: an information-processing approach to the 'good language learner' problem. *Applied Psycholinguistics* 7, 41–56.

NEMSER, W. 1971: Approximative systems of foreign language learners. *International Review of Applied Linguistics* 9, 115–23.

OCHS, E. 1982: Talking to children in Western Samoa. *Language in Society* 11, 77–104.

PARADIS, M. (ed.) 1983: *Readings on aphasia in bilinguals and polyglots.* Montreal: Didier.

PETERS, A. 1983: *The units of language acquisition.* Cambridge: Cambridge University Press.

PIKE, K. 1960: Nucleation. *Modern Language Journal* 44, 291–295.

POINCARÉ K. 1913: *The foundations of science.* New York: The Science Press.

POPPER, K. 1959: *The logic of scientific discovery.* New York: Basic Books.

PORTER, J. 1977: A cross-sectional study of morpheme acquisition in first-language learners. *Language Learning* 27, 47–62.

POSNER, M.I. and SNYDER, C.R.R. 1975: Attention and cognitive control. In Solso, R.L. (ed.), *Information processing and cognition: the Loyola symposium* (Hillsdale, NJ: Lawrence Erlbaum).

PRESTON, M. and LAMBERT, W. 1969: Interlingual interference in a bilingual version of the Stroop Color-Word task. *Journal of Verbal Learning and Verbal Behavior* 8, 295–301.

RICKFORD, J.R. 1983: What happens in decreolization. In Andersen, R. (ed.) *Pidginization and creolization as language acquisition* (Rowley, MA: Newbury House).

RITCHIE, W. 1978: The right-roof constraint in an adult acquired language. In

Ritchie, W. (ed.), *Second language acquisition research: issues and implications* (New York: Academic Press).

ROSANSKY, E.J. 1976: Methods and morphemes in second language acquisition research. *Language Learning* 26, 409–25.

ROSSMAN, T. 1981: *The nature of linguistic processing in reading a second language*. Unpublished Thesis, Concordia University.

RUMELHART, D.E. and NORMAN, D.A. 1978: Accretion, tuning, and restructuring: three modes of learning. In Cotton, J. and Klatzky, R. (eds.), *Semantic factors in cognition* (Hillsdale, NJ: Lawrence Erlbaum).

RUTHERFORD, W. 1982: Markedness in second language acquisition. *Language Learning* 32, 85–108.

——1984: Description and explanation in interlanguage syntax: state of the art. *Language Learning* 34, 127–55.

RUTHERFORD, W.E. and SHARWOOD SMITH, M. 1985: Consciousness-raising and universal grammar. *Applied Linguistics* 6, 274–82.

SACHS, J. 1967: Recognition memory for syntactic and semantic aspects of connected discourse. *Perception and Psychophysics* 2, 437–42.

SAJAVAARA, K. 1978: The monitor model and monitoring in foreign language speech communication. In Gingras, R.C. (ed.), *Second language acquisition and foreign language teaching* (Washington, DC: Center for Applied Linguistics).

SANKOFF, G. 1983: Comments on Valdman's 'Creolization and second language acquisition'. In Andersen, R.W. (ed.), *Pidginization and creolization as language acquisition* (Rowley, MA: Newbury House).

SATO, C. 1984: *The syntax of conversation in interlanguage development*. Unpublished dissertation, University of California, Los Angeles.

SCHACHTER, J. 1974: An error in error analysis. *Language Learning* 24, 205–14.

——1983: A new account of language transfer. In Gass, S. and Selinker, L. (eds.), *Languages transfer in language learning* (Rowley, MA: Newbury House).

——1984: A universal input condition. In Rutherford, W.E. (ed.), *Language universals and second language acquisition* (Amsterdam: John Benjamins).

SCHACHTER, J. and CELCE-MURCIA, M. 1977: Some reservations concerning error analysis. *TESOL Quarterly* 11, 441–51.

SCHACHTER, J. and RUTHERFORD, W.E. 1979: Discourse function and language transfer. *Working Papers on Bilingualism* 19, 1–12.

——1982: Simplification, transfer and relexification as aspects of pidginization and early second language acquisition. *Language Learning* 32, 337–66.

SCHMIDT, M. 1980: Coordinate structures and language universals in interlanguage. *Language Learning* 30, 397–416.

SCHNEIDER, W. and SHIFFRIN, R.M. 1977: Controlled and automatic processing. I: detection, search, and attention. *Psychological Review* 84, 1–64.

SCHUMANN, J. 1978a: *The pidginization process: a model for second language acquisition*. Rowley, MA: Newbury House.

——1978b: Social and psychological factors in second language acquisition. In Richards, J. (ed.), *Understanding second and foreign language learning: issues and approaches* (Rowley, MA: Newbury House).

——1981a: Discussion of 'Two perspectives on pidginization as second language acquisition'. In Andersen, R.W. (ed.), *New dimensions in second language acquisition research* (Rowley, MA: Newbury House).

——1981b: Reaction to Gilbert's discussion of Andersen's paper. In Andersen, R.W. (ed.), *New dimensions in second language acquisition research* (Rowley, MA: Newbury House).

——1982: Simplification, transfer and relexification as aspects of pidginization and early second language acquisition. *Language Learning* 32, 337–66.

——1983a: Art and science in second language acquisition research. *Language Learning* 33, 49–76.

——1983b: Reaction to Eckman and Washabaugh's discussion of Schumann and Stauble. In Andersen, R.W. (ed.), *Pidginization and creolization as language acquisition* (Rowley, MA: Newbury House).

SCHUMANN, J. and STAUBLE, A.-M. 1983: A discussion of second language acquisition and decreolization. In Andersen, R.W. (ed.), *Pidginization and creolization as language acquisition* (Rowley, MA: Newbury House).

SEGALOWITZ, N. 1986: Skilled reading in the second language. In Vaid, J. (ed.), *Language processing in bilingual psycholinguistic and neuropsychological perspectives* (Hillsdale, NJ: Lawrence Erlbaum).

SELIGER, H. 1979: On the nature and function of language rules in language teaching. *TESOL Quarterly* 13, 359–70.

SELINKER, L. 1969: Language transfer. *General Linguistics* 9, 67–92.

——1972: Interlanguage. *IRAL* 10, 209–31.

SELINKER, L., and LAMENDELLA, J. 1976: Two perspectives on fossilization in interlanguage learning. *Interlanguage Studies Bulletin* 3, 144–91.

SELINKER, L., SWAIN, M. and DUMAS, G. 1975: The interlanguage hypothesis extended to children. *Language Learning* 25, 139–91.

SHARWOOD SMITH, M. 1981: Consciousness raising and the second language learner. *Applied Linguistics* 2, 159–68.

——1985: Modularity in muddy waters: linguistic theory and second language developmental grammars. Paper Presented at MIT Working Conference on Second Language Acquisition.

SHIFFRIN, R.M. and SCHNEIDER, W. 1977: Controlled and automatic human information processing. II: perceptual learning, automatic, attending, and a general theory. *Psychological Review* 84, 127–90.

SLOBIN, D. 1983: What the natives have in mind. In Andersen, R. (ed.) *Pidginization and creolization as language acquisition* (Rowley, MA: Newbury House).

SMITH, F. 1971: *Understanding reading*. New York: Holt.

STAUBLE, A.-M. 1978: The process of decreolization: a model for second language development. *Language Learning* 28, 29–54.

——1980: Acculturation and second language acquisition. In Krashen, S. and Scarcella, R. (eds.), *Issues in second language research* (Rowley, MA: Newbury House).

STRONG, M. 1984: Integrative motivation: cause or result of successful second language acquisition? *Language Learning* 34, 1–14.

SWAIN, M. 1985: Communicative competence: some roles of comprehensible input and comprehensible output in its development. In Gass, S.M. and Madden, C.G. (eds.), *Input in second language acquisition* (Rowley, MA: Newbury House).

TAKALA, S. 1984: A review of *Language two* by Heidi Dulay, Marina Burt, and Stephen Krashen. *Language Learning* 34, 157–74.

TARONE, E. 1979: Interlanguage as chameleon. *Language Learning* 29, 181–91.

——1982: Systematicity and attention in interlanguage. *Language Learning* 32, 69–84.

——1983: On the variability of interlanguage systems. *Applied Linguistics* 4, 142–63.

TAYLOR, B.P. 1975: Adult language learning strategies and their pedagogical implications. *TESOL Quarterly* 9, 391–99.

TAYLOR, G. 1984: Empirical or intuitive? A review of *The Natural approach: language acquisition in the classroom* by Stephen D. Krashen and Tracy D. Terrell. *Language Learning* 34, 97–105.

TRUBETZKOY, N.S. 1936: Essai d'une theorie des oppositions phonologique. *Journal de Psychologie* 33, 5–18.

VALDMAN, A. 1983: Creolization and second language acquisition. In Andersen, R. (ed.), *Pidginization and creolization as language acquisition* (Rowley, MA: Newbury House).

VIHMAN, M. 1982: The acquisition of morphology by a bilingual child: the whole-word approach. *Applied Psycholinguistics* 3, 141–60.

VIHMAN, M. and McLAUGHLIN, B. 1982: Bilingualism and second-language acquisition in preschool children. In Brainerd, C.J. and Pressley, M. (eds.), *Progress in cognitive development research: verbal processes in children* (Berlin: Springer).

WASHABAUGH, W. and ECKMAN, F. 1980: Review of J.H. Schumann, *The pidginization process: a model for second language acquisition. Language* 56, 453–6.

WHINNOM, K. 1971: Linguistic hybridization and the 'special case' of pidgins and creoles. In Hymes, D. (ed.), *Pidginization and creolization of languages* (Cambridge: Cambridge University Press).

WHITE, L. 1981: The responsibility of grammatical theory to acquisitional data. In Hornstein, N. and Lightfoot, D. (eds.), *Explanation in linguistics: the logical problem of language acquisition* (London: Longman).

——1983: Markedness and parameter setting: some implications for a theory of adult second language acquisition. Paper presented at the University of Wisconsin-Milwaukee Linguistics Symposium, March.

——1985a: Against comprehensible input: the Input Hypothesis and the development of L2 competence. Paper presented at Language Acquisition Research Symposium, Utrecht, September.

——1985b: Island effects in second language acquisition. Paper presented at the Workshop on Linguistic Theory and Second Language Acquisition, MIT, October.

——in press: The principle of adjacency in second language acquisition. In Gass, S. (ed.), *Second language acquisition: a linguistic perspective* (Cambridge: Cambridge University Press).

WODE, H. 1981: *Learning a second language: 1: an integrated view of language acquisition.* Tübingen: Narr.

——1984: Some theoretical implications of L2 acquisition research and the grammar of interlanguages. In Davies, A., Criper, C. and Howatt, A.P.R. (eds.), *Interlanguage* (Edinburgh: Edinburgh University Press).

WODE, H., BAHNS, J., BEDEY, H., and FRANK, W. 1978: Developmental sequences: an alternative approach to morpheme orders. *Language Learning* 28, 175–85.

WOLFE, S. 1981: *Bilingualism: one or two conceptual systems?* Unpublished thesis, San Francisco State University.

WONG FILLMORE, L. 1976: *The second time around: cognitive and social strategies in second language acquisition*. Unpublished dissertation, Stanford University.

——1982: The development of second language literacy skills. Statement to the National Commission on Excellence in Education, Houston, Texas.

——1985: Second language learning in children: a proposed model. In Eshch, R. and Provinzano, J. (eds.), *Issues in English language development* (Rosslyn, VA: National Clearinghouse for Bilingual Education).

ZOBL, H. 1979: Systems of verb classification and cohesion of verb-complement relations as structural conditions on interference in a child's L2 development. *Working Papers on Bilingualism* 18, 43–57.

——1982: A direction for contrastive analysis: the comparative study of developmental sequences *TESOL Quarterly* 16, 169–83.

——1983: Markedness and the projection problem. *Language Learning* 33, 293–313.

——1984a: Cross-language generalizations and the contrastive dimension of the interlanguage hypothesis. In Davies, A., Criper, C. and Howatt, A.P.R. (eds.), *Interlanguage* (Edinburgh: Edinburgh University Press).

——1984b: The Wave Model of linguistic change and the naturalness of interlanguage. *Studies in Second Language Acquisition* 6, 160–85.

Index

181

182   *Index*

Kaplan, A., 3, 5, 12, 15, 17
Karmiloff-Smith, A., 134, 137–8, 144
Kasper, G., 145–6, 151, 156
Keenan, E., 85
Keller-Cohen, D., 77
Kellerman, E., 79–81, 87, 89, 97, 102, 105, 159
Klein, W., 114
Kolers, P., 138, 152
Krahnke, K., 47, 48
Krashen, S., ix, 6, 9, ch. 2, 91, 149, 152, 153, ch. 7 *passim*
Kuhn, T., 158
Kumpf, L., 87

Labov, W., 109
Lambert, W., 126, 153, 160
Lamendella, J., 6, 160
Lance, D., 67
Language Acquisition Device, 23–58 *passim*
language proficiency, 13
language-learning ability, 126–7
Larsen-Freeman, D., 34, 66
learnability, 105, 128
learning strategies, 60–3, 128, 145–6, 160, 164–5
learning, 20–58 *passim*
Lehtonen, J., 141
Lenneberg, E., 96
Levelt, P., 133, 135
Lewin, K., 16, 162
Lightbown, P., x, 2, 4, 34, 143, 148, 155, 159, 160–1
linguistic universals, x, 2, 10, 67, ch. 4, 150, 159
Linton, E., 110
Littlewood, W., 164
Long, M., 10, 19, 45, 50, 74, 75, 80, 157–8, 160, 163
Lord, C., 88

Macedo, D. P., 120
Markedness Differential hypothesis, 89–90
markedness, 79–80, ch. 4 *passim*, 120, 150, 158
Mazurkewich, I., 97–8
McLaughlin, B., 22, 29, ch. 6 *passim*, 162, 165
McLeod, B., 133, 146
Meara, P., x

Meisel, J., 35, 73, 75, 77, 114–15, 116, 120, 126, 129–30, 160
methodology, 2, 4–6, 33–4, 80–1, 87, 101–2, 158–62
Monitor Model, ix, 9, ch. 2, ch. 7 *passim*
morpheme studies, 2, 31–4, 66–9, 76, 159
Mulford, R., 104
multidimensional scaling, 105
multilinguals, 142
Muñoz-Liceras, J., 87, 99
Mühlhäusler, P., 121, 132

Nagel, E., 8
Nation, R., 142
nativization, 112–13, 120–1, 128–30, 131, 146
negative input, 106
negative transfer, 13
Nemser, W., 60
neurolinguistics, 6, 160
non-systematic variation in the interlanguage, 72–3, 125–6, 144
Norman, D., 138

Ochs, E., 44–5
Odo, C., 117, 122, 129
operationalism, 13
output, 50

Paradis, M., 160
parameters, 24, 92, 94–5, 100–1, 163
permeability, 63
Peters, A., 41
pidginization, 109, 111–12, 115, 116–19, 125, 127–32, 159
Pike, K., 143
Poincaré, H., 15
Popper, K., ix, 3, 15, 158
Porter, J., 67
Porter, P., 50
pro-drop principle, 95
procedural knowledge, 138, 145
Protestant ethic, 13
proto-theory, 10–11, 151
psychoanalytic theory, 17
psychological distance, 110–12, 125–7, 132, 160

reading, 13, 42–3, 142–3, 147–8
relative clauses, 85–6, 93